W9-AYP-549

UNDER FIRE
The Story of American War Correspondents
by M. L. Stein
Photographs

Lexington and Concord . . . Bull Run and Appomattox ts
. . . San Juan Hill . . . Vera Cruz . . . Chateau Thierry
. . . Ethiopia . . . Nanking . . . Madrid . . . Poland . . .
Pearl Harbor . . . North Africa . . . Normandy . . .
Guadalcanal . . . Hiroshima . . . Saigon . . . Hanoi . . .
the Sinai . . . American reporters have never failed to
go where the action was. Today when we read newspaper
accounts of fighting in some global hot spot, or view on
TV the devastation of war, we are witnessing the latest
chapter in a great journalistic tradition.

From the American Revolution onwards, American
war correspondents have overcome every obstacle and
faced death itself to bring the American public vital information. This extraordinary breed of men and women
not only reported battles but fought their own: against
the enemy, against rival papers, against the hazards of
communication and even, in their desire to report the
facts, against their own government's censorship.

Charged with the fascination of history come alive,
this is the story of the many colorful, daring correspondents who let neither man nor circumstance stand between
them and the news. Such literary greats as Stephen Crane
and Ernest Hemingway were war reporters, as well as
such immortal newsmen as Ernie Pyle, Robert Capa
and Edward R. Murrow, the pioneer war photographer
Matthew Brady, the legendary Richard Harding Davis
and the uninhibited Floyd Gibbons.

This book is filled with tales of heroism, humor and
tragedy, of great events and vivid personalities involved
in exploits that read like fiction. Most of all, it is filled
with a sense of what the finest brand of journalism really
is—not a way of making a living but a way of life, with
its own code, its own courage, its own unshakable
integrity.

Books by M. L. Stein

Freedom of the Press
A Continuing Struggle

Under Fire
The Story of American War Correspondents

Your Career in Journalism

Under Fire

The Story of American War
Correspondents

by
M. L. STEIN

Illustrated with Photographs

JULIAN MESSNER  NEW YORK

Published simultaneously in the United States and Canada
by Julian Messner, a division of Simon & Schuster, Inc.,
1 West 39 Street, New York, N.Y. 10018.

Printed in the United States of America
Library of Congress Catalog Card No. 68-14950

For
Phillip, Aaron and Larry

ACKNOWLEDGEMENTS

I am grateful to a number of persons and organizations who contributed to this book.

Several newsmen and women were kind enough to donate their time for interviews about their war reporting experiences. Among them are Hal Boyle, William Ryan, Stanley Swinton and George Esper, Associated Press; Bob Bryant, *San Francisco Examiner;* Joe Rosenthal, *San Francisco Chronicle;* Frank Bartholomew, United Press International; Barry Cunningham, *New York Post;* Robert Magidoff, New York University; Marlene Sanders, ABC News; Frank Holeman, *New York Daily News;* Howard Taubman, *The New York Times;* Sigrid Schultz, Dick Phelan, Lewis Merrim and Tony Chapelle.

Special material and pictures were made available to me by the Associated Press, United Press International, the *Chicago Tribune, The New York Times,* the American Broadcasting Company, the National Broadcasting Company, the Columbia Broadcasting System, the Scripps-Howard Newspapers, the *Los Angeles Times, Newsday,* the Department of Defense, *Stars and Stripes,* the Marine Corps Combat Correspondents and Photographers Association and the Overseas Press Club of America.

The research took me through hundreds of books and other sources. A selective bibliography is provided at the end.

Most of all I am grateful to my wife, Irene, for her highly competent and enthusiastic research assistance. Her ability to track down an obscure but fascinating item made my job more rewarding.

M. L. Stein

CONTENTS

CONTENTS

1

From Lexington to Gettysburg

JOURNALISM HAS SOMETIMES BEEN CALLED INSTANT HISTORY. SUCH a definition certainly could be applied to war reporting. The combat correspondent cannot wait for the tide of events to pass so that he may see the whole panorama of the battle and write about it with the depth and perspective that time can bring. He must tell his story under fire or immediately after the bullets and bombs have stopped flying. The world does not want to wait for the assessment of history; it wants information from the battlefield at the time history is being made. The victories, defeats, casualties, heroism and stupidities of war are hurled from the correspondent's typewriter and carried to the farthest corners of the earth as fast as modern communications can speed them. Often this is measured in seconds.

The historian years later may quarrel with the daily account or interpretation of a battle or war and set things right with the benefit of his additional knowledge and new insight. Nonetheless, judge not the war correspondent too harshly. In most instances he did his job well under hazardous conditions. Sometimes he died doing it.

The American combat correspondent can be traced back to the Revolutionary War. One reporter of that conflict was Isaiah Thomas, a patriot who was forced to move his newspaper, the *Massachusetts Spy,* from Boston to Worcester to escape arrest and hanging by the British. Thomas, who was probably America's first war correspondent, reported the Battle of Lexington from the best possible vantage point—as a member of the militia. His account appeared in the May 3, 1775, issue of the *Spy.* Here is part of it:

> Americans! forever bear in mind the Battle of Lexington!
> —where British troops, unmolested and unprovoked, wantonly and in a most inhuman manner, fired upon and killed a number of our countrymen, then robbed, ransacked, and burnt their houses! nor could the tears of defenseless women, some of whom were in pains of childbirth, the cries of helpless babes, nor the prayers of old age, confined to beds of sickness, appease their thirst for blood—or divert them from their Design of Murder and Robbery!
> . . . The body of the troops . . . under the command of Lieutenant Colonel Smith, had crossed the river and landed at Phipp's Farm. They immediately to the number of 1000, proceeded to Lexington, about six miles below Concord, with great silence. A company of militia, of about eighty men, mustered near the meetinghouse; the troops came in sight of them just before sunrise. The militia, upon seeing the troops, began to disperse. The troops then set out upon the run, hallooing and huzzaing, and coming within a few rods of them, the commanding officer accosted the militia, in words to this effect,
> "Disperse, you damn'd rebels!—Damn you, disperse!"
> Upon which the troops again huzzaed and immediately one or two officers discharged their pistols, which were instantaneously followed by the firing of four or five of the soldiers; and

then there seemed to be a general discharge from the whole body. It is to be noticed they fired on our people as they were dispersing, agreeable to their command, and that we did not even return the fire. Eight of our men were killed and nine wounded. The troops then laughed, and damned the Yankees, and said they could not bear the smell of gunpowder . . .

An unknown correspondent was responsible for this dispatch in the *New York Journal* of August 2, 1779:

The detachment marched in two divisions, and about one o'clock came up to the enemy's pickets who, by firing their pieces, gave the alarm and . . . ran to the fort, from every quarter of which in a short time they made an incessant fire upon our people. They, with fixed bayonets and uncharged pieces, advanced with quick but silent motion through a heavy fire of cannon and musketry till, getting over the abatis and scrambling up the precipes, the enemy called out, "Come on ye damn'd rebels! Come on!"

Some of our people softly answered, "Don't be in such a hurry, my lads. We will be with you presently."

Lively Revolutionary War reporting also appeared in the *Pennsylvania Journal,* the *Newport Mercury,* the *New Jersey Gazette,* the *New York Packet* and others. Colonial editors were hardly objective correspondents, but it was not a time for objectivity.

The Mexican War of 1846-1847 was well reported by such men as George Wilkins Kendall and James L. Freaner, who rode with General Zachary Taylor and his troops. At that time the telegraph was just coming into use as a conveyor of news, and newsmen used it freely to report from Mexico. Kendall, who established the *New Orleans Picayune,* had three virtues that are as important to a journalist today as they were then: intelligence, daring and enterprise. When he had trouble getting his dispatches home, he beat the time problem by purchasing a small and fast steamer for a press boat and outfitting her with typesetters and printing equipment. He then hired tough horseback riders who sped his war front stories to

Vera Cruz, where they were set in type and rushed to New Orleans by boat. Several of Kendall's express riders were killed or captured by bandits, but the system worked. Kendall himself was wounded in the knee during one engagement.

Freaner, who signed his stories "Mustang," killed a Mexican officer at the battle of Monterey and seized his horse, an act which gave him the idea for his pen name. The New Orleans correspondent also served twice as an official bearer of dispatches from General Winfield Scott to Washington.

Some Mexican War reporters managed to print one-page news sheets on the battlefield. The papers carried such names as the *American Star,* the *American Eagle* and the *Tampico Sentinel.* The Mexican War gave birth to what was probably the first organized effort at correspondence by professional newspapermen.

At the battlefield of South Mountain, Maryland, there is a stone arch memorializing 147 reporters and artists who covered the Civil War. The inscription reads: "To the Army correspondents and artists 1861-1865 whose toils cheered the camps, thrilled the fireside, educated provinces of rustics into a bright nation of readers and gave incentive to narrate distant wars and explore dark lands."

Actually the tablet bears the names of less than half the number of men who reported that momentous conflict. The Civil War drew more newsmen than any previous event in history. And with good reason. It was the biggest story of the day by far. A great nation was ripped apart and was settling its differences in blood. The fate of the Union was at stake and the entire world watched the struggle.

The outbreak of the war also coincided with the beginning of a new era in journalism. Even before 1861 newspapers were increasing in size and circulation in the United States. Between 1840 and 1860 the number of dailies jumped from 138 to 372. People turned more and more to the printed word for information. And for millions, their only link with the Civil War was through the newspapers.

ything and the other correspondents took issue with the Army or
was "suitable." The military, meanwhile, prepared to invoke the
Article of War against newsmen. It stated that anyone commu-
ing information to the enemy "by any means whatever" could be
nced to death. So tight did the security become that reporters for
York papers resorted to requesting official reports from friendly
oyees of the War and Navy Departments. This is still the practice
ashington today.

October, 1861, Secretary of State William H. Seward issued a
order: The censor was to forbid all telegraphic dispatches from
ington which related to the military and civil operations of gov-
ent. The following year Secretary of War Stanton, another of-
who took a hard line with the press, decreed that newspapers
not publish the "number, position or strength of the military
of the United States." *Harper's Weekly* lost its right to circulate
e Northern camps for printing sketches of McClellan's siege
s. General Henry W. Halleck ordered more than thirty corre-
ents out of his area.

porter George Alfred Townsend, twenty-one, of the *New York*
d, was arrested for joining a cavalry scouting patrol. Major
al William Tecumseh Sherman, who had a violent temper to
his red hair, tried his best to hang another *Herald* corre-
ent, Thomas W. Knox, for his report of Sherman's defeat at
burg. Knox, a twenty-eight-year-old former schoolteacher, was
ly court-martialed as a spy; but a board of officers ruled only
nox had defied orders "without criminality" and ordered him
the operations zone. The judgment failed to mollify Sherman,
ad an abiding hatred for newsmen, calling them a "dirty set of
ers who have the impudence of Satan."
ey come into camp," Sherman continued, "poke about among
y shirks and pick up their camp rumors and publish them as
and the avidity with which these rumors are swallowed by the
makes even some of our officers bow to them. I will not. They
est and shall not approach me and I will treat them as spies,
in truth they are."

The Civil War correspondents, an army in themselves, came from
all over the states and from abroad. Some were raw cubs and others
were experienced hands. Of the more than three hundred reporters
who followed the Northern armies, several had reported other wars.
Richard C. McCormick, of the *New York Evening Post,* had covered the Crimean campaign and George F. Williams, of *The New
York Times,* the action against the Mormons in 1858. An Associated Press correspondent, James O. Noyes, had filed dispatches from
Turkey, Palestine and Egypt. Edward H. House had written about
John Brown's raid in Virginia for the *New York Tribune* before the
war.

There were such journalistic stars as Henry M. Stanley, of the
Tribune, who achieved new fame eleven years later when he found
explorer David Livingstone in the jungles of Africa. A young German
immigrant, Henry Villard, represented three newspapers for a total
of fifty dollars a week, a handsome journalistic salary in that day.
After the war Villard became a millionaire railroad tycoon. Ains-
worth Spofford, of the *Cincinnati Commercial,* and John Russell
Young, of the *Philadelphia Press,* had both been Librarians of
Congress.

The Civil War correspondents were generally in their late twenties,
although about six were nineteen or less in 1861. Some were college
graduates, while others had not finished high school. Like other reporters in other wars, some were conscientious and enterprising
while others were timid and inept. A few flamboyant individuals lent
color to the scene. Perhaps the most notable was William Howard
Russell, of the *Times* of London, already a celebrated correspondent by 1861. Stout and middle-aged, Russell arrived on the battlefield in a khaki "Himalayan" suit, with a set of pro-Northern opinions. The Britisher was received in a manner befitting his eminence.
He dined at the White House and was invited to make speeches in support of the North. The proper Englishman covered the first battle of
Bull Run after turning down General Irwin McDowell's suggestion
that all correspondents wear white uniforms "to indicate the purity
of their character."

Russell, who fancied himself a military tactician, was disgusted by the Union rout at Bull Run and tried to regroup the panicky troops. *The New York Times* wrote: "We scarcely exaggerate the fact when we say the first and foremost thought in the minds of a very large portion of our people after the repulse of Bull Run was 'What will Russell say?'"

Russell had plenty to say about the retreat at Bull Run. ". . . disgraceful conduct of the troops . . . a miserable causeless panic . . . scandalous behaviour" were among his comments. The *New York Herald* accused him of being a Confederate agent who led the retreat. Russell also drew the wrath of the *New York Illustrated News,* whose cartoonist caricatured him as a "swinish boozer who viewed the battle from a safe remove through bleary eyes and a spyglass." By this time Russell had fallen almost completely out of favor with the Army. He applied for permission to accompany the troops to Fortress Monroe but at the last minute Edwin Stanton, Secretary of War, had him pulled off the steamer. Russell returned to England, frustrated and bitter.

The correspondents were headquartered in Washington, where War Department officials were at some loss as to how to deal with them. There had been newsmen in Washington since Andrew Jackson's administration but they were a special problem for a nation at war. A journalist can be a curse or blessing to the military, depending on the nature of his reports. The Army has never appreciated public accounts of its battlefield losses or blunders.

However, the Civil War correspondents were at first well received in Washington. Although they had no official status, they were wined and dined at officers' mess and were given elaborate briefings by Army commanders. Several were allowed to accompany troops into the field.

The honeymoon did not last long. The brass was dismayed at the speed by which news items could be telegraphed to newspapers around the land. Reporters' copy also was carried by locomotive. A story filed in the morning would be in print by the following afternoon and often the information found its way into Southern papers

as well. Communication between the Union ... was not difficult. General Robert E. Lee once c... ally scanned the Yankee papers for useful inf...

Before the war, news often ran as much as a ... appeared not to mind. But in 1861 there was ... for fresh information. Telegraph wires were co ... dispatches from Washington, and correspon... other for their use. Competition became so fier... would instruct operators to punch out chapters ... were ready to send their dispatch. In this way t... open for their exclusive use. Opposition repor... ting the wire. The telegraph companies final... limit for any one correspondent at a time. Eve... seized control of the telegraph lines to regula... tion.

The military, stung by some newspaper cri... more hostile to the press as the war dragged ... posed and some correspondents were order... zones. General Winfield Scott complained th... patches were keeping the Confederates info... ments. In an interview with Murat Halstead, ... *mercial,* General Benjamin Butler snapped: '... not accomplish much until it hanged a half ... one newspaper reporter." Later, after Gener... itician, had issued a censorship order, the N... in an editorial:

"Why, dear Major General. The newsp... epaulettes and all! Without the newspapers ... ment, have been a petty attorney in a petty ...

An attempt at a truce was made by Major ... McClellan, a young, handsome officer with a ... He proposed to the reporters that they no ... "furnish aid and comfort to the enemy" and ... tee the Army's help in obtaining facilities fo... stories. The agreement fell apart when the ...

The situation became worse for newsmen after the Knox trial. Not only were they denied official reports but they even had trouble getting mess privileges, food for their horses and travel passes. The *New York Herald,* which fielded the largest number of correspondents, was forced to set up its own logistic support for them. The reporters were provided with a supply-laden wagon with the paper's name emblazoned on the side.

The press fared no better in the South. Southern reporters were frequently barred from the front and censorship was severe. In January, 1862, the Army of the Potomac expelled all correspondents. At the same time the Confederate Congress made it a crime to publish any news of troop or naval movements. Many of the Southern papers were supplied by The Press Association of the Confederate States of America, headed by J. S. Thatcher. Even so, clients got little news because of censorship. A Kentucky editor observed in 1862 that Southern publishers were "in happy ignorance" of what was happening, except for three Confederate victories. Poor mail and telegraph service also hampered the flow of information in the South.

One of the more enterprising Southern papers was the *Memphis Daily Appeal,* which kept three staff correspondents with the main Confederate armies throughout the war. According to historian George Sisler, the *Appeal* operated like a folding tent show, keeping just one step ahead of the Yankee armies. The editor often transported his presses by railroad car, publishing at various times in Atlanta, Jackson, Grenada, and other Southern towns. The paper shifted location so often it was nicknamed the "Moving Appeal."

Among the *Appeal's* reporters was John H. Linebaugh, who signed his stories "Shadow." It was Linebaugh's misfortune to fall afoul of rebel General Braxton Bragg, who had him arrested on a treason charge because of the newsman's critical appraisal of Bragg's generalship. Bragg, whose distaste for newspapermen was well known, couldn't make the charge stick, however, and Linebaugh was released. He rejoined Bragg's army and the two declared an uneasy truce for the remainder of the war.

Another *Appeal* correspondent was Robert Ette, assigned to the

Army of the Mississippi. Ette covered the Battle of Shiloh and filed a memorable first-day story, which began: "We slept last night in the enemy's camp."

The roving *Appeal* was finally captured by Union forces two days after Lee surrendered to Grant at Appomattox.

The Southern press was crippled by newsprint and manpower shortages. Many of its papers were printing only half sheets by 1863. Earlier, the *New Orleans Daily Picayune* announced that all of its reporters had enlisted in the army.

Despite restrictions, Northern Civil War correspondents managed to feed the public an amazing amount of news from the battle zones. Often their dispatches were obtained under extremely adverse or hazardous conditions.

George W. Smalley, of the *New York Tribune,* covered McClellan's victory at Antietam and was twice grazed by bullets. After the battle he mounted a horse and rode thirty miles to a telegraph office, where he filed a short bulletin. He then caught a train, made connections with another and wrote his story in a rattling coach under the light of an oil lamp. At 7 A.M. the next morning Smalley, near exhaustion, rushed into the *Tribune* news room and handed the editor his copy.

Whitelaw Reid, of the *Cincinnati Gazette,* was the only correspondent at the battle of Shiloh. He was later hired by the *Tribune,* for which he wrote brilliant accounts of the carnage at Gettysburg.

One of the great scoops of the war was credited to Henry Villard, who, after the battle of Fredericksburg, rode for miles to send his story of the disaster, despite General Burnside's order that no news of it be released. Villard persuaded a steamer captain to take him to Washington but there he found the wires to New York closed down. He nonetheless got the story to the *Herald* office by train.

Albert D. Richardson, of the *Tribune,* lived as dangerously and as adventurously as any hero in fiction. In the spring of 1861 he volunteered to travel through the South, where he risked hanging if recognized. His dispatches were sent in code to a New York bank, which relayed them to his paper. Later he witnessed the bombardment of

Fort Henry from a tree which stood between the fort and the gunboats. Richardson and another *Tribune* reporter, Junius Henri Brown, asked for and received permission to board a Union boat attempting to run the blockade at Vicksburg. The craft was torn by cannon balls and the captain killed. The two newsmen dived into the water and were pulled out by Confederates. Both were imprisoned but escaped and trekked northward, wading icy streams and fleeing howling dogs. Negroes, mountaineers and an unknown girl helped guide them to safety. When they reached the Union lines, Richardson, tears in his eyes, saluted the flag and then dashed for the telegraph office. His story began: "Out of the jaws of death; out of the mouth of hell."

A *New York Herald* reporter, Finley Anderson, was on a Union gunboat when it ran aground in the Louisiana River in 1863. He was captured and spent a year in a Confederate prison. On his release he wrote a four-column story of his experiences.

There were casualties among the correspondents. Phineas Homans, of the *Herald,* died when he fell from the deck of a gunboat. Another *Herald* man, J. P. Dunn, suffered a fatal illness after covering the battle of Vicksburg. One *Chicago Journal* reporter was killed by gunfire at Fort Henry and another was struck by a cannon ball at Shiloh. Arthur B. Fuller, of the *Boston Journal,* fell at Fredericksburg. Eight newsmen were known to have died of camp diseases.

Bradley S. Osbon, of the *New York World,* a naval war specialist, was under fire more than twenty times and was wounded in action during seven different battles. He reported the fall of Fort Sumter in an exclusive eyewitness account. Osbon had been at sea most of his life and was a signal officer on the U.S. revenue cutter *Harriet Lane.* In the battle of Port Royal a shell fragment snipped off most of his bushy red beard.

Many Northern reporters were on the front line despite criticism of some generals that they were gleaning most of their news in Washington taverns. David R. Conyngham, of the *Herald,* once rode into battle and met a general who expressed mock surprise that a correspondent should be so far up front. Before the reporter could reply, their position was raked by artillery and the general fell wounded. Conyngham looked down at the officer and remarked, "You see, sir, that correspondents go farther than generals here." He then galloped off in search of news.

A few editors also ventured into the field. One was Henry J. Raymond, of *The New York Times,* who had covered the Austro-Italian War of 1859. His Civil War service, however, was less than distinguished. He left the battle of Bull Run before it was over, convinced that the North had won. He wired his paper to that effect and then returned to the battlefield to find the Union troops in confused retreat. He filed a substitute story but it was delayed by the censor and the *Times* was beaten by rival papers. Raymond went back to New York, leaving the war correspondence to regular *Times* reporters.

The competition was hottest among the New York newspapers. The *Herald* at one time had sixty-three correspondents in the field. Running close behind were the *Times* and *Tribune,* which had as many as twenty reporters each covering a major battle. The *Herald*'s war corps was directed by the paper's brilliant but eccentric editor, James Gordon Bennett, who had changed the face of American journalism by giving the common reader straight local news of crime, corruption, politics and disasters in language geared to the masses. Bennett spent more than half a million dollars covering the Civil War, giving his reporters expense accounts unheard of in that day. J. Cutler Andrews, in *The North Reports the Civil War,* wrote:

> To employ an army or navy correspondent cost the paper between one and five thousand dollars a year. Special messengers received smaller wages but were accorded travel allowances which frequently exceeded the salaries of the correspondents. Expenditures for horses and campaign outfits were by no means a negligible item: some correspondents used up as many as a half dozen campaign mounts a year.

The New York Times reported the Civil War from the time of the first shell burst over Fort Sumter in Charleston Harbor. The *Times* correspondent there, Dr. George H. C. Salter, who wrote under the name of "Jasper," wired a one-word dispatch to his newspaper: "War."

A number of *Times* men later distinguished themselves in the field. Lorenzo Crounse covered many of the great battles, had two horses shot under him, was wounded and was briefly a Confederate prisoner. William Swinton was so keen a news gatherer that he was almost shot as a spy for eavesdropping on a military strategy huddle between Generals Grant and Meade. Poet Walt Whitman filed articles to the *Times* on the wounded in hospitals. A skilled and fast-moving reporter, Ben C. Truman, presented the *Times* with the news of the battle at Franklin, Tennessee, four days before the War Department heard about it. Henry Raymond, the *Times* editor, thought so highly of Truman that he paid him $100 a week, a magnificent sum in those days. According to biographer Francis Brown, Raymond always paid well for top newsmen and was constantly on the lookout for additions to the *Times* staff. One of them was a youth named Franc B. Wilkie, who, in the summer of 1861, was reporting the war in Missouri for a Dubuque, Iowa, paper. Raymond happened to see one of Wilkie's "letters," liked it and lured him to the *Times* with an offer of $7.50 a column and expenses. Raymond's judgment paid off. Wilkie got an exclusive story of the Union defeat at Lexington after slipping over to the Rebel lines for an eyewitness view of the siege. The young reporter remained loyal to the *Times* even though the *Tribune* offered him $125 in gold for his article. Raymond was so pleased with the report that he gave Wilkie a generous bonus and raised his salary.

The *New York Tribune* was published by Horace Greeley, who a few years earlier had issued what was to become a famous piece of advice: "Go west, young man, and grow up with the country." A devout abolitionist, Greeley felt a keen personal interest in the war and was said to have urged the Union to move into Virginia even though its forces were unprepared. The advance led to the defeat at Bull Run, for which some critics blamed Greeley.

The strongest competition for the New York papers was provided by the *Philadelphia Inquirer,* which sent out a large number of war correspondents and whose owner, William W. Harding, had a close connection with the War Department. Reporters also represented papers in Boston, Chicago and Cincinnati. The *Cincinnati Commercial* was known as the "soldier's paper" because it was so widely read in the western armies of the Union. J. Cutler Andrews writes of the war correspondents:

> They were a picturesque lot with their fancy vests, their stiff collars, and their beards of all shapes and sizes. The *New York Tribune* took a special pride in having its correspondents outshine those employed by the other papers, and so they commonly wore knickerbockers of the finest corduroy, buckskin jackets, high-topped boots of top grain leather, conspicuous gauntlets and broad-brimmed hats.

Many of the reporters were colorful individualists and a far cry from the restrained, objective newsman of today. Swinton, of *The New York Times,* for example, freely criticized generals, a habit that kept him in almost constant hot water with the Union high command. At one time General Grant intercepted Swinton's dispatch and threatened to put him before a firing squad.

An elegant *New York Herald* newshawk, DeBow Randolph Keim, declared that he never read Shakespeare because he was afraid it would influence his own style.

Henry E. Wing, a frail cub reporter for the *Tribune,* traveled freely between the lines disguised as a plantation owner. Wing was the first to bring news of the Battle of the Wilderness. This was after President Lincoln had waited for three days without any word from General Grant. Wing appeared at the tiny settlement of Union Mills, Virginia, and tried to wire his story but was blocked by Secretary of War Stanton, who labeled him a spy and ordered him shot the next morning. However, Lincoln heard of the incident and telegraphed Union Mills, asking if Wing truly had information about the battle. Assured that he did, Lincoln asked Wing if he would come to Washington and tell him what he knew about the fate of the Army of the

Potomac. The reporter agreed if the president would allow him to send 100 words to the *Tribune*.

"Write your hundred words and we will send it at once," Lincoln replied. A few hours later Wing told his story to the president and his cabinet. Then in a private audience with Lincoln, the journalist gave him a message from Grant. "He told me I was to tell you, Mr. President, that there would be no turning back," Wing related. Lincoln kissed the reporter, who, instead of being shot the following morning, rode back to the battlefield. Thereafter, Wing became known as "Lincoln's reporter." In one skirmish Wing, who had lost two fingers at Fredericksburg, seized a rifle and joined the ranks.

Always the enterprising reporter, Wing made arrangements to get the first news of Lee's surrender. He persuaded a member of Grant's staff to come out of the house in which the ceremony took place and wipe his forehead three times with a handkerchief if the Confederate leader did capitulate as expected. When Wing got the signal he dashed off on his horse to file his last dispatch: "War over." He later bought a paper in Connecticut and lived until 1925.

Civil War correspondents were not particularly well paid, even by salary standards of the day. Bernard A. Weisberger, in *Reporters for the Union,* says:

". . . The army's reporter's job . . . was hard and occasionally dangerous, and its pay had no special allurements. Salaries hovered around $25 weekly, with expenses sometimes thrown in."

Stories ran as high as 7,000 words and were frequently written on portfolios carried by the newsmen. If these were not available, any kind of scrap paper was used. When a correspondent returned to his home office he was usually bone-tired from his work in the field. And like the soldier, he frequently suffered shell shock to the point where he was too shaken to function effectively and had to be taken off the line to recuperate. Another nerve-wracking fear was that of being captured and treated as a spy. Joseph B. McCullagh, of the *Cincinnati Enquirer,* was captured by Confederate guerrillas, who forced him to remain with them for several days. He hiked seventy miles back to the Northern lines after his release. A *New York*

Tribune reporter was about to be lynched by Confederate irregulars when he was rescued by a Union patrol.

By today's standards, Civil War newswriting tended to be somewhat formal and opinionated. Yet many of the battlefield accounts were detailed and accurate despite the multiple problems reporters had in getting the story. The dispatches lacked the crispness of modern journalistic writing but readers nevertheless got a graphic description of events. The articles usually had a headline followed by as many as seventeen subheads, a practice that has disappeared among newspapers. Here is a report of the battle of Bull Run from the *New York Tribune* of July 22, 1861.

Our troops, after taking three batteries and gaining a great victory, were eventually repulsed and commenced a retreat on Washington.

The retreat is in good order with the rear well covered by a good column.

Our loss is 2,500 to 3,000.

The fortifications around Washington are strongly reenforced by fresh troops.

ADDITIONAL

It is reported that late yesterday afternoon after the Rebels had been driven from their strongholds at the Run, they were reenforced by Gen. Johnston's forces when the Union army was attacked and driven in disorder from the ground.

The Rebel army numbered 90,000.

THE RETREAT

Washington, Monday, July 22, 1861

After the latest information was received from Centreville at 7½ o'clock last night, a series of events took place in the intensest degree disagreeable. Many confused statements are prevalent but enough is known to warrant the statement that we have suffered in a degree which has cast a gloom over the remnants of the army, and excited the deepest melancholy throughout Washington.

The carnage is tremendously heavy on both sides, and on ours it is represented as frightful. We were advancing and taking their masked batteries gradually, but surely, and driving the enemy toward Manassas Junction when the enemy seemed to have been reenforced by Gen. Johnson [sic], who, it is understood, took command and immediately commenced driving us back, when a panic among our troops suddenly occurred and a regular stampede took place. . . . The panic was so fearful that the whole army became demoralized, and it was impossible to check them either at Centreville or at Fairfax Courthouse . . .

. . . The road from Bull Run was strewed with knapsacks, arms, &c. Some of our troops deliberately threw their guns and appurtenances, the better to facilitate their travel.

The story was unsigned. It may have been put together by a rewrite man in the *Tribune* office from information collected from various sources. The same practice is used by newspapers today.

The *New York Herald*'s account of the fall of Fort Sumter was presented chronologically. Thus, it is not until the thirtieth paragraph of the story that the reader learns that Major Anderson surrendered the fort to the Confederates. The lead or first paragraph said, "The cannonading is going on fiercely from all points—from the vessels outside and all along our coast.

"Fort Sumter is on fire . . . "

These events took place in the morning. The fort gave up in the afternoon of the same day. Today, such a story would be written with the surrender in the lead or first paragraph. The action leading to the fall would have been described in succeeding paragraphs.

Southern newspapers were similar in style but some inclined toward emotionalism in reporting the war. The *Daily Richmond Examiner* on June 2, 1864, said:

We have reliable intelligence from Norfolk that the Confederate boat A.C. White has been surrendered to the enemy by the treachery of its commander, Captain Byers. . . . The traitor is supposed to have conveyed to the enemy full infor-

mation of the disposition and condition of our forces at Norfolk and on the Peninsula . . .

Another communication in that same paper:

We have received by mail some later advices from New
Orleans. The people of New Orleans bow to the brute force
of the conquerer, but do not cringe before it, still maintaining in their perilous and helpless position a lofty dignity and
patriotism.

This dispatch appeared in the June 2, 1864, issue of the *Charleston Daily Courier:*

The Georgia Front—Sherman's career, and the Yankee
hopes built upon it, have ended. The army, which he com-
mands, has at length reached a point whence further flank
movements upon Atlanta may not be executed and cannot be
attempted without great hazard. The confederate commander
has his back upon that city, and is in possession of all the
roads leading to it, and says to the robber host, "thus far shalt
thou come and no further."

Many of the battle stories were eyewitness accounts. One of the
most vivid reports of Gettysburg was written by Whitelaw Reid, who
watched the struggle from Cemetery Hill, a clear observation point
but also the most dangerous one. The following is a section of Reid's
dispatch:

. . . Hancock was wounded; Gibbon succeeded to command—a proved soldier, and ready for the crisis. As the
tempest of fire approached its height, he walked along the
line, and renewed his orders to the men to reserve their fire.
The rebels—three lines deep—came steadily up. They were
in pointblank range. At last the order came! From thrice six
thousand guns there came a sheet of smoky flame, a crash of
leaden death. The line literally melted away; but there came
a second, restless still. It had been our supreme effort—on the
instant we were not equal to another. Up to the rifle pits,
across them, over the barricades—the momentum of their

charge, the mere machine strength of their combined action swept them on. Our thin line could fight but it had not weight enough to oppose this momentum. It was pushed beyond the guns. Right on came the rebels. They were upon the guns, were bayoneting the gunners, were waving their flags above our pieces. But they had penetrated to the fatal point . . .

The Civil War correspondent could also wield a scathing pen when he thought he saw blundering and confusion. Here is what Samuel Fiske, of the *Springfield* (Massachusetts) *Republican,* wrote about the battle at Antietam:

Troops didn't know what they were expected to do, and sometimes in the excitement, fired at their own men. Generals were the scarcest imaginable article, plentiful as they are generally supposed to be. We neither saw nor heard anything of our division commander after starting on our first charge early in the morning, but went in and came out here and there, promiscuously, according to our own ideas, through the whole day.

George Williams, of *The New York Times,* wrote a remarkably accurate account of a Shenandoah Valley battle he had *not* seen. Frustrated in his effort to get to the scene, Williams fashioned his story from interviews with wounded soldiers being transported from the field and with an old farmer who had seen the fight. He paid the farmer ten dollars for his help and rushed off to file the story. The *Times* was the only New York paper to carry anything about the battle. The report was so precise that General Wallace, of the Union force, wondered why he had not seen Williams on the battlefield.

Although the Civil War was fought more than a hundred years ago, reports of battles appeared in the newspapers within forty-eight hours after they happened, which was noteworthy even by twentieth-century standards. That achievement was largely due to the fact that generally the Civil War correspondents were dedicated, conscientious and brave men. They created for American journalism a great tradition which has been carried on to this day.

One of the most colorful war correspondents in history emerged in the post-Civil War period. He was a strapping, adventure-loving Ohioan named Januarius Aloysius MacGahan, who hadn't planned on being a newspaperman at all. In 1868 at the age of twenty-four he went to Europe to improve his general education and study law. He was contentedly at his books in Brussels when Louis Napoleon declared war on Prussia. A *New York Herald* representative happened to be in Brussels and MacGahan offered his services as a correspondent. It was the beginning of a remarkable career. He covered the fighting in the streets of Paris, once getting arrested and then released through the intervention of the American minister in France.

But it was in the conflict between Russia and the Turcoman tribes in Central Asia that MacGahan performed his most remarkable exploit. Ignoring a general's order not to follow Russian troops in their march, MacGahan tramped 900 miles through a blazing desert, where he lived in daily danger of death by sunstroke, thirst or massacre. Some days he slogged through sand up to his knees. On the twenty-ninth day he reached the camp of the Russian column and was promptly arrested. Later, the general relented and allowed him to cover the fighting and he joined the Russian forces in their seizure of the Turcoman stronghold of Khiva.

MacGahan, six feet three and able to speak in a dozen tongues and dialects, remained in Europe for other battles. In the Russian-Turkish war his horse slid over a bank and fell on him, breaking his ankle. He was put on a gun carriage but was thrown off that, injuring himself even more severely. He once rode forty-five miles to deliver one of his dispatches to a courier, who carried it to Bucharest, the nearest place it could be telegraphed. MacGahan died of typhoid fever in 1878. His body was returned to the United States after the Ohio legislature appropriated money for the passage. He was buried with military honors.

In the United States, the Indian Wars in the 1860s and 1870s were reported by a band of newsmen who shocked and thrilled readers with tales of scalpings, massacres and heroic deeds by our soldiers in remote western outposts. The accuracy of the stories depended on the correspondent. Some of these men were rank amateurs who sent wildly exaggerated accounts of the fighting to newspapers in the east. Still others were Army officers whose reports of Indian encounters were heavily biased in favor of the military. But also in the field were experienced reporters who turned out excellent copy on the frontier conflicts. One of them, John F. Finnerty of the *Chicago Times,* wrote:

> Let no easy-going journalist suppose that an Indian campaign is a picnic. If he goes out on such business he must go prepared to ride his forty or fifty miles a day, go sometimes on half rations, sleep on the ground with small covering, roast, sweat, freeze and make the acquaintance of such vermin or reptiles as may flourish in the vicinity of his couch; and finally, be ready to fight Sitting Bull or Satan when the trouble begins, for God and the United States hate noncombatants.

Finnerty covered the Sioux War of 1876, the Ute uprising in 1879 and a campaign against the Apaches in 1881.

Historian Elmo Scott Watson lists twenty-four professional Indian War correspondents, including the famous Henry M. Stanley of "Stanley and Livingstone" fame.

Mark Kellogg, a frontier correspondent serving several papers, was killed with Colonel Custer and all his troops in the historic battle at the Little Big Horn. Ridgeway Glover, the first photographer to take pictures of the Indian hostilities, was killed, scalped and mutilated by Sioux Indians after he had left the safety of Fort Kearney in Wyoming to look for subject matter. He had also written for various publications, including *Leslie's Weekly.*

One of the most outstanding of the Indian correspondents was Charles Sanford Diehl, of the *Chicago Times* and later the Associated Press. Diehl, who started his newspaper career at age fourteen in Illinois, not only covered the Indian campaigns but got an exclusive interview with Chief Sitting Bull, who gave the reporter his autograph. The Indian leader also revealed that he was asleep in his teepee when Custer (Sitting Bull called him Long Hair) attacked and said he did not even take part in the historic battle at the Little Big Horn. The newsman also made friends with William F. "Buffalo Bill" Cody, who carried his dispatches to the telegraph office at Bismarck, North Dakota. Diehl took part in some of the fighting as well. Once an officer, seeing him crouched behind a barricade with a rifle aimed at hostile Indians, shouted: "Come out of that. You are not paid to be killed. We are."

Diehl survived, as did most of his colleagues covering the Indian Wars. Some lived to report America's next major conflict in the nineteenth century, the Spanish-American War.

2

The "Little" War

ON THE NIGHT OF FEBRUARY 15, 1898, THE UNITED STATES BATTLE-ship *Maine* was blown up in Havana harbor, killing 260 crewmen. The cause of the explosion was never satisfactorily explained, but most Americans at the time blamed Spanish agents. Less than three months later Congress declared war on Spain. The conflict lasted 113 days.

It is quite probable that we would have fought Spain even without the *Maine* incident. A wave of sympathy had been building up for Cuba, which was under Spanish rule and torn by civil strife. The newspapers, particularly those in New York, were whipping up sentiment for the Cuban rebels and hatred for the Spanish "oppressors." Some historians claim the press was actually responsible for the war, but it's more likely that the papers fanned a flame that was already white hot. America was young and beginning to feel its muscles. It looked with envy at the great nations and wanted to emulate them in military power. And there also was the United States' traditional support of the underdog. After all, we had won a mighty struggle to free ourselves from a colonial yoke.

In any event, the press played a bizarre and spectacular role in the war. One of the most rabid war advocates was William Randolph Hearst, publisher of the *New York Journal*. The *Journal* began a campaign several months before the war on behalf of a Cuban patriot, Evangelina Cisneros, who faced a Spanish court-martial on a charge of treason. So vivid was the *Journal's* appeal that prominent persons appealed to the Pope and the Queen Regent of Spain for the girl's release. Then one day the *Journal* announced in huge black headlines:

EVANGELINA CISNEROS RESCUED BY THE JOUR-NAL; AN AMERICAN NEWSPAPER ACCOMPLISHES AT A SINGLE STROKE WHAT THE RED TAPE OF DIPLOMACY FAILED UTTERLY TO BRING ABOUT IN MANY MONTHS.

And indeed *Journal* hirelings had spirited Miss Cisneros out of a Havana prison. The newspaper taunted its rivals with an "ear" which read: "The *Journal's* Motto: While Others Talk, the *Journal* Acts." Even before the Cisneros escapade the newspaper had supplied its readers with copious accounts of alleged Spanish cruelty to the Cubans. Top newsman Richard Harding Davis and artist Frederic Remington had provided graphic examples of starving Cuban children. The story is told that Hearst, having sent Remington to Cuba to illustrate the conflict, was unimpressed when the artist cabled back that he could find no war. The publisher, the account goes, fired off the following reply: "You furnish the pictures and I'll furnish the war."

The *Journal's* chief competitor, Joseph Pulitzer's *World*, was not far behind in generating war hysteria. Editorially it took a more moderate tone than the *Journal*, but its headlines sometimes outdid the other in size and shrillness. The entire front page of one issue was devoted to the *Maine* explosion. The circulation of each paper ran well over a million as eager readers snapped up copies. The cry "Remember the *Maine*" became a national slogan. For both newspapers there also was a ready-made villain—Spanish General Don Valeriano Weyler y Nicolau, who was dubbed "Butcher Weyler" by correspondents. This was not the finest hour of American journalism. Neither was our military effort exemplary. Students of the Spanish-American War generally agree that it was ill-conceived, badly planned and loosely fought by the United States. Our biggest advantage, historians say, lay in the fact that the Spaniards made even more mistakes. Frank Freidel wrote: "Shocking revelations of the inadequacies of the War Department and even the Navy, ridiculous quarrels among rival commanders, and the brevity of the conflict gave the . . . war something of a disreputable and quasi-comic opera aspect."

Still, the campaign in Cuba produced an array of high-caliber and colorful correspondents, including the redoubtable Richard Harding Davis, famed novelists Stephen Crane and Frank Norris, J. L. Stickney, Stephen Bonsal, Tommy Dieuade, Sylvester Scovell, James Creelman, Charles M. Pepper and many others. They came from all over the United States and from abroad. More than one hundred reporters converged on Tampa, Florida, the staging area for troops being shipped to Cuba. On the night of June 9, 1898, most of them were given Army permission to board the headquarters ship *Seguranca* for the ninety-mile trip to Cuba. They were dressed in an assortment of olive hunting suits, white ducks and business suits. Some carried revolvers, canteens, bed rolls, machetes, cameras, binoculars and, of course, notebooks. The old Army game of "hurry up and wait" was in force even then. It was not until June 14 that the ship finally sailed. An estimated four hundred other newsmen and artists found their way to Cuba during the hostilities. It was a well-covered war, however brief.

Surely the star of this journalistic parade was Richard Harding Davis, who had already gained fame as a roving correspondent and adventurer. No fiction writer could have produced a more dashing figure. Davis was so handsome that the renowned illustrator Charles Dana Gibson used him as a model. His manners were impeccable, his ideals high and his personal courage beyond question. He was also something of a snob and possibly the most opinionated reporter in the history of American journalism.

According to biographer Fairfax Downey, Davis "was born with a silver pen in his mouth." His father was an editorial writer for the *Philadelphia Inquirer* and his mother wrote fiction for the *Atlantic Monthly*. Richard inherited their literary gifts but he was not a scholar. He flunked out of three colleges—Swarthmore, Lehigh and Johns Hopkins—the victim of mathematics and chemistry. Even so, young Davis was a commanding figure on campus. In his freshman year he wrote two professional stories for the local newspaper and a national magazine. He also contributed to college publications, taking stands against cheating, hazing and fraternities. He compiled these articles in a privately printed volume entitled *Adventures of My Freshman Year* and sold it at twenty-five cents a copy.

In 1886, Davis, without a degree but with a budding reputation as a writer, got a job as a reporter on the *Philadelphia Record* through the help of his father. Ink-stained staffers stared wordlessly when Richard Harding Davis appeared for his first day of work. His suit was of the most fashionable English cut and he carried a cane so huge that his colleagues later named it "Davis' railroad tie." An elegant pair of yellow gloves completed his ensemble. The young cub quickly raised the blood pressure of the *Record*'s crusty city editor, James S. Chambers Jr., who referred scornfully to cane-carrying reporters as "journalists." Davis and Chambers were on a collision course from the start. For one thing, the editor resented having Davis hired "over his head." But what galled him most was the yellow gloves. Davis claimed he only wore them in cold weather but Chambers was convinced they were an affectation unbecoming a newspaperman. For three months Davis chased fire wagons, covered murders and handled other stories as a general assignment reporter at seven dollars a week. Through it all he maintained his debonair manner and stylish attire while Chambers seethed behind his desk.

Then one night the editor saw the opportunity for which he had been waiting. He spotted Davis lounging in the sports department, the notes for an unwritten story sticking out of his pocket.

"Take off your gloves and coat and get to work," Chambers bellowed. Davis turned away from the football scores, sauntered over to his desk and began writing the story—with his gloves on. Chambers' face reddened in rage. When he finally got the copy he blue-penciled it unmercifully and then called Davis over. "You're through here," he told him, his face at last breaking into a smile of sheer delight.

"Well," the young man replied, "I suppose that's the way it must be." He then offered the city editor his gloved hand for a farewell shake. Chambers' reaction is unprintable.

Richard Harding Davis was not long jobless. He landed on the new *Evening Sun* in New York at thirty dollars a week. Fourteen months later he was getting fifty dollars. At this period he also began writing short stories which were widely popular among college students and other young people. Davis was only twenty-six years old and already the talk of the literary world. He was named managing editor of *Harper's Weekly* but left that magazine to go abroad as a free-lance writer. An admirer of the British style, he lived for a time at Oxford University but not as a student. He began to make a lot of money, writing travel pieces, fiction and anything else that promised a fat fee. Back in America, William Randolph Hearst offered him $500 to cover the Yale-Princeton football game, a record price for a single assignment. In 1897, Scribners published his greatest financial success, the novel *Soldiers of Fortune,* which sold more than a half million copies. Davis spent his earnings lavishly, acquiring a reputation as a man about town and fashion plate. He became a celebrity.

Davis and other newsmen were already in Key West, Florida, trying to get to Cuba when Hearst offered him $3,000 and expenses to cover the insurrection against the Spaniards for the *Evening Journal.* Davis joined the Cuban rebels and soon became one of the most ardent champions of their cause. His copy was studded with examples of "Spanish brutality" and he demanded United States intervention. Such sensationalism was made to order for Hearst, who was whipping up war frenzy at home while running a neck-and-neck circulation race with Pulitzer's *World*. The Hearst-Davis combine appeared to be an outstanding instance of publisher-reporter solidarity. Then came the "Olivetti Affair."

Spanish officials boarded an American ship, the *Olivetti,* in Havana harbor and supposedly searched three Cuban women for "treasonable papers." Davis cabled a story of the incident to the *Journal,* which must have regarded it as heaven sent. Huge black banner headlines proclaimed:

DOES OUR FLAG PROTECT WOMEN? INDIGNITIES PRACTICED BY SPANISH OFFICIALS ON BOARD AMERICAN VESSELS. RICHARD HARDING DAVIS DESCRIBES SOME STARTLING PHASES OF CUBAN SITUATION. REFINED YOUNG WOMEN STRIPPED AND SEARCHED BY BRUTAL SPANIARDS WHILE UNDER OUR FLAG ON THE OLIVETTI.

There was also a half-page illustration by Frederic Remington, who had returned from Cuba weeks before. It showed a nude young woman cowering while Spanish soldiers searched her clothing.

This was too much even for Davis. He cabled a denial of the *Journal* version, declaring that the women had been searched by a police matron in the privacy of their staterooms. His story had not made that point clear, he admitted. Hearst published Davis' disclaimer but the two parted company and the reporter never again worked for the *Journal.*

Richard Harding Davis left Cuba in February of 1897 and returned to London, where he got wind of a Greek-Turkish war. Hired by the *London Times,* Davis sailed for Greece to report the outbreak.

Davis' first battle was with the aide-de-camp of Crown Prince Constantine of Greece. The officer, who was anti-*Times,* refused at first to accredit Davis, who was both shocked and angry. The idea of not granting Richard Harding Davis press credentials was unthinkable. So he challenged the aide to a duel, giving him the choice of swords, pistols, clubs, fists "or any weapon you choose." The Greek official blanched and issued Davis his papers. He soon put them to use. While other correspondents ran off on a wild goose chase, Davis and John Bass of the *Journal* were the only press witnesses to an eight-hour infantry and artillery battle, which proved to be the major engagement of the war. The two reporters lay in a muddy trench with Greek soldiers, Davis calmly taking pictures and making notes amid a deadly cross-fire.

When he returned to London, Davis was acclaimed the foremost war correspondent of his day. Legends began to circulate about his front-line activities. It was reputed that he said his prayers every night, wrote his mother every day and always carried a dinner coat in his field kit. Some less favored reporters pointed to his amazing luck in always being where the action was. This was true of Davis' journalistic career, but he also had a sharp sense of news and was never afraid to go after it.

Less than a year later the United States was at war with Spain. A number of newspapers and magazines bid for Davis' service in Cuba, including the *London Times, Scribner's* and James Gordon Bennett's *New York Herald Tribune,* which got him. As usual, Davis went in style. A letter from the Navy Department secured him a berth aboard Admiral Sampson's flagship blockading Havana. But this was too tame for a man of Davis' temperament. He left the "luxury cruise" and went to Tampa, where American troops were gathering. With the arrival of Theodore Roosevelt and his "Rough Riders," a crack cavalry unit, Davis saw his story. The newsman liked the Rough Riders' discipline, crisp khaki uniforms and well-kept rifles. They were in sharp contrast to the run-of-the-mill volunteers who poured into Florida. There was one sour note in Davis' favorable appraisal of the new outfit. He had met Teddy Roosevelt before and the two were not taken with each other. Roosevelt, a hearty, outdoor type, regarded Davis as a dude and also suspected him because of his pro-British attitude. The newspaperman felt that

Roosevelt was not military enough, a conviction that was confirmed in his mind when he saw him dining with two of his sergeants. Such familiarity violated Davis' rigid sense of caste.

Nonetheless, Davis was not one to let a personal feeling interfere with a good story. He attached himself to the Rough Riders, followed them to Cuba and then joined them in the first major battle of the war at Las Guasimas. In the thick of the firing, the newsman grabbed a carbine dropped by a wounded man and charged through the brush, emptying the weapon and reloading. At one point he directed fire on a group of Spaniards and at another he ordered a dazed lieutenant and his troops to push on. Men fell beside Davis and bullets whizzed past his head. When Edward Marshall of the *Journal* was hit, Davis found stretcher bearers for him. The wounded correspondent was hauled off, still scribbling notes for his story.

It was Davis, more than any other reporter, who was responsible for the reams of publicity American newspapers gave to the Rough Riders. He also covered the decisive battles of San Juan Hill and El Caney, despite frequent attacks of sciatica, a lower back ailment that afflicted him most of his life. In addition to his combat coverage, Davis wrote several pieces denouncing United States authorities for bad management of the war. He complained, among other things, of the lack of tomatoes in the troops' standard ration of hardtack and bacon. His outspoken criticism earned him a number of enemies in and out of government.

Richard Harding Davis covered four wars before he died on April 11, 1916, at the age of fifty-two. He was a legend in his own lifetime and was perhaps the most romantic figure in the annals of journalism. His correspondence and books, novels and plays made him rich and famous. He had two wives, the second a chorus girl, and spent money as fast as he made it. He was nearly penniless when he died. Even his field trips were expensive. In the Boer War, for example, his entourage and equipment consisted of three servants (one did nothing but polish his boots), three ponies, two oxen, a green tent with windowpanes and ventilators, a bathtub, folding bed, two tables, a cart and his wife.

Davis, of course, did not have a monopoly on bravery and enterprise in the Spanish-American War. James Creelman, of the *New York Journal,* led an attack on a fortification in the El Caney skirmish, seizing a Spanish flag as a trophy for his paper. At that second he was wounded in the back and arm and fell unconscious. In his memoirs Creelman wrote:

> Someone knelt in the grass beside me and put his hand on my fevered head. Opening my eyes, I saw Mr. Hearst, the proprietor of the *New York Journal,* a straw hat with a bright ribbon on his head, a revolver at his belt, and a pencil and notebook in his hand.
>
> The man who had provoked the war had come to see the result with his own eyes, and, finding one of his correspondents prostrate, was doing the work himself. Slowly he took down my story of the fight. Again and again the tingling of Mauser bullets interrupted, but he seemed unmoved. The battle had to be reported somehow.
>
> "I'm sorry you're hurt"—and his face was radiant with enthusiasm—"wasn't it a splendid fight? We must beat every paper in the world!"

Creelman wasn't delirious. William Randolph Hearst actually was in Cuba, the leader of a team of twenty writers, artists and photographers who came on his yacht *Buccaneer.* The boat also contained a small printing plant which produced a four-page edition of the *Journal* for distribution to the troops. After one naval battle, a "task force" from the *Buccaneer* went ashore in a launch and captured about twenty-five soaked and unresisting Spanish sailors who had fled their sinking ship. Hearst himself strapped on a six-shooter and waded into the surf to assist in the seizure. Later, the publisher signaled the American flagship that "We have prisoners for the fleet." The *Journal,* of course, ran a full account of the "feat" the next day.

That was not Creelman's first attempt at derring-do. In the Greek-Turkish war he was captured by the Turks but turned the experience into a triumph by getting an exclusive interview with their field marshal. He was freed in time to cover the famous battle of Meluna Pass, where he found himself in competition with an English reporter who was as gutty and enterprising as he was. They both raced back to the Greek city of Larissa to file their stories, Creelman on a small pony and the Britisher on a splendid cavalry mount. The American's horse was sturdy but the mountains and the mud proved too much for it and the newsman was forced to walk. He was attacked by a pack of savage dogs, which he tried to fend off by setting fire to the grass around him. It was wet and would not burn. Just when he seemed doomed two Greek soldiers in starched skirts appeared and rescued him. When he got to the telegraph office the Englishman was leisurely dictating his dispatch. A lesser man might have thrown up his hands in defeat but not Creelman. Somehow, he persuaded the telegraph superintendent to interrupt his rival's message and send his story instead.

Wars always have had a strong attraction for those with a literary bent, and the conflict with Spain was no exception. Among the correspondents were men who were not so much interested in the hard news as they were in what the common soldiers felt. One of these reporters was Stephen Crane. Crane was only twenty-six when he shipped to Cuba for the *New York World,* but he had already covered the Greek-Turkish war and had scored a critical success with his novel *The Red Badge of Courage.*

Stephen Crane was born in 1871, the fourteenth child of a New Jersey minister. The family moved to Port Jervis, New York, when he was a small child. His mother wrote articles for Methodist papers and did some corresponding for the *New York Tribune.* He attended Syracuse University but did not receive a degree. His early newspaper career was unpromising; the *New York Herald* fired him at nineteen and for a while he lived a hand-to-mouth existence as a free-lance writer.

Rejected by the Navy as physically unfit, Crane signed on with the *World* as a means of getting to Cuba. He was sick with tuberculosis during most of his time there, sometimes to the point of not knowing where he was. He dragged his thin, wasted body into the jungles and once made a reconnaissance of a Spanish outpost forty miles from the American lines. Crane also waded ashore with the marines at Guantánamo Bay and even ran errands for the lieutenant of his unit. On one occasion, the young correspondent received official notice for his coolness under fire.

Crane's dispatches were filed sporadically, but that mattered little. Few of his stories concerned actions, victories or defeats. He wrote mostly about the human interest side of the war—the thoughts of the common soldiers, anecdotes, etc. Many of his articles were really essays rather than news reports. But when he dealt with the immediate side of the war he did it in a brisk, readable and professional manner. Here is one of his *World* accounts of a Rough Rider engagement:

PLAYA DEL ESTE, June 25—Lieut. Col. Roosevelt's Rough Riders, who were ambushed yesterday, advanced at daylight without any particular plan of action as to how to strike the enemy.

The men marched noisily through the narrow road in the woods, talking volubly, when suddenly they struck the Spanish lines.

Fierce fire was poured into their ranks and there began a great fight in the thickets.

Nothing of the enemy was visible to our men, who displayed much gallantry. In fact, their bearing was superb, and couldn't have been finer.

They suffered a heavy loss, however, due to the remarkably wrong idea of how the Spanish bushwhack.

It was simply a gallant blunder.

Crane also wrote a moving description of his encounter with the wounded correspondent Edward Marshall.

. . . Meanwhile, a soldier passing near me said: "There's a correspondent up there all shot to hell."

He guided me to where Edward Marshall lay, shot through the body. The following conversation ensued:

"Hello, Crane!"

"Hello, Marshall! In hard luck, old man?"

"Yes, I'm done for."

"Nonsense! You're all right, old boy. What can I do for you?"

"Well, you might file my despatches. I don't mean file 'em ahead of your own, old man—but just file 'em if you find it handy."

R. W. Stallman and E. R. Hagemann said that Crane filed Marshall's stories, trudging six miles to the coast in 100-degree heat to find a cable. As a result he missed out on most of the fighting at Las Guasimas.

Crane and other correspondents had a great deal of trouble sending their stories back to the States. There was no telegraphic communication between Cuba and the United States mainland, which meant that reporters had to use all their ingenuity to relay their copy to their offices. Several of the major newspapers had their own dispatch boats for use by correspondents. The dispatch boats usually took reporters' copy to Key West, where it was telegraphed to the newspaper offices. Correspondents chartered yachts, tugs, steamships and any other kind of craft that could make the run to Florida. The Associated Press had five such vessels and the New York papers had from two to six ships each for carrying correspondents and messages. The larger newspapers filed as many as 5,000 words a day from Key West at a cost of five cents per word. The *New York Journal* said it paid $3,000 a day in cable costs during the war, a sum even today's editors would consider high. Pulitzer's *World,* in attempting to compete with Hearst's *Journal,* nearly went bankrupt.

J. L. Stickney, of the *New York Herald,* who witnessed the battle of Manila Bay from the bridge of an American warship, sent his copy to Hong Kong by steamer because the Manila cable was down. The *Herald* published his story under a six-column banner headline but gave him no by-line—even though Admiral Dewey himself had congratulated the paper on Stickney's work. According to historian-journalist Gregory Mason, Stickney and Tommy Dieuade, of the *New York Evening Sun,* produced some of the best writing of the war. Mason added: ". . . it never occurred to the newspapers of

Spanish-American War days that staff men like Dieuade deserved the recognition of a by-line."

However, by-lines were heaped lavishly on the special writers, such as Davis, Crane, Stephen Bonsal, Julian Hawthorne, John Fox and Frank Norris, who later became an important novelist. The works of such artists as Frederic Remington, Harry Grant Dart and Howard Chandler Christy were also signed. The practice of not giving by-lines to staff writers virtually disappeared by World War II, when most combat correspondents received recognition for their work.

By Civil War standards, reporters in Cuba were bothered little by censorship. Newspapers suffered no restrictions in publishing reports of American military movements and troop locations. Grant Squires, a former *New York Tribune* reporter, was appointed a military censor in New York early in the war, but the effort had little success. Generals and naval officers sometimes tried to keep newsmen out of certain areas, but even this had small effect. On one occasion, however, General Shafter, the American commander in Cuba, ordered all Hearst reporters out of captured Santiago and made it stick.

But news was not handed on a platter to the correspondents. After all, the Army and Navy were fighting a war and had to give that their primary attention. Newsmen, for example, were not kept informed of the movements of warships and had to stay with the fleet day and night. This was dangerous because fighting vessels in a war zone douse their lights at night. It was not only hard to see them but the correspondents in their dispatch boats ran the risk of being fired upon as enemy craft. George Kennan, of *Outlook* magazine, recalled a conversation with a destroyer deck officer, who told him, "We can't afford to take any chances of torpedo boats. If you show up at night in the neighborhood of this ship, we shall fire on you first and ask questions afterward."

"But how are we to know where you are?" another correspondent inquired.

"That's your business," the officer retorted.

Generally, the correspondents lived with the troops, enduring the privations and lack of proper medical and sanitary facilities which characterized the Spanish-American War. Of the 306,000 troops in Cuba, 5,400 died in service; but less than 400 of these were combat casualties. Most were victims of disease caused by filthy living conditions. A number of newsmen also fell ill, some fatally.

Correspondents also had the problem of getting their own food. In a letter to a friend, Stephen Bonsal, *New York Herald,* wrote:

Some time ago you were good enough to inquire what the war correspondents did during the few moments that were left them from their daily task of running the army, and at times of putting under necessary discipline the Commander-in-Chief. Your inquiry is almost too direct, but I think you will find it in a measure answered in my reply to the question you marked No. 2 in order of importance, and which—I think I recall the way you put it—read, "And did you really have to eat the soldier's food?"

Honestly, we did not have to eat it. We were not forced to, we were but rarely invited to, and to tell you the truth, we only did it when the soldiers were not looking . . .

To be perfectly frank, from the day of landing, we, too, have had our own little troubles with the Commissary Department. Upon our passes issued by the War Department we were informed that we could draw rations if we paid for them; but, as a matter of fact, we could not. How many times we went to the commissary's store and returned—well, empty-handed! . . . During the two sad days after San Juan we were most of us living upon the charity of the army, picking up the unconsidered trifles that fell from the tables (this is a figure of speech of course, as they ate on the ground) of our generous army friends. We all had, of course, great fat rolls of greenbacks in our pockets, mouldy with rain, and small coins until our pockets bulged out and filthy lucre ran upon the ground. Who would stop to pick the stuff up? Not I, though I have been very pennywise in my day. Money was dirt cheap on the road to Santiago. We shied nickels and dimes at the landcrabs, which they picked up and carried away in their "strikers." It was our only sport.

North American, John T. McCutcheon, *Chicago Daily Tribune,* and Julian Ralph, who was sent by the *London Daily Mail.* Censorship was strict, particularly on the British side. Ralph discovered that one British censor had tossed his dispatches in the wastebasket for ten days without even telling him about it. Later, the reporter was informed that the only message he could file to England was a description of a sandstorm. In time, however, regulations were eased to permit battle accounts to be transmitted abroad.

For Davis, the Boer War was also a wedding trip, as his bride accompanied him to South Africa. But because of regulations she was permitted only to go as far as Cape Town. Davis joined a British unit and promptly earned a rebuke by officers when he returned salutes, a gesture forbidden to civilians by custom. Later, the doughty reporter got into even more hot water with the English because of a dispatch he filed from the Dutch side.

While in Pretoria, Davis visited British officers locked up in a schoolhouse serving as a makeshift prisoner-of-war camp. Davis, who had rather Victorian ideas of proper behavior, was shocked when the officers shouted to girls passing by their barred windows. He wrote: "Personally, I cannot see why being a prisoner would make me think I might speak to women I did not know, but some of the English officers apparently thought their new condition carried that privilege with it." Davis also objected to "offensive" caricatures of Boers the captives had drawn on the walls.

Among the British correspondents in the Boer War was a sandy-haired young man named Winston Spencer Churchill, whose mother was an American. Churchill, then twenty-five, served in South Africa both as a correspondent for the *London Morning Post* and as an officer aide to three British generals. The scion of a distinguished family and already a veteran of war reporting in India, Winston Churchill was eager for his new assignment. A few days after he arrived, an armored train on which he was riding was derailed and shelled by Boers. Churchill helped clear the wreckage at the risk of his life and almost made his escape in the engine. But he hopped off to help an officer in trouble and was captured. Several days later

Bonsal went on to explain that the soldiers guarding the commissaries usually told correspondents there was only enough food for the soldiers, a fact which was all too true. The correspondent said he was once able to get food by giving a supply sergeant a Turkish coin in exchange. The sergeant had disdained American money as being worthless in Cuba.

Correspondents set up their headquarters at Siboney, a coastal town that served as the military supply base for the assault on Santiago. The reporters took over three buildings, naming the street "Newspaper Row." They wrote their dispatches in Siboney after returning from the front. Before the Santiago campaign, several of the correspondents became restless for action and talked about organizing a press battalion to seek out the enemy. The fighting came soon enough, however, and the newsmen marched in with the troops.

One of the most colorful correspondents in Cuba was Sylvester Scovel, of the *World,* who had covered the rebel insurrection on the island long before America declared war on Spain. Once he was jailed by the Spanish and freed only after his newspaper had waged a strong campaign in his behalf. During the war, Scovel reportedly won the favor of American officers by spying behind the Spanish lines. But whatever consideration this had gained him was lost at the flag-raising ceremonies in Santiago.

As the flag was being hoisted, the photographers aimed their cameras upward. Scovel began climbing to the headquarters roof so he would be in the pictures. General Shafter spotted him and thundered, "Throw him off." The nimble newsman clambered down before the soldiers got to him, marched up to General Shafter and swung a punch at his nose, missing it by an inch. Shafter ordered Scovel locked up, but this proved difficult since there was no jail nearby. A lieutenant solved the problem by forcing Scovel to mount an empty pedestal which had supported the statue of a Spanish patriot knocked down by Cubans. Menaced by bayonets, the unfortunate newsman had to stand in the blazing sun until the Army found a prison cell for him.

But despite such incidents, the Spanish-American War elevated the combat correspondent to a high place in American journalism. The reporters in Cuba were a tough, nervy bunch of men who would go anywhere for a story. Their accounts were not always objective but through their efforts, often under fire, the American people knew what our troops were doing in Cuba. Several of the correspondents had covered other wars and would, like Richard Harding Davis, report still more. As wars go, the Spanish-American conflict was small. But for the correspondents who were there, it was a great experience.

3

Dateline:
The World

FOR THE RESTLESS AND ADVENTUROUS AMERICAN NEWSMAN T period between the Spanish-American War in 1898 and the outbr of World War I in 1914 offered plenty of action. Reporters from United States fanned out to cover the Boer War in South Africa 1899, the Boxer Rebellion in China, 1900, the Russo-Japanese V 1904, and the Balkan Wars in 1912-1913. In addition, Ameri correspondents reported the Mexican revolution from 1910 thro United States intervention in 1914.

The Boer War was fought between Dutch settlers in South A and the British who were attempting to establish commercial r there. American journalists on the scene included the roving Ric Harding Davis, Jack London, Hugh Sutherland of the *Philade*

he escaped from a Dutch prison stockade and made his way through 300 miles of hostile territory to safety in Portuguese Africa, despite one of the biggest manhunts in history. Churchill was said to have disguised himself as a woman, a Dutch policeman and a waiter to escape detection. He crossed the border in a freight car, reported to the British consul and then returned to the British forces in South Africa until the end of the war.

The Dutch had issued this "wanted" poster after Churchill's escape:

"Englishman, twenty-five years old, about five feet eight inches high, indifferent build, walks a little with a bend forward, pale appearance, red-brownish hair, small moustache, hardly perceptible, talks through his nose, cannot pronounce the letter S properly, and does not know any Dutch."

Churchill was hailed as a hero in England. After the war he became a member of the British parliament. In 1914, F. Lauriston Bullard wrote:

". . . But whatever he [Churchill] is and whatever he may become, it is certain that this man of versatility and industry, with his passion for being in the midst of things, will never enjoy life more than did he when he was winning the attention of the world as a newspaper special and a soldier."

Winston Churchill, of course, went on to become prime minister of England during her gravest hour in World War II. His inspiring leadership was a major factor in Britain's final victory.

The Boxer Rebellion, a short-lived but bloody affair, produced one of the great journalistic scoops in history. The Boxers were a nationalist Chinese force. They mounted a murderous attack on the city of Peking, which was under international control. The world knew little or nothing of the fighting which threatened the lives of many foreigners, including Americans. Robert Coltman, correspondent for the *Chicago Record,* was inside the besieged city. While bullets spattered around him, he wrote his dispatch. He then gave it to a ragged beggar, who smuggled it through the Boxer lines to a cable office. The story electrified the world.

American and other correspondents were severely hamstrung by censorship and other controls in the Russo-Japanese War. The Associated Press became so desperate for news that it commissioned two Russians as correspondents. *The New York Times* evaded censorship by using wireless to report a naval battle. Radio was so new that neither side had figured a way to control it. Other reporters were not so lucky. John Fox, an American correspondent, wrote: "Of this war in detail I know no more than I should have known had I stayed home—and it has taken me seven months to learn that it was meant that I should not know more."

A cartoon in the British magazine *Punch* at that time shows a Japanese officer and a correspondent. The officer is saying to the reporter: "Abjectly we desire to distinguish honourable newspaper man by honourable badge." At the same time he is tying a cloth marked "censorship" over the newsman's eyes.

Richard Harding Davis also was on hand for the Russo-Japanese conflict but since most correspondents were kept far from the fighting, he spent most of his time covering Japanese festivals. He finally left in disgust; Davis was no man to sit idly by while armies fought. Jack London, already renowned as a novelist, saw some action in Manchuria.

On Easter Sunday 1914, headlines in the *New York Sun* announced:

WILSON TO ASK CONGRESS TODAY TO SANCTION INTERVENTION; NORTH DAKOTA SAILS FOR MEXICAN WATERS: THOUSANDS CHEER THE BIG DREADNOUGHT

The headlines were accurate. The United States had jumped into a revolution in Mexico that began in 1910. President Woodrow Wilson sent troops after the bandit-general Pancho Villa raided Texas border towns and killed eighteen American engineers who had been invited to operate mines in Mexico.

There was more involved than Villa, however. American financial interests were believed threatened and President Wilson was under pressure to throw United States weight around in Mexico. An excuse for such action came when Mexican troops arrested a boatload of American sailors in the port of Tampico on April 9, 1914. General Victoriana Huerta, the Mexican leader, later apologized; but he turned down a request for a formal salute of the American flag as demanded by custom. War fever and indignation swept through the United States. A few days later Wilson was informed that a German ship planned to unload arms for Huerta's government at Vera Cruz. The president ordered American troops to take the port.

It wasn't much of a war but it was the closest one at hand, and scores of American reporters beat a path to Mexico. Some of these men—like Frazier Hunt, John Reed, Richard Harding Davis and William G. Shepherd—later covered the Western Front in World War I.

American warships shelled Vera Cruz and marines occupied the city. Dudley Harmon, special correspondent for the *New York Sun,* cabled back a rather florid account of the battle under the headline:

ALL VERA CRUZ UNDER CONTROL; 6 MORE AMER-
ICANS WOUNDED; GUNS OF WARSHIPS SILENCE
MEXICAN SHARPSHOOTERS—OCCUPATION FORCE
SEARCHES EVERY HOME FOR ARMED CITIZENS

Harmon's story read in part:

. . . A great many of the snipers were convicts, released from the local prison by General Maass before he fled. Armed with rifles from the Mexican armories and inflamed by liberal draughts of mescal, they were dangerous and treacherous adversaries. With them intense excitement prevailed. Half crazed peons ran hither and thither, shouting out aimlessly and apparently not knowing where to seek refuge. With them were a few civilians who hate the "gringos" and fight them whenever they can. The remainder of the resistance was composed of riffraff of the city, criminals and degenerates of all sorts, with a few ignorant peons really actuated by love of their country and trying to do their patriotic duty.

In strange contrast to the Mexicans were the advancing marines. They marched to their work like a skilled surgeon to an operation. Angered to a fever heat by the killing of their comrades yesterday they nevertheless preserved every decorum of discipline and seemed to bear no malice or desire for revenge. The parade-like line marched across the great square with the natives fleeing before them.

A young and quick-witted United Press reporter, William Shepherd, beat everybody on the Vera Cruz landing and he wasn't even there! As the UP's Mexico City correspondent, Shepherd was friendly with the Western Union operator there. When he learned that the United States fleet was enroute to Vera Cruz he headed at once for the telegraph office. Happily for Shepherd, the Mexico City operator was a pal of his counterpart in Vera Cruz, who transmitted a play-by-play account of the American seizure of the port. The Vera Cruz telegrapher told of Mexican forces firing on American ships, the marines going ashore and the fighting in the streets. Every nerve of Bill Shepherd's body tingled as the messages continued. It's the excitement that every reporter feels when he knows he's close to a big story.

Finally, the Vera Cruz operator signed off, saying, "They're now shooting through this building. Good-by."

Shepherd hurriedly wrote a story of the invasion but the Mexico City operator wouldn't send it because of censorship. Shepherd shrugged amiably and walked out. A few minutes later he was at the censor's office, where he penciled another message—in code. It was addressed to Margaret Howard, the wife of UP manager Roy Wilson Howard, in New York. The telegram read: FILMS FORWARDED VERACRUZ STOP JOHNSON RETURNING VIA-RAILROAD MEXICITY.

The censor was nervous over the words Vera Cruz but Shepherd convinced him the missive was harmless. The wire was dispatched and as soon as she received it, Mrs. Howard telephoned her husband, who knew exactly what to do with it. Minutes later United Press moved this bulletin over its wires:

MEXICO CITY, April 21 (United Press) American troops are in Vera Cruz and will report their occupation of the city to Washington from there over cable lines to which they now have access. Mexican forces are retiring by rail toward Mexico City.

Despite the UP scoop, the United States government denied the marine landing at Vera Cruz and the rival Associated Press sent out a story implying that UP's dispatch was a phony. Seven hours later Washington officially announced the seizure of Vera Cruz. Shepherd, meanwhile, caught a train for that city to report the fighting. At first he was a bit put out because his office had not sent him a congratulatory note on his clean beat. But then he realized that such a cable would have probably placed him before a Mexican firing squad, since it would have tipped off officials to the coded story. "I'm much obliged to New York for being alive," he observed later.

Shepherd was often commended for his simple and moving style. When asked how he did it, Shepherd explained: "Why, there's nothing to it. I just write for the milkman in Omaha. I figure if he can understand what I'm writing, then everybody can understand it." The Omaha milkman became a standard target for UP newswriters.

As marines mopped up snipers on the streets of Vera Cruz they were treated to an incredible sight. Dining in regal splendor at an outdoor cafe was Richard Harding Davis, a split of champagne by his side. Davis, who was covering the war for a news syndicate, later joined other newsmen on a cross-country trek to the front at El Tejar. Their caravan was intercepted by a detachment of Mexican soldiers who, for a few tense moments, seemed on the verge of shooting the correspondents. But Jimmy Hare, a photographer, had a brilliant inspiration. He suggested that the Mexican Federals pose for a picture, a gesture that brought smiles of pleasure to their faces. They proudly lined up for the shot and the reporters were allowed to continue after good wishes were exchanged all around. Some of the Mexicans even served as guides to El Tejar.

Davis' troubles were not over, however. Several days later he and Frederick Palmer and Medill McCormick were taken off a train and arrested while they were en route to Mexico City to interview dictator Huerta. Palmer, an Associated Press man, was soon released; but Davis and McCormick, of the *Chicago Tribune,* spent an uncomfortable twenty-four hours in a lice-ridden provincial jail.

Among the American correspondents in Mexico none was more complex than John Reed, who rode with the revolutionary general Pancho Villa in 1913, a year before the United States became involved in that country's affairs. The son of wealthy parents and a Harvard graduate, Reed later became a dedicated communist and died in Moscow at the age of thirty-three, a hero in Russia.

He was twenty-six when the *New York World* and *Metropolitan* magazine sent him to cover the exploits of Villa, who had captured the imagination of many Americans. At least one historian believed that Reed faked some of his stories, but there is no question that he lived with the rebel troops and accompanied them in battle. John Reed also was a vivid writer, as is illustrated by this account of his foray with the Mexican "tropa."

. . . Then there was Captain Fernando, a grizzled giant of a man in tight trousers who had fought twenty-one battles. He took the keenest delight in my fragmentary Spanish, and every word I spoke sent him into bellows of laughter that shook down the abode from the ceiling. He had never been out of Durango, and declared that there was a great sea between the United States and Mexico, and that he believed all the rest of the earth to be water. Next to him sat Longinos Guereca, with a row of decayed teeth across his round, gentle face every time he smiled, and a record for simple bravery that was famous throughout the army. . . . Then came Patricio, the best rider of wild horses in the state, and Fidencio next to him, a pure-blooded Indian, seven feet tall, who always fought standing up . . .

This was the Tropa when I first saw them. About a hundred they were, in all stages of picturesque raggedness; some wore overalls, others the charro jackets of peons, while one or two sported tight vaquero trousers. A few had shoes, most of them only cowhide sandals, and the rest were barefooted.

Sabas Gutierrez was garbed in an ancient frock-coat split up the back for riding. Rifles slung at their saddles, four or five cartridge belts crossed over their chests, high flapping sombreros, immense spurs chiming as they rode, bright colored serapes strapped on behind—this was their uniform.

Captain Fernando invited Reed to ride with him at the head of the column, offering him a half-bottle of strong liquor which the reporter drank in one gulp in response to the officer's challenge to "show that you're a man." The feat brought cheers from the troops, who now accepted Reed as one of them.

Another correspondent who rode with Villa was Timothy G. Turner, who came from a well-known newspaper family. His grandfather, with Horace Greeley, established the *Cleveland Leader* and his father was city editor of the *Jackson* (Michigan) *Patriot* and the *Chicago Journal.*

Turner, elegantly attired in cape, English riding breeches, South African-type felt hat and a walking stick, employed two Indians to carry his typewriter and luggage as he accompanied the Mexican rebels for the *El Paso Herald* and the Associated Press. He was with the troops when they took Torreon, dodging machine gun bullets that killed men all around him. But his worst ordeal was still to come.

In Torreon, Turner, with other correspondents, submitted his dispatch to the censor for telegraphing to his paper. The censor, an army major, ripped up his copy and flung the pieces in his face. It seems that the Villista forces were smoldering over an AP story which hinted at a split between Pancho Villa and Venustiano Carranza, acting president of Mexico.

The enraged major wasn't through. He hired a sniper to pick Turner off on the streets of Torreon, and only poor aim kept the reporter alive. He was fired upon several times as he rode in an open carriage. When he learned of the plot Turner decided his usefulness in Mexico was at an end, and he departed for El Paso on the first train out.

The Mexican revolution had its share of picaresque newspapermen, and one of the most striking of the breed was Edward S. O'Reilly, a tall Texan, who fought as well as reported the war for the Associated Press. He was shot off his horse while leading an insurgent band against government forces. Before getting his wounded leg bandaged he limped thirteen miles to a telegraph office to file his story. Throughout the revolution O'Reilly functioned as both newsman and participant, a role that would horrify today's American journalist but which seemed to bother him not at all. At one point he was even personal bodyguard to a provincial governor.

O'Reilly became a close companion of Pancho Villa, riding in the general's private railroad coach and telling him about President Woodrow Wilson and the United States. Finally, the vagabond correspondent became disenchanted with the revolution and called on Villa to bid him good-by.

"You must not leave us now," the rebel chieftain protested. "I will make you a major." O'Reilly was commissioned on the spot and remained with Villa for a few more months. Then he quit Mexico for good, drifting to Chicago for a conventional news job with AP. There weren't many newsmen like him, even in his day.

Then as now, newspapers often hired "specials" to cover major events. Some of these persons are not primarily newspapermen but are assigned to a story because of their special background or knowledge. In 1914, the *Chicago Tribune* enlisted V. Blasco-Ibáñez, the Spanish novelist (*The Four Horsemen of the Apocalypse,* etc.), to report from Mexico. Blasco-Ibáñez filed what today would be considered "think pieces," analytical or interpretive treatments of events. Here is one of his accounts:

> In its whole history, Mexico militarism shows only a series of civil wars, resulting in execution for private citizens, plundering for towns, destruction for the national railways. . . .
> In former times, there were, in Mexico, only such generals as belonged to the regular army, soldiers by profession, like the professional soldiers of every other country. Now there are Generals and Generals! There are Generals appointed by Carranza. There are generals created by Villa. There are

Generals manufactured by Felix Díaz. There are Generals counterfeited by Zapata. Who is not a General down there? . . . The Mexican General in the make-up supplied by the revolution does not know what a sword is. He never wore one. He carries a revolver in his belt. . . . Mexico City since the revolution has lived the life of a dime novel. Often the generals are mere boys, and often have only a small lapel pin or other designation to tell them apart from the armed citizenry. As a popular method of cutting down the number of generals and a means of occupying themselves, there are shoot-outs in the streets of cities between these generals.

The United States withdrew from Mexico shortly after the Vera Cruz campaign; but in 1916 President Wilson ordered General John J. Pershing to hunt down Villa in Mexico after the Mexican leader had raided Columbus, New Mexico, killing sixteen Americans. The punitive expedition broke up Villa's army, but he escaped. Several reporters tagged along with Pershing, including Floyd Gibbons of the *Chicago Tribune* and Robert Dunn of the *New York Tribune,* who had jointly purchased an ancient wreck of a car by signing a note on wrapping paper. The chase produced little news and correspondents grew bored with the whole thing. So did President Wilson, who called off the pursuit because he had more important plans for Pershing. The United States was nearing entrance into the First World War and the general was to head the American forces in France, which also would be the main arena for the newsmen.

4

The Big Action: 1914-1918

ON A JUNE DAY IN 1918, FLOYD GIBBONS WAS ADVANCING WITH A marine regiment in the battle of Belleau Wood in France. Machine gun fire cut down an American officer and Gibbons went to his aid, getting hit himself by three bullets. The newsman lost an eye, received the French Croix de Guerre for valor and continued reporting from the Western Front.

It was World War I and Gibbons, a genial Irishman who began his newspaper career in Milwaukee, was one of sixty American correspondents accredited by the United States Army alone during that gigantic conflict. But Americans had covered the war even before this country's entrance into the hostilities. For some of these reporters it was their first war, for others the third, fourth or fifth. Old hands like Richard Harding Davis, Frazier Hunt and Karl von Wiegand competed with fledglings like Westbrook Pegler, who, at twenty-three, was the youngest correspondent accredited to the American forces. Many of the newspapermen had eagerly abandoned routine, city-side assignments to write the biggest story of them all. Some, like Pegler, John T. McCutcheon, Gibbons and Damon Runyon, were to be familiar by-lines to American readers for years afterward. Others had their moment in history and faded into obscurity following the armistice in 1918.

The political and economic forces which produced World War I had simmered for years before they erupted in June, 1914, when a Serbian revolutionary assassinated Austrian Archduke Franz Ferdinand in the obscure Bosnian town of Sarajevo. Austria-Hungary declared war on Serbia (now part of Yugoslavia) and the great powers of Europe took sides for what was to become a world-wide conflict. Allied against Austria and Germany were England, France and Russia and later Italy. Two months later Germany launched an attack on France through neutral Belgium.

American correspondents were on both sides of the line in the early years of the war. The first one accredited by the British forces was Frederick Palmer, a crack veteran of the Greek-Turkish War, the Philippine insurrection, the Russo-Japanese conflict and the Mexican border campaign. Palmer, who later was to become the chief American Army censor with the rank of major, was in 1914 the official correspondent for the three big American news services—the Associated Press, United Press and International News Service. This meant that he was virtually the only Allied war reporter for just about every newspaper in the United States.

With the German armies was Karl H. von Wiegand, who had been sent to Berlin by United Press in 1911. His first dispatches from the eastern front were realistic enough to make readers shudder. A sample:

> . . . Today I saw a wave of Russian flesh and blood dash against a wall of German steel. . . . From the outset of the

advance the German artillery began shelling the onrushing mass with wonderfully timed shrapnel.

On came the Slav swarm—into the range of German trenches, with wild yells and never a waver. Russian battle flags, the first I had seen, appeared in the front of the charging ranks.

Then came a new sound. First I saw a sudden, almost grotesque melting of the advancing line. It was different from anything that had taken place before. The men literally went down like dominoes in a row. . . . Almost in the second that I pondered, puzzled, the staccato rattle of machine guns reached us.

Raymond Gram Swing, who later was to become a prominent radio newscaster, was another European correspondent who covered the German side. A *Chicago Daily News* man, Swing was permitted to visit Liège, Belgium, which had fallen to the Germans in two weeks of siege. The victory was attributed to Germany's huge new artillery pieces dubbed "Big Berthas." This was a good story and Swing wanted to get it past the censor. By chance, the reporter ran into a traveling University of Chicago student, who was persuaded to memorize the dispatch as Swing dictated it. When he got to the *Chicago Daily News* office in London, the student typed out the story and it was published around the world.

In his autobiography, Swing told of another occasion when a German baroness helped him get to the front line by outfitting him as a surgeon's assistant, even arranging for him to get a short course in first aid. The ruse didn't work, but a German lieutenant escorted him back to Berlin through Belgium, permitting Swing to see the action he had gone for. Swing also was one of the few correspondents to witness the Dardanelles naval battle in Turkish waters.

Both the Allies and the Austrians and Germans were suspicious of reporters, most of whom had trouble getting to the fighting zones and then filing their copy. Some Allied censors even suggested that the correspondents' private letters be tested for invisible ink. In 1915, the British finally permitted six correspondents, including Frederick

Palmer, to stay at army headquarters. For a time the reporters were accepted by the officers. Then, according to Joseph J. Mathews (*Reporting the Wars*), a change of censors canceled all of the newsmen's hard-won privileges. They were in the doghouse again.

"There ensued," wrote Mathews, "what was probably the strangest incident in the history of the relations between war correspondents and military censors: the correspondents went 'on strike,' refusing to write a word until the news restrictions had been relaxed. . . . the correspondents won their point."

Another battler against censorship was Herbert Bayard Swope, war correspondent for the *New York World*. In 1914, the Allies cut the only cable line linking Germany and the United States. Swope, covering the German forces, filed his material through a courier service to London via The Hague. This by-passed the German censors but not the British, who had a crack at his copy. After the United States entered the war, Swope was just as disturbed by American restraints on newsmen.

Despite restrictions, more American correspondents poured into Europe to satisfy a swelling curiosity about the war back home. Among them were the famed humorist Irvin S. Cobb, Will Irwin, McCutcheon, Harry Hansen of the *Chicago Daily News,* Roger Lewis of Associated Press, and Henry Suydam, *Brooklyn Eagle*. Richard Harding Davis crossed the Atlantic in an elegant suite on the *Lusitania* and reached Brussels in time to report the German capture of that city, one of the most brilliant accounts of the war. The Germans later arrested Davis as a spy when he tried to get through the lines to Paris. The American ambassador to Belgium finally obtained his freedom. Eventually he got to Paris on a train loaded with wounded soldiers.

Arresting correspondents as spies was a fairly common practice in the early years of the war. McCutcheon, Hansen and Irwin were caught in the German push through Belgium and locked up for several hours as suspected spies after they accidentally wandered into German headquarters.

The policy of all the combatants was to take correspondents to the front in carefully arranged tours. Official communiqués told little, putting an added burden on the newsmen. This meant that they were forced to use their wits in breaking through this wall of censorship. Some did it by establishing key contacts in various headquarters. Will Irwin, a Stanford graduate and one of the leading newspapermen of his day, got a world scoop on the crucial Battle of Ypres at a fashionable dinner party in London. Certain influential Americans and Britons were seeking a reliable American reporter to tell the United States of Britain's victory in that sixteen-day battle in 1915. Irwin, a *New York Tribune* writer, had seen some of the fighting at Ypres but had not realized its immense scope at the time. English sources gave him the whole picture, largely because of his outstanding reputation. Irwin also was one of the few American reporters with the Italian army. He was given deferential treatment, and the army provided him with an automobile and driver. While touring the Austrian front, Irwin was knocked over by a shell concussion but was unhurt. In fact, American correspondents in World War I were a remarkably lucky lot; only two were injured and none was killed in combat.

The French were slow to set up accreditation for foreign newsmen and when they did the requirements were so stringent as to be absurd. The reporter had to be French or a citizen of an Allied nation. In addition, he had to have complete fluency in the French language and take a tough test to prove it. No one qualified. Later, the French army relented a bit and allowed a few correspondents at the front. So smothering was the censorship that a number of newsmen carried stretchers and acted as ambulance orderlies to learn what was going on. Emmet Crozier wrote:

> . . . The winter of 1914-15 was the beginning of the Dark Age of war correspondence. Many of the newspapermen gave up . . . and returned to the United States. . . . Late in March and in April, three parties of newspaper correspondents were permitted by the War Office to make short tours behind the lines in France. They were accompanied by Army officers, and their movements were closely restricted, but they

saw how the troops lived, they waded in muddy trenches, and they took back to London a first-hand glimpse of the front.

Paris almost fell in the early war years, and employees of the Paris edition of the *New York Herald* worried about their fate should the Germans enter the city. Following a staff meeting, they sent a wire to *Herald* owner James Gordon Bennett, asking what measures he had taken for their safety. The irascible Bennett cabled back that if they were that concerned they could all quit and he would get out the paper himself. A few accepted his suggestion and departed for London that night.

But Paris was saved when a "taxicab army" was rushed to the front and turned back the Germans in the Battle of the Marne. Frederick Palmer and Elmer Roberts, of the Associated Press, were the first to see the area and filed stories which got through the censors.

Censorship was not the only problem of the correspondents. World War I was a trench war. The year 1915 brought a stalemate in which both sides dug in for months at a time. Attacks were computed not in miles but in yards, and a drive of a few thousand yards constituted a major action. After the German slash through Belgium, correspondents were hard-pressed to come up with exciting stories. Spectacular advances such as those of General George Patton in World War II were unheard of in 1914-15.

For newsmen, the story was not in the meager pushes but in the grimly mounting casualties. Hundreds of thousands of lives were sacrificed as vast armies clashed across "no man's land." Here is how Richard Harding Davis described the aftermath of the Battle of Soissons:

> . . . The four miles of countryside over which for four days both armies had ploughed the earth with these shells was the picture of complete desolation. The rout of the German army was marked by knapsacks, uniforms, and accoutrements scattered over the fields on either hand as far as you could see. Red Cross flags hanging from bushes showed where

there had been dressing stations. Under them were blood-stains, bandages and clothing, and boots piled in heaps as high as a man's chest, and the bodies of those German soldiers that the first aid had failed to save.

Both sides disguised their losses in a cloud of propaganda which did not fool experienced correspondents at the front. Wilbur Forrest, of United Press, commented cynically:

> A heavy defeat in the field was often described as a strategic withdrawal, or even more boldly, the occupation of a new position in accordance with plan. Communiqués minimized defeat and exaggerated victory . . .

Forrest had won laurels for the United Press for his enterprise in getting the full story of the German sinking of the British liner *Lusitania* on May 7, 1915, with the loss of 1,153 lives, including 128 Americans. As a cub reporter in UP's London bureau, Forrest had heard reports of the torpedoing and also rumors that the survivors had been taken to Queenstown, Ireland. He hurried there and went for three days without sleep as he interviewed the passengers and compiled a list of the dead. The young newsman was the first press association man to get on the wire with the complete account of the disaster. He then fell into bed and slept for eighteen hours.

Another alert London correspondent was William G. Shepherd, who was fresh from his exploits as a UP reporter in the Mexican border campaign. Like other newsmen, Shepherd burned to file the story of the German Zeppelin bombing of London in September, 1915. The British War Office, however, forbade a word to be printed about the attack and was not even accepting stories for censorship. Shepherd talked to London residents, visited the bombed sections and then sat down to write his story. The article praised Londoners for their calm under "trying circumstances," noting how the city's routine continued smoothly—all without once mentioning Zeppelin or air raid. The censor passed the story, which gave Americans at least a fair inkling that London had undergone some kind of ordeal. But Shepherd was to enjoy an even greater triumph. The next day he kept an interview with Guglielmo Marconi, the inventor of the wireless. The Italian was hollow-eyed from lack of sleep but was in a high state of excitement. He had stayed up all night watching bombs drop over London and had even journeyed to the devastated areas in a taxi.

Shepherd decided at once to change the drift of the interview, which originally was planned as an assessment by Marconi of the effects of his radio. The reporter instead got the inventor's reaction to the Zeppelin raid and the details of what he had seen. The newsman then wrote his story, clearly referring to the attack and also noting Marconi's indignation that the dirigible was used as a weapon. By that curious logic known only to censors the dispatch was allowed to be sent to the United States on the grounds that it was an interview, not an account of the air raid. The censor-frustrated London newspapers had to pick up Shepherd's story, which was the first public report of the historic bombing.

Meanwhile, another ambitious newspaperman was impatiently marking time as a copyreader on the *Paris Herald*. After editing his high school paper in New Rochelle, New York, Henry Wales held jobs on newspapers in San Francisco, Salt Lake City, Reno and New York City. In 1915 he went to Paris on his own, hoping to connect as a war correspondent. James Gordon Bennett gave him the *Herald* spot, which paid his rent but did little to satisfy his longing for action. On his day off young Wales obtained the first interview with the first Allied air ace, Georges Guynemer, a Frenchman who had shot down five German planes. The reporter could speak no French but the flier's mother spoke English and acted as translator. Wales sold his story to Lincoln Eyre, *New York World* correspondent, who also hired him on the spot. Later, Wales became a war reporter for International News Service and eventually was named chief of the *Chicago Tribune*'s Paris bureau. After the war he covered such events as the Versailles peace conference, Mussolini's march on Rome, Charles Lindbergh's historic solo flight across the Atlantic, Hitler's rise in Germany and World War II. He hobnobbed with kings and statesmen and was considered a friend by General

John J. Pershing, commander of the American Expeditionary Force in France, who was known for his general coolness to the press.

Floyd Gibbons was certainly one of the most colorful World War I correspondents and also one of the most daring. He was the perfect example of the swashbuckling newspaperman, ready at all times to go anywhere and do almost anything to get a story. In February, 1917, the *Chicago Tribune* decided it needed another man on the Western Front and Gibbons was picked. The newspaper scheduled passage for the reporter on a ship carrying Count von Bernstorff, a German diplomat, who had been asked to leave Washington. According to Ward Greene, another World War I correspondent, Gibbons canceled the reservation on the theory that the Germans would not torpedo a vessel containing one of their own officials. Gibbons *wanted* a ship that was likely to get hit so he could write a first-hand account of the disaster. So the newsman booked passage on the British liner *Laconia,* thinking it would be a more likely submarine target. It was. On a calm ocean on the night of February 25, 1917, a German U-Boat commander spotted the ship off the coast of Ireland and fired two torpedos which sent her to the bottom. Gibbons, who had been playing cards at the time, was rescued at sea. A few hours later he filed his story from Queenstown, Ireland, while he was still wet and chilled to the bone. The account, which Ward Greene included in his book on star reporters and their great stories, was a compelling narrative of death and destruction at sea. It appeared in the *Tribune* and read in part:

> . . . The Cunard liner *Laconia,* 18,000 tons burden, carrying seventy-three passengers—men, women and children—of whom six were American citizens—manned by a mixed crew of 216 bound from New York to Liverpool and loaded with foodstuffs, cotton and war material was torpedoed without warning by a German submarine last night off the Irish coast. The vessel sank in about forty minutes . . .
>
> The torpedo had hit us well astern on the starboard side and had missed the engines and the dynamos. . . . The illumination of the upper deck, on which I stood, made the dark-

ness of the water, sixty feet below, appear all the blacker when I peered over the edge at my station boat, No. 10. . . . Up and down the deck passengers and crew were donning lifebelts, throwing on overcoats and taking positions in the boats. There were a number of women but only one appeared hysterical—little Miss Titsie Sikosl, a French-Polish actress, who was being cared for by her manager . . .

We rested on our oars, with all eyes on the still lighted *Laconia*. The torpedo had struck at 10:30 p.m., according to our ship's time. It was thirty minutes afterward that another dull thud, which was accompanied by a noticeable drop in the hulk, told its story of the second torpedo that the submarine had despatched through the engine room and the boat's vitals from a distance of 200 yards. . . . The ship sank rapidly at the stern until at last its nose stood straight in the air. Then it slid silently down and out of sight like a piece of disappearing scenery in a panorama spectacle.

In describing the rescue, Gibbons wrote:

. . . We had been six hours in the open boats, all of which began coming alongside one after another. Wet and bedraggled survivors were lifted aboard. Women and children first was the rule.

The scenes of reunion were heart-gripping. Men who had remained strangers to one another aboard the *Laconia* wrung each other by the hand or embraced without shame. The frail little wife of a Canadian chaplain found one of her missing children delivered up from another boat. She smothered the child with ravenous mother kisses while tears of joy streamed down her face.

On land Americans produced some of the finest combat correspondence in the history of such journalism. Wythe Williams' report of the battle of Verdun is one example. Williams, of *The New York Times*, and John Bass, *Chicago Daily News*, walked six miles through intense cannon fire to Fort Douaument at a time when no one knew whether the French occupants were alive or dead. They found numbed, shell-shocked survivors who, in the words of Burnet Hershey, another newsman, looked like "animated ghosts." Somehow the two newsmen got back to the main citadel at Verdun and reported what they had seen. Fresh troops were rushed in to Douaumont in time to save it from falling to the Germans. This was the turning point in the Verdun struggle.

The United States declared war on Germany on April 6, 1917. With the arrival of American troops in France newspapers in this country began sending more correspondents to the battle zones. General Pershing persuaded Frederick Palmer to handle the press section, which was operated on a more relaxed basis than those of France and England. Major Palmer issued one memorandum which declared that "under no circumstances shall correspondents be required to write or make any statement contrary to their opinions or inclinations." The American Expeditionary Force (AEF) initially accredited twelve correspondents, with preference given to the press associations and large newspaper organizations. Each reporter was required to deposit $3,000 with the War Department to pay for his overseas transportation and other expenses. If the newsman broke any military rules the money would be forfeited. As a newspaperman, Major Palmer took pains to see that the correspondents covered the war in style. He requisitioned automobiles for their use and even tried to obtain Army chauffeurs for them, a move that was killed by the brass. He did manage, however, to convince General Pershing to hire civilians for the driving job.

The new crop of American correspondents included Heywood Broun, *New York Tribune,* a huge, unkempt man who was to become a famous columnist after the war. In the 1930s, he was one of the principal founders of the American Newspaper Guild, in which editorial employees were unionized for the first time in the United States.

The American war correspondents of 1917-18 wore the Sam Browne belts of officers and jaunty peaked caps piped with red and green braid. Their outfits were usually completed with whipcord riding breeches and tunics bearing the red letter "C" on the left sleeve.

AEF headquarters had the idea initially that the American public could be kept informed about the war through three or four regional newspapers. Staff officers were appalled at the number of correspondents who appeared in France. But according to Raymond S. Tompkins, who was there, the American press corps never reached much above forty, a very small number by the standards of World War II, Korea and Vietnam.

Writing in the *American Mercury* magazine in 1928, Tompkins noted with a touch of jaundice: "The basis of all the war correspondents of the Great War was a simple credo which none of us realized we were following, but which all of us actually followed . . ."

He then listed the credo as follows:

That all the Americans were natural-born fighters.

That in any engagement between Americans and Germans, the German force was always from 5 to 10 times as large as the American force.

That it was difficult in our army to keep the wounded from getting up and rushing back into the fighting.

That lemonade was the popular French drink for American soldiers.

That next to reaming a German with his bayonet, the American soldier loved best to play with the little French children back of the lines or help the aged French farmer get in his wheat.

Indeed, the headlines of the day bore out Tompkins' theory:

YANKEES' GO-GET-'EM SPIRIT CURBS U-BOATS

CHICAGO YOUTH THRIVES ON RISKS AT BATTLE FRONT

YANK ATTACK WRECKS WHOLE HUN DIVISION

HUMOR IS MIXED WITH TRAGEDY ON WAY TO FRONT: MARCH OF THE AMERICANS FAILS TO DAMPEN THEIR SPIRITS.

A glance at today's newspaper war headlines and stories reveals a more mature and sophisticated reporting and editing. Most contemporary battle correspondents write about war as they see it—not as a sport, but as a grim, bloody business in which the enemy is often just as tough and heroic as our men.

American press headquarters in World War I were set up at Neufchâteau, about 200 miles from Paris. An AEF bulletin advised correspondents to have telegraph credit cards, typewriter, copy paper, terrain maps and a small rubber bathtub. "Black Jack" Pershing remained virtually unapproachable, however, holding few press conferences and telling reporters little. Once Westbrook Pegler, a brash UP man, rode over to the commander's headquarters, hoping for an exclusive interview. He actually got inside Pershing's office, where he announced: "I'm Pegler of United Press. Can you give me a statement on the general situation?"

"Pegler," Pershing replied coldly, "get the hell out of my office."

In a few weeks American censorship tightened, to the disgust of correspondents who had endured such treatment for almost four years. Broun reacted by mailing articles to the *New York Tribune* without submitting them to the censors. Similar steps were taken by Pegler, Reginald Wright Kauffman, *Philadelphia North American,* and Wythe Williams, *The New York Times.* All lost their army credentials, and Pegler was sent out of France. He promptly joined the United States Navy and after the war became a controversial sportswriter and columnist. Broun, who delighted in taking jabs at generals, was suspended and fined after he slipped a story past the censor which read, "General Pershing completed his tour of inspection yesterday morning. The American Army is doing as well as could be expected."

As the war continued, more correspondents attached themselves to the AEF. Among them were such well-known newsmen as Edwin

L. James of *The New York Times,* another flamboyant type; Webb Miller, United Press, veteran of the Mexican affair; and Frazier "Spike" Hunt, *New York Sun* and later the *Chicago Tribune,* a handsomely rugged man who later did an outstanding job in covering the Russian Revolution.

Although censorship rules were strict, accredited correspondents could visit the front. And many did, living with the troops or in farmhouses, cellars, etc. One imaginative UP reporter, Fred S. Ferguson, scooped his rivals on the momentous battle of Saint-Mihiel by writing his story *before* the engagement. Prior to the attack, military intelligence officers briefed the press corps on the entire plan for the operation. The correspondents then left to observe the battle. But not Ferguson. He remained to write the story based on the outline given by the briefing officers, typing it in "short takes," one or two paragraphs to a page. He then handed his copy to a friend at headquarters with instructions to file the takes if they were confirmed by incoming battle reports. If the battle did not go according to plan, the friend was to "kill" the dispatch. The Saint-Mihiel drive went exactly as laid out by army intelligence and Ferguson's story reached the United States before any other.

The first American to enter Saint-Mihiel after the Germans abandoned it was George Seldes, correspondent for the Marshall Syndicate. The French populace hailed him as a hero and liberator and was wining and dining him when General Pershing and Secretary of War Newton D. Baker arrived several hours later.

In February, 1918, the AEF headquarters did another about-face and loosened controls on correspondents, permitting them to list casualties and note the activities of front-line units. They could even go "over the top" if they desired. James Hopper, of *Collier's* weekly, was among those who accepted the invitation in the American attack on Cantigny. He went over with the first assault group and returned with a batch of German prisoners who had surrendered to him, thinking he was an officer. Wilbur Forrest, Edwin James, Paul Scott Mower, *Chicago Daily News,* and Don Martin, former *Herald* political reporter, covered the much bigger battle at Château-Thierry—

which was followed by another fight with the censors over releasing the news. American marines and infantry had been key factors in halting the German advance on Paris and the correspondents wanted to write about it, especially since the French already had issued a communiqué. Crozier wrote that the issue was finally resolved when the United States Army censors allowed American correspondents to write that the Americans had stopped the German drive on the Marne and saved Paris.

Two factors motivated the correspondents in their never-ending struggles with the censors. One was their fierce pride in their work. When a newspaperman is assigned to a story he is expected to get it and he wants to get it. The payoff for a newsman is in getting published. Censors try to blackout publication entirely or so water down the copy that it comes out with only a pale resemblance to the original. The other factor in World War I was the hot competitive situation among American newspapers and wire services. Carr Van Anda, *The New York Times* managing editor, posted every available military map in his office and by charting the course of battles was able to have reporters on the scene even before the first attack. He also instructed Walter Duranty in the *Times* Paris bureau to cable everything at "double urgent" message rate of seventy-five cents a word. This was expensive but it enabled the *Times* to get up-to-date information on various war actions. The *New York World* offered Frederick Palmer $40,000 a year to go to France but he turned it down for $175 a month as an army major. United Press, which normally was close with a dollar, put on extra men all over Europe and increased its cable flow of news. Roy Howard, UP head, asked Ed L. Keen, London office manager, if he needed funds and because of a garbled reply sent him $15,000 in gold by steamer. Keen had actually said that he did not need money.

Keen, who dressed conservatively but thought dramatically, consistently beat the opposition at the beginning of the war with a simple but brilliant idea. Knowing that cable lines would be crowded with hundreds of other dispatches, Keen filed a duplicate UP flash on every other available route from London to New York. Thus, if the original was delayed on the main route there was a good chance that one of the others would get through even if it had to travel farther.

The Associated Press, the now-defunct International News Service and other press associations also beefed up their operations, diverting their best men to the war.

It was not surprising that the New York newspapers would spend a great deal of money covering the war but midwestern and western papers also tried to provide their readers with staff reports from the fronts. The *Chicago Tribune* fielded some of the best correspondents in the business. Besides Floyd Gibbons, there were Ring Lardner, who became famous as a short story writer; John T. McCutcheon, noted writer and cartoonist; Parke Brown; and Frazier Hunt.

Besides professional pride and competition, there was another consideration in the press's opposition to censorship, particularly when there was no military justification for it. The news organizations and their correspondents believed the American public had a right to know what was going on. Their sons were dying on the battlefields and they were making sacrifices at home. It was their war, too. Richard Harding Davis spoke for every correspondent when he wrote:

> This is a world war, and my contention is that the world has the right to know, not what is going to happen next, but at least what has happened. If men have died nobly, if women and children have cruelly and needlessly suffered, if for no military necessity and without reason cities have been wrecked, the world should know that. . . . Some men are trained to fight, and others are trained to write. The latter can tell you of what they have seen so that you, safe at home at the breakfast table, also can see it. . . . This war is a world enterprise, and in it every man, woman, and child is an interested stockholder. They have a right to know what is going forward. The directors' meeting should not be held in secret.

World War I ended officially on November 11, 1918, but four

days earlier United Press had startled the world with a flash report announcing the armistice. The story triggered wild celebrations in the United States; but it was false and created one of the great journalistic arguments in history. To add to the uproar, the November 7 message was filed by no less a personage than Roy Wilson Howard, the president of United Press.

As Joe Alex Morris recounts the incident, Howard, a small but dynamic man, had made a tour of European UP installations and left Paris on November 6 for Brest, France, where he was to get a ship to New York. Peace talks were in the wind.

The next day in Brest, Howard was met by an American intelligence officer who told him the armistice had been signed, but there had been no official announcements. Tingling with excitement but also skeptical, the UP chief sought confirmation. Someone suggested he call on Admiral Henry B. Wilson, commanding officer of all United States naval forces in France.

Howard found the admiral in a buoyant mood and his office in a flurry of activity.

"By God, major," Wilson said to Howard's officer escort, "this is news, isn't it!" The admiral then handed out copies of a telegram to his orderlies, telling them to distribute them to the local newspaper and to the city at large.

After he was introduced to the admiral, Howard asked what the news was.

"The armistice has been signed," the navy commander replied, and gave Howard a copy of the telegram.

"Is it official?" the newsman inquired.

Assured that it was, Howard asked if the admiral objected to his filing the announcement to United Press.

"Hell, no," Wilson boomed. "Here's a copy. Go to it."

Howard lost no time in getting to the Brest telegraph office, where he sent this bulletin:

UNIPRESS NEWYORK
URGENT ARMISTICE ALLIES GERMANY SIGNED

ELEVEN SMORNING HOSTILITIES CEASED TWO
SAFTERNOON SEDAN TAKEN SMORNING BY
AMERICANS

The cable was rewritten in UP's New York office and millions of
Americans read this translation in their hometown newspapers:

> PARIS, November 7 (United Press) The war is over.
> Germany and the Allies signed an armistice at 11 a.m. to-
> day, hostilities ceasing three hours later. As Marshal Foch's
> terms are known to include provisions which will prevent
> resumption of hostilities, the greatest war of all time has come
> to an end.

United Press editors in New York were delighted with their scoop
over their chief adversary, the Associated Press, but there was worry
over the fact that Howard's flash was not confirmed by any other
source. The concern was well founded. Two hours later Howard filed
another bulletin, saying that Admiral Wilson had admitted that his
information could not be supported. To compound UP's misery, the
message was delayed en route and it was some time before a correc-
tion could be put on the wire. Instead of enjoying a triumph, United
Press was forced to eat crow. It was with no little satisfaction that
the Associated Press moved the following story the next day:

> NEW YORK, November 8 (Associated Press) Millions of
> Americans realized today that they had been hoaxed into
> celebrating the end of the war by publication of the United
> Press dispatches declaring the armistice signed and fighting
> ended.

The mistake undoubtedly stained what was a fine UP war reporting record, but a subsequent investigation established that the error
was the fault of the military authorities. Admiral Wilson later issued
a statement absolving Howard or the United Press from any re-
sponsibility in the matter.

The United Press partly recouped on Armistice Day when ace
reporter Webb Miller turned out a remarkable first-hand story of

the cease-fire on the front line. An American army pilot flew Miller over the line, where he saw Germans and Americans playing games in their respective positions. Retreating German soldiers waved at the plane as it passed over them. Miller also saw graves being dug for those killed in the final minutes of the fighting.

World War I ended, but war correspondence did not. Already the distant sound of guns was being heard and there were reporters to heed their call.

5

Between World Wars

In 1936, Webb Miller, the great foreign correspondent, wrote a book called *I Found No Peace*. The title was an accurate description of the stormy, fateful years between world wars. While the United States returned to what President Warren G. Harding termed "normalcy," the clash of arms continued around the globe. Any American who wanted to read about a war had only to open his newspaper.

The armistice silenced the guns on the Western Front, but Russia remained torn by a bloody revolution by the Communists against the Czarist government. In 1919, the United States sent an expeditionary force to Siberia to help the White Russian (Czarist) troops battling the rebels. One of the first American reporters on the scene was vet-

eran Frazier Hunt, *Chicago Tribune,* who rode a thousand miles by
sled through the civil war areas. His series of stories were read in the
United States Senate and were influential in bringing about the with-
drawal of our soldiers from Russia.

Hunt, dressed in a fur-lined trench coat against the brutal Siberian
winter, persuaded partisans to let him ride an armored troop train
attacking Vladivostok, a key seaport still held by the Whites. However, other Reds had taken the city the previous night and Hunt
found everything quiet as the train steamed in. Several American
army officers along the track spotted Hunt and shouted gaily:

"We surrender. Will you accept our unconditional surrender?"

Equal to the occasion, the newsman yelled back:

"I will . . . and may God have pity on your miserable souls."

Later, Hunt wrote in humor:

"It isn't every war correspondent who can capture a city."

While Hunt and other correspondents continued to report from
abroad, a sensitive eighteen-year-old student at the University of
Chicago yearned to see the places they were writing about. He was
Vincent Sheean, who was to become one of the best newsmen of his
time.

Sheean quit college and went to work for the *Chicago Daily News*
shortly after World War I. The job lasted only a few weeks and he
moved on to the *New York Daily News.* In 1922, he got his long-
sought chance at foreign correspondence when the *Chicago Tribune*
hired him for its European edition. Sheean kept traveling for years,
reporting wars, revolutions and other events.

In 1924, Spain was engaged in a campaign to quell Rif tribesmen
in Morocco, and Sheean went there despite the disapproval of Spanish authorities, who had previously arrested him as a spy in Madrid.
To avoid Spanish agents, he stayed in the international city of Tangier, from which he could hear the sound of the fighting in the hills.

Every newsman dreams of the exclusive story, and Sheean was no
exception. He conceived the idea of interviewing the Rif leader, Abd
el-Krim, who was hiding in the mountains. The young correspondent
began looking around for a guide to take him into the forbidden ter-

ritory. He was warned many times that such an expedition was dangerous. In his *Personal History,* Sheean recalled that one friend told him:

"You don't know this country. Your life isn't worth a sou once you get beyond the French outposts. . . . There are border tribes between here and the Rif that think nothing of robbing and killing. That's how they live."

Instead of abandoning the plan, Vincent Sheean sent a letter to Abd el-Krim, asking for permission to visit him. And the request was granted!

In preparing for the trip, Sheean donned Arab clothing so he wouldn't attract attention in the hills. His other gear consisted of an old overcoat for a blanket, a toothbrush, a French-Arabic dictionary and a prayer rug to be offered as a gift to the Rif leader. The reporter then set off an a two-and-one-half-day trip, alternately riding a "stinking mule" and walking. At Abd el-Krim's headquarters, Sheean waited ten days before he got his interview. The Rif chief grandly proclaimed his terms for making peace, but in the end he was exiled and his tribes defeated. But still Sheean had his exclusive story, which he filed on his return to Tangier after a trek that was often conducted under fire from Spanish positions. Tangier was the base for a number of other war correspondents, including the old campaigner Floyd Gibbons and Paul Scott Mowrer, *Chicago Daily News.* Sheean, however, was the only one reporting from the Rif side, a fact which made his dispatches stand out. He was frequently under fire from Spanish planes and, as if this weren't trouble enough, one of his Arab guides threatened to kill him with a knife. He ran from the man and hid in a cornfield until friendlier Arabs found him. Later, Sheean covered the Chinese revolution which brought Chiang Kai-shek to power in 1927.

American correspondents also told readers about the Japanese invasion of Manchuria in 1931. Demaree Bess, the United Press man in Peking, got a pre-dawn call from Chiang Kai-shek's top aide about the Japanese attack, which he quickly confirmed. The Japanese eventually moved against Shanghai, bombarding the city for several hours. As the battle raged, a young, fashionably dressed UP man, H. R. Elkins, strolled nonchalantly between the lines, jauntily swinging a gold-headed cane. He lost his poise a few minutes later when bullets whistled past his head. He dived for a ditch and crawled safely to the Chinese barricades, where soldiers took him to their commander. As the fighting continued outside, the commander offered Elkins a cup of tea and the two discussed the progress of the battle.

About this time Floyd Gibbons, a patch covering his eye, stood on the roof of the Cathay Hotel in Shanghai, watching Japanese planes bombing a railway station. It was the newsman's seventh war, and this time he was reporting for International News Service instead of the *Chicago Tribune*. Another INS man in China was Edward Hunter, who spent weeks gathering evidence of the slaughter of Chinese farmers by Japanese troops. His report became a part of the League of Nations records.

Few of the thousands of words filed by correspondents from various war zones created much of a stir in the United States. We were still comfortably wrapped in isolation, unaware that these "small wars" were leading to the biggest war of all time. However, two wars in the middle 1930s, the Italian-Ethiopian conflict and the Spanish Civil War, aroused some interest here, at least enough for newspapers and press associations to send some of their top men to cover them. Those clashes proved to be weapons-testing grounds for World War II. In both Ethiopia and Spain the airplane, as a means of terrible destruction, came into widespread use.

In the summer of 1935, Premier Benito Mussolini had more than 250,000 well-armed troops in Italy's East African colonies adjoining the primitive kingdom of Ethiopia, ruled by slight, bearded Haile Selassie, the "Conquering Lion of Judah." The dispute centered on ownership of a strip of territory between Ethiopia and Italian Somaliland where opposing patrols had fought the year before. The world shuddered at the thought of a modern army attacking a backward country. The League of Nations threatened to invoke sanctions against Italy if it invaded Ethiopia, whose troops consisted largely of tribesmen armed with spears and bows and arrows. Mussolini ignored world opinion and sent his legions against Ethiopia on October 3, 1935.

One of the reporters who covered the first stages of the Italian thrust was Jim Mills. Earlier, Mills, who had covered with distinction the civil disobedience movement in India, got wind of a fantastic plan by Haile Selassie to avert the war. Francis W. Rickett, a big British promoter, arrived in the Ethiopian capital of Addis Ababa on what was supposed to be a secret mission for the emperor. Selassie signed away valuable holdings in his country to British and American financial interests represented by Rickett. The Ethiopian leader thought that Mussolini would hold back his troops if England and America had a stake in his land.

Alerted to the scheme, Mills and a London reporter tagged after Rickett for a week, covering him in shifts. Finally, the exasperated visitor promised both newsmen an exclusive on his plan if they left him alone for a few days. The reporters agreed, the deal went through and they got their story as promised. It was a satisfying dispatch for the AP man, but the negotiations did not impress the Italian dictator, who launched the war anyway.

Mills was in the thick of action. Oliver Gramling, in his history of the Associated Press, said the correspondent witnessed the first Italian air raid on Ethiopia and was almost a casualty of it. Three bombs fell near Mills, setting fire to a Red Cross tent and killing scores of panic-stricken natives. Mills also took pictures which he rushed back to Addis Ababa, where he filed his story. His AP colleagues were not so fortunate. Edward J. Neil was stricken by tropical fever and later suffered a chest hemorrhage from overwork. He recovered only to injure his leg in the crash of a bomber on which he had hitched a ride to see the war from the air. Mark Barron was felled by a virulent jungle disease and was removed from the battle zone on a stretcher.

Meanwhile, United Press was not idle. Edward W. Beattie, transferred from the Berlin bureau, got the first interview with Haile Selassie on his reaction to the League of Nations' efforts to prevent the war. Beattie also informed the world that the Lion of Judah's air force consisted of four ancient biplanes and that only his small imperial guard was equipped with uniforms and modern weapons. The UP man then left for the front, outfitting himself with provisions for which he submitted the following expense account to his office:

"Canvas bag for camping, 48 thalers; provisions in field, 201 thalers; mule, 240 thalers; boy's wages, 60 thalers; feed for mule, 9 thalers; Mauser rifle, and ammunition, 280 thalers; 3 pack and riding mules and feed, 210 thalers." An Ethiopian thaler was worth 35 cents.

Other UP reporters who hurried to Ethiopia included the seasoned pro Webb Miller, who scored a world beat on the Italian invasion; his story reached Rome even before the official message to Mussolini from the Italian high command.

The 200 correspondents attached to the Italian army soon ran into the curse of all war reporting: censorship. General Pietro Badoglio summoned them all to a press conference at which he announced they had been indulging in too many "picnic excursions." He accused them of sending stories damaging to the Italian military effort and ordered them all confined to the town of Asmara, where they were to write articles based only on official handouts. As a final blow, he informed the correspondents that he planned a long period of reconstruction and road building, during which there would be little news. The number of reporters shortly dwindled to twenty, with most of the major American newspapers and wire services maintaining coverage. Newsmen covering the Ethiopian side received more or less the same treatment from Haile Selassie, who ordered them all back to Addis Ababa for spoon-feeding of information. It is an axiom of war that some commanders fear the press more than the enemy.

Next to censorship, heat was the principal foe of the reporters. Temperatures often reached 120 degrees, swiftly debilitating even the toughest man. Even rugged Floyd Gibbons collapsed while trying to reach Adowa after its capture by the Italians. Webb Miller, who was with him, pushed on, hiking thirty miles to get the story, which he shared with his old friend Gibbons.

Will Barber, *Chicago Tribune* correspondent, was hospitalized with malaria. Fellow reporters filled him in on the war's progress and he dictated his last story from his hospital bed. It was about the pitiful efforts of the spear-carrying Ethiopian army to defend itself against planes, tanks and cannons. Barber, thirty-two years old and married one year, died three days later and was buried on a hill overlooking Addis Ababa. His obituary was written by his father, Frederick C. Barber, who also had been a war correspondent.

Only brief stories were accepted over the cable lines. Longer material had to be sent out by any means available—a courier, an ambulance driver, a friendly pilot, etc. The AP's Eddie Neil remarked: "Once you finished a story, it was like putting it in a bottle and throwing it overboard in the middle of the ocean. All you could do was to hope somebody would find it and send it along to New York."

The Italo-Ethiopian war lasted a little over seven months. It ended with the triumphant entry of Italian columns into the capital of Addis Ababa. Neil was in the lead unit. He had one more war to cover before "30" was written on his fine career.

That same year, 1936, saw the outbreak of one of the bloodiest internal conflicts in history, the Spanish Civil War. It raged for three years and aroused strong emotions throughout the world. Many volunteers from other countries, including the United States, fought for both sides, and a few newspaper correspondents became politically involved in the conflict. The struggle pitted an established, leftist government against forces supported by wealthy landowners, the former monarchy, the Catholic church hierarchy and elements of the regular army. Communist Russia provided military aid to the government loyalists and the rebels were helped by Nazi Germany and Fascist Italy, both of which sent troops and arms.

Scores of American correspondents were assigned to Spain. Some came with the smell of gunpowder still fresh in their nostrils from other wars. Others would hear shots fired in anger for the first time in their lives—and the last. The "old pros" included Webb Miller, Vincent Sheean, Reynolds Packard, Eddie Neil, Herbert Matthews and Alexander Uhl. One of the "specials" was Ernest Hemingway, who later wrote a memorable novel of the Spanish Civil War, *For Whom the Bell Tolls.* He covered the fighting for the North American Newspaper Alliance and was a familiar figure around Madrid—a huge, sloppily dressed man who liked to shoot rabbits when the front was quiet. Hemingway counted himself as a combat veteran. In World War I he drove an ambulance for the Italian army and was wounded four times.

Correspondents filed their stories each night from the Telephone Building on the Gran Via, the tallest structure in Madrid. The Republican Army used the roof as an observation post, which made it a legitimate target for enemy shells. In one month the building received more than one hundred direct hits. A newsman risked his life every time he entered to send a dispatch.

Alexander Uhl, Associated Press correspondent, was waiting for a telephone line when a six-inch shell ripped through the wall and exploded a few feet over his head. It was experiences like this which produced "bomb jitters" among many newsmen and accounted for their frequent replacement in Spain. A slammed car door or the sound of an airplane motor could be nerve-wracking for men who often had to work under constant fire.

That wasn't the only communications problem. Newspaper stories were telephoned to London and Paris, where they were cabled to various parts of the world. But there were only two outside lines from Madrid, and the competition for them was fierce since it often took six hours to get a connection. Some newsmen slept on cots in the telephone room, leaving instructions to be awakened when their calls went through. Censorship was rigid and the government operator simply cut the line when anything unauthorized was transmitted. Reporters tried American slang to beat the rules but the Spanish got a Canadian girl operator who understood their game. Trips to the front were hazardous. On a bitter, December day in 1937, an insurgent major led an automobile caravan of newsmen up to the Teruel front, which was under murderous artillery fire. One shell landed a foot from a car occupied by Eddie Neil, of AP, Bradish Johnson, of *Newsweek* magazine, and two British correspondents. Johnson, a twenty-three-year-old Harvard graduate covering his first war, was killed instantly, as was one of the Englishmen, Richard Sheepshanks, of Reuters. Neil, his body pierced by thirty-four shell splinters, was rushed to a field hospital, where he died three days later. Neil had once written to a friend:

"One nice thing these wars do teach you—when your number comes up, you grin, shrug, and make the best of it. No one has time to listen to a bleat."

The cities also could be dangerous for correspondents. The government looked everywhere for suspected spies, and sentries were inclined to be trigger happy. H. E. Knoblaugh, of the Associated Press, was walking along a Barcelona street one day when a man just ahead of him was shot dead when he failed to heed a guard's order to halt. Another time Knoblaugh and a government official were riding in a car which was riddled with bullets from an unseen sniper. Both escaped injury.

Among those who covered the rebel side was Edmond Taylor, a native of St. Louis, Missouri, who had been in Europe since 1928 for the *Chicago Tribune*'s foreign news service. With the help of a devil-may-care French chauffeur, Taylor slipped into Spain over a narrow dirt road, talked his way past several armed patrols and got to Pamplona, where he got an exclusive story on an insurgent uprising. Later he was arrested by Falangist (rebel) troops and interrogated for hours before being released. He promptly cabled this dispatch: "This civil war or insurrection, or whatever you want to call it is something like a crusade, something like a Chinese bandit war, something like a family feud in the Kentucky mountains, or an ax murder in a basement."

Taylor, a resourceful reporter, often evaded censorship by smuggling out his copy and filing from a French border town. When news was scarce the insurgents obligingly organized junkets to the front. On one of these excursions, Taylor's car reached a village just as loyalist troops were storming it. He and other reporters were trapped in a stream of rifle and machine gun fire from both directions. At the same time, two government planes strafed the fleeing Falangist militia. The aircraft chased Taylor's car along a road, forcing him and his driver to leap from the auto and dive over a stone wall. The correspondent later recalled that "we . . . lay very small among the boulders for a quarter of an hour while the two airmen put in some much-needed machine gun practice on the car . . ."

Aerial warfare on such a large scale was a new element, even for veteran war correspondents. For example, planes pounded Barcelona for three days in a row, flying over every hour on the hour. Irving B. Pflaum, a United Press man who survived the assault, wrote prophetically:

> That is the one real fear I remember out of my two war years in Spain. It is that methodical, systematic, terroristic bombing of crowded metropolitan centers that may be one of the decisive factors in future wars. With me it was decisive. It licked me.

Pflaum left Barcelona for two days but returned and continued reporting from that stricken city. Earlier, he had covered most of the important battles in Spain and got a scoop of the famous siege of the Alcazar in Toledo. He was the only newspaperman to enter the rebel-held fortress until it was rescued by the troops of General Francisco Franco, the insurgent commander-in-chief.

Vincent Sheean, who had undergone bombing by five planes in Morocco thirteen years before, counted more than fifty as he lay in a ditch with Spanish loyalists under fire. The German and Italian aircraft rained down hundreds of explosives around Sheean, but he emerged unscathed and returned to the meal of chestnuts and champagne cider he had left when the raid warning sounded.

Air defense improved with air power, a factor that affected correspondents who used planes to observe ground action and to fly in and out of Spain with their reports. Jay Allen, *Chicago Tribune,* arranged to take a French plane to Bilboa, the scene of a major battle. The rebels sent word they would shoot the craft down and the French ambassador in Spain warned that they meant it. Allen, however, figured the rebels wouldn't fire on a plane that contained a foreigner. He recounted later:

". . . They [the rebels] always knew who was aboard. There was no other way to get in to Bilboa." The plane landed safely.

Several correspondents were jailed and at least one was threatened with death. H. R. Knickerbocker, of the Hearst Press, and Webb Miller, United Press, were imprisoned by Franco's lieutenants despite the fact that both had been more than fair to the insurgents in their writings. Another UP man, Henry Gorrell, was clapped behind bars by government soldiers in Madrid because he had been in Fascist Italy and spoke Spanish with an Italian accent. What followed was a nightmarish experience. Before thrusting him in a cell a guard attached a tag with the number sixty-one to his coat. The reporter noticed that all the other prisoners also had numbers. A guard regularly called out a number and someone, his hands bound, was then led away. Gorrell realized to his horror that the numbered inmates were being taken to the execution grounds and shot. He also became aware that the numbers were being called in order and that they had reached the forties. Like the strokes of doom, the voice intoned: "forty-one . . . forty-two . . . forty-three." The count had reached forty-eight when Gorrell's colleagues from the UP's Madrid bureau found him and obtained his release. Gorrell learned later that only he and his chauffeur had left the jail alive.

The *Chicago Tribune*'s Alex Small was seized by Falangist troops in Irun and taken before the military commander, who told him:

"You will be shot."

"What is my crime?" Small asked.

"You said that Madrid would not fall," the general retorted.

Fortunately, a photographer friend heard of Small's predicament and staged a big shouting scene at headquarters. Small was freed.

American correspondents devised various ways to outwit the heavy censorship. A former Oregonian, Lawrence A. Fernsworth, of *The New York Times,* hit upon a scheme that enabled him to file almost every story from France. Operating from Barcelona, Fernsworth would go aboard a British cruiser in the harbor at night to "visit the captain." About an hour later the ship would speed him to Marseilles, where he posed as the vessel's interpreter. Two days later the warship would return to Barcelona and Fernsworth would casually stroll off, his "visit" concluded. British cooperation was obtained because the correspondent also was covering the war for the *London Times*.

Charles Nutter, of the Associated Press, was able to file a story completely free from censorship from Madrid, but it almost cost him his life. The copy had been approved by the censor and Nutter prepared to telephone it to London from the press room of the Foreign Office building. As usual, the censor listened on an extension phone to make sure that only the authorized message was sent. Suddenly, the newsman heard the whine of a shell and a heavy crash against a church a few yards away. Fragments whistled through his window, narrowly missing his head. The next shell smashed into the Foreign Office building, which was the real target. The structure shook as the bombardment continued. Nutter, shaken but determined to file, began his recitation. But the shelling was too much for the censor. He dropped his phone and ran for the basement where others were fleeing. As he dashed by Nutter's desk he yelled:

"Tell them anything you like about this attack."

Nutter dictated a story of the cannonade as it happened. He was on the line for almost an hour while shells burst all around him. Miraculously, he suffered not a scratch, although six persons were killed by shrapnel. When he had finished, his London colleague hung up with a "Cheerio!"

In the winter of 1939, when Franco's legions were nearing final victory, Harold Peters, the UP manager in Barcelona, sent out a story which, despite the censor's alterations, managed to indicate that the war was almost over. It read:

> BARCELONA, January 23 (UP)—The entire Spanish Republic was placed under a state of war, equivalent to martial law, today as Barcelona prepared to defend the city against General Franco's army of Spaniards, Moors, Italians and Germans. It was reported that the town of Martorell, ten miles to the west, had fallen.

But Peters' greatest coup came the next day while he was on the telephone to London, dictating a long, dull dispatch based on official government handouts. He had reeled off 700 words in a flat monotone when, without altering his voice pitch, he said: "Big shots scrammed Franceward." Then, without interrupting his flow, he continued droning out the approved account. The censor missed the injected sentence but the London UP office did not and Peters had the scoop of the year. United Press flashed a bulletin to the world that the Republican government had fled Barcelona for France and that the war was all but finished.

One American reporter traded his pencil for a gun. He was James Phillips Lardner, twenty-four-year-old correspondent for the Paris edition of the *Herald Tribune*. In the fall of 1938, he gave up his job and joined the Abraham Lincoln Brigade, a loyalist unit composed of American volunteers. One day he was sent out on a patrol and never returned. He had been shot, the last American to die in Spain. His press credentials were found on his body.

Because some newsmen felt strongly about the conflict, their writing frequently took on a vivid, personal quality. Jay Allen filed this story to the *Chicago Tribune:*

> I have just come from Badajoz, several miles away in Spain. I have been up on the roof to look back. There was a fire. They are burning bodies. Four thousand men and women have died at Badajoz since General Francisco Franco's rebel foreign legionnaires and Moors climbed over the bodies of their own dead through its many times blood-drenched walls.

Ernest Hemingway wrote:

> The dead sleep cold in Spain tonight. Snow blows through the olive groves, sifting against the tree roots. Snow drifts over the mounds with the small headboards. (When there was time for headboards.) The olive trees are thin in the cold wind because their lower branches were once cut to cover tanks, and the dead sleep cold in the small hills above the Jarama River. It was cold that February when they died there

and since then the dead have not noticed the changes of the seasons.

The Spanish Civil War ended in 1939, but for many American correspondents who covered it, the terrible conflict was only a prelude to the bloodiest war in the history of mankind.

6

World War II—
Massive Coverage

A ROUTINE DAY APPEARED TO BE SHAPING UP IN THE WASHINGTON
bureau of the Associated Press on Sunday, December 7, 1941. Editor
W. T. "Bill" Peacock had sent a reporter to cover a press conference
with the Russian ambassador, Maxim Litvinoff, but little news was
expected from it. Ed Bomar was musing over a "think piece" on the
worsening relations between the United States and Japan but he decided to go out for a cup of coffee before writing it. Other staffers
drifted in and out on various assignments.

When the telephone rang at 2:20 P.M. no one got excited. Phones
ring frequently in news offices. But this was the White House switch-
board operator, who told AP to stand by for an important call from
Steve Early, President Roosevelt's press secretary. Peacock instructed

the teletype operator to hold the circuit open for a bulletin. In a few moments Early came on . . .

"I have an announcement from the President. . . . The Japanese have attacked Pearl Harbor and the island of Oahu from the air . . ."

The message was heard simultaneously by United Press and International News Service.

Peacock shouted "flash" to the operator and then wrote seven startling words. In a few seconds the operator was punching them out and in minutes they would be shooting around the world.

FLASH
WASHINGTON—WHITE HOUSE SAYS JAPS ATTACK
PEARL HARBOR

The *AP World,* the wire service's house magazine, recalled:

> The flash cleared, Peacock then started to write a bulletin, but his hands were shaking so badly he thought he might have to give up. He recalls that Bomar and Lear (who didn't know what the flash said) were staring at him as if he had gone crazy.
>
> "I think *you* had better write this bulletin, Ed," Peacock told Bomar.
>
> "What do you want me to say?"
>
> "We're at war, that's what," said Peacock, even as—somehow—he managed to write his own bulletin.

In a matter of hours the world-wide facilities of AP and other press associations were focused on the biggest story of the century. Newspapers, too, mobilized their forces—from New York to California there was one main front-page story: the war.

World War II had the most immense coverage in the history of warfare. A total of 1,646 American news correspondents were accredited by the United States War and Navy Departments. This figure does not include reporters accredited by Allied and neutral countries. The Associated Press alone had 179 correspondents and photographers on various fronts. In addition to the press associations, thirty newspapers and twelve magazines had their own reporters and cameramen in fighting theaters. The leading radio networks also had their men in combat zones.

The price for this massive coverage came high. Thirty-seven correspondents were killed and 112 wounded. The Associated Press and United Press each lost five men, International News Service, two, and *The New York Times* and *Time-Life,* three each. Seventy-eight newsmen waded ashore with the first wave of infantry on D-Day in Normandy. Correspondents flew on bombing missions, rode destroyers, went on patrols, were strafed and shelled and frequently became the targets for snipers.

American newsmen and women covered World War II from the time German troops had marched into Poland in September, 1939, setting off the most terrible conflict in history. Most of these reporters were old European hands, such as Leland Stowe, *Chicago Daily News,* and Louis P. Lochner, Associated Press.

Lochner was a University of Wisconsin graduate who began his newspaper career in Milwaukee before he knew how to operate a typewriter. On his second day on the job he rented a typewriter and taught himself to use it overnight. A foreign correspondent since 1914, he was in Berlin at the outbreak of the Second World War and with Pierre Huss and Frederick C. Oechsner, of UP, rode into Paris with German troops. After the Japanese attack on Pearl Harbor, Lochner and other American correspondents were interned by the Germans and held for five months before being transported out of the country in a sealed train.

Leland Stowe moved from the Spanish Civil War to World War II fronts without breaking stride. He got a clean beat on the Nazi seizure of Oslo, Norway, reporting that "Less than 1,500 German soldiers had occupied Norway's capital while thousands of dazed, bewildered citizens looked dumbly on." Earlier Stowe had covered the Russian-Finnish War in weather that was 30 degrees below zero. He wrote:

I had lain in the snow and watched Russian bombs coming down on me when I was nearly one mile away from the only legitimate target anywhere around. I had talked with passengers whose train had been machine-gunned on the Turku-Helsinki line. I had been in bombed Finnish towns and villages . . .

Stowe also was the first American correspondent with the Russian army after Germany invaded that country. He later became a journalism professor at the University of Michigan.

Another highly experienced combat correspondent at the outset of World War II was John T. Whitaker, *New York Herald Tribune,* who was almost shot as a spy along with two other American reporters.

Whitaker, H. R. Knickerbocker and Virginia Cowles were the only journalists to witness the entry of the German army into Czechoslovakia. They were arrested by the Gestapo, charged with being Czech spies and sentenced to death. With machine guns pressed against their stomachs, the three started arguing with their German captors. The Gestapo officer had foolishly given them his name, and the correspondents, with a great show of outrage, tossed out the names of high German officials from Hitler on down. A dire fate would befall the officer if anything happened to them, they warned him. The upshot was that the Gestapo leader not only freed them but apologized and gave them half a tank of precious gasoline for their car!

Meanwhile, twelve American newsmen were receiving accreditation in London by the British Army for a trip to the Western Front. Among them were William Chaplin, INS; Norman Denny, *New York Times;* William H. Stoneman, *Chicago Daily News;* Bill Henry, *Los Angeles Times;* and Arthur Mann, Mutual Broadcasting System.

The British, always sticklers for propriety, brooded over the issue of what kind of uniforms the Americans would wear. The question was: Would American neutrality be violated if they were outfitted in British officer garb? It was finally decided to dress them in an olive drab officer's uniform with no indication of nationality. Most American newsmen suffered through this debate without caring one way or another about what they wore. They wanted to get to the front and would have gone there in street cleaners' uniforms. They managed far better, however, and their final ensemble was dashing indeed. It included a military cap with a two-inch circle of green felt topped by a gold "C" for correspondent. On the newsman's left shoulder was another green felt strip with Foreign War Correspondent emblazoned in gold letters. Thus bedecked, they went off to France with seventeen British correspondents and a few from other countries.

Censorship was in full force for correspondents on all fronts. The delay in dispatches from London climbed from an hour to five hours a month after hostilities started. Italy, Poland and Germany also subjected stories by neutral reporters to a rigid screening, which meant that they were sometimes not sent at all. The *Herald Tribune* was forced to abandon its direct telephone line from London to New York and had to rely on regular cable.

Newsmen in London and Paris worked out of buildings protected by sandbags and stocked with food, cots, lanterns and candles. Both the Associated Press and United Press, working on a twenty-four-hour shift, moved 80,000 words a day in the first two weeks of the war. This was twice their normal average, but American readers were devouring the reports. Newspaper circulation shot up immediately with a number of dailies increasing the number of pages and their press runs. The *New York Daily News* picked up 200,000 new readers a day and a thirty-two-page "War Crisis Extra" of the *Chicago Times* was sold out minutes after it hit the streets.

What made this war different and more difficult for the press to cover was the fact that it was fought on many different fronts, each with its own communications problem. In the Spanish-American War, and even World War I, there was usually only one major battle going on at one time. Correspondents generally covered the same actions and developed a camaraderie akin to club membership. They could make unified requests of the brass and could be of great help to each other in the problems of news gathering. World War II reporters, on the other hand, were scattered around the world and many of them never met. In the early part of the war, for example, the British fought in France, Scandinavia, Greece, North Africa and Turkey.

Many of the American correspondents were young—in their twenties and thirties. Robert St. John, at thirty-seven, was told by his AP superiors in New York in 1939 that he was "too old" to be a war correspondent when he applied for European duty. St. John disagreed and, taking his wife, shipped off to Paris as a free-lancer. Luck was with him. He walked into the AP's Budapest bureau the day Germany invaded Poland. The bureau chief, Robert B. Parker, Jr., told St. John to take off his coat and go to work. He never stopped until the end of the war, becoming one of the outstanding newsmen in Europe.

Sporting a luxuriant beard which caused some persons to suspect him as a spy, St. John roved over Europe during the war years, piling up a series of adventures which he later put into two highly readable books. He was in Belgrade when German bombers hit the city and fled just ahead of Nazi troops. With Leigh White of the *New York Post* and Russell Hill, *New York Herald Tribune,* St. John hired a fishing boat to get them across the Adriatic to Greece. They made it, although their pilot was killed by German dive bombers. In Greece they hopped a troop train which also was sprayed by Nazi aircraft fire. Machine gun bullets found both St. John and White, and the latter was wounded critically. Crawling out of the wrecked train, the three newsmen crouched under a truck as the planes screamed over again and again, dropping bombs and spattering the roadbed with machine gun fire. After the ordeal, St. John and Hill ripped a shutter off a nearby house and used it as a stretcher to haul the badly bleeding White to an aid station. They were picked up by a British truck which took them to a makeshift hospital at Corinth. The truck was strafed twice on the way, and the hospital area was the scene of another air raid. St. John leaped into a trench, where he was buried under a mass of wreckage, but he survived. White underwent four operations to save his shattered leg. He wrote later: "There never was a better comrade than Bob St. John."

Working out of the Budapest AP office with St. John was a handsome, blond Arizonian named Daniel DeLuce, thirty, who filed a memorable story from stricken Poland. When the Nazis invaded that country, the New York AP headquarters lost contact with its two bureau men in Warsaw. The Budapest office was ordered to find the two missing correspondents and DeLuce was picked for the job. With no press credentials, uniform or gun, DeLuce set off for a strange country that was being battered to pieces by German military might. Three days later the two Warsaw AP men phoned in that they were safe and with the fleeing Polish government. But no word from De-Luce. On the sixth day the Budapest AP phone rang and it was DeLuce, speaking calmly against a background roar of falling bombs. He was brimming over with hot, front-line news. He was in Lwow, Poland, reporting that "there are at least twenty-one Nazi bombers over my head. The table the phone's on is shaking like a leaf." The story, as eventually filed to New York, won DeLuce a commendation from Kent Cooper, head of Associated Press at the time.

There is always danger for the combat correspondent but there are other factors that make his job a tough one. Harold Denny, a newsman in Europe in the early days of World War II, wrote in *The New York Times:*

> . . . No, danger is not the greatest worry of the war correspondent. What breaks the correspondent down is physical exhaustion and sometimes the hardships of living in primitive places under wartime conditions. Often a correspondent must lose a whole night's sleep in an air raid, then start early in the morning on a long trip to the front, plod for miles and return in the evening with good stories, but too tired to write them properly . . .

The war from the German side was covered by thirty American correspondents in Berlin. Their toughest foe was Nazi censorship, which included tapped telephones and the constant threat of expulsion for violating any of the press rules. Among the newsmen ordered out of the country were the scholarly Otto Tolischus, *The New York Times;* Beach Conger, *Herald Tribune;* and his successor,

Ralph Barnes, a strapping, well-liked veteran correspondent who was later killed in the crash of a British bomber in Yugoslavia.

One of the Berlin newsmen, Ernest R. Pope, recalled that they saw only what the Germans wanted them to see, which was not much. The correspondents were periodically taken on guided tours by Nazi officers, who explained the fighting as they rode along. Once a bullet shattered the windshield of an automobile carrying a group of American newspapermen through France.

Pope said press briefings were conducted by a Professor Boemer, adding:

> During conferences we may ask Boemer any questions we please. He may answer them, or he may merely smile. The smile is a form of censorship. It means "I shan't tell you and I shan't say I won't tell you, and if you find out elsewhere, send the story at your own risk."

American correspondents ran into similar frustrations in Italy, Hitler's Axis partner. In October, 1940, the Italian army invaded Greece from Albania, but newsmen were refused permission to visit the front. The UP's Rome bureau manager, Reynolds Packard, and his wife, Eleanor, also a UP staffer, worried that some rival would somehow get to the battle area and beat United Press on the story. Then Mrs. Packard got an idea. She remembered an old pass for Albania issued to her husband by a high government official. The pass had been invalidated by the Greek war but the Packards, with the aid of a few rubber stamps, doctored it up to make it look current. The scheme worked and Reynolds Packard got a front-row seat for the fighting. In fact, his seat was too close. Caught under a Greek artillery barrage, he scrambled into a ditch almost on top of an Italian soldier who had got there a second before. The next shell ripped off the arm of the soldier and Packard wormed his way to a new position. He next hitched a ride in an Italian correspondent's car, but the auto was struck by machine gun bullets before it made two miles. Still, the determined newsman filed several dispatches from Greece via the Italian reporter who had access to a plane to Rome.

They were the first eyewitness accounts of the invasion and a scoop for United Press. Packard narrowly missed being tossed out of Italy; the government let him off with a stern reprimand.

To a dedicated reporter this is simply part of the game. His job is to get the story and he will get it almost any way he can. Fascist and Nazi regulations on news made the correspondents' task harder, but it also gave them an opportunity to stretch their wits and ingenuity to the limit. To the newsman, rules aimed at suppressing information are fair game if there is no convincing reason for them. It should be noted, however, that American correspondents attached to United States troops cooperated fully with authorities in holding back facts that might have jeopardized our forces.

Correspondents in London did not have to leave the city to find the war. It was there. In 1940, England endured a terrible ordeal that came to be known as the Battle of Britain. Night after night, thousands of Nazi bombers rained tons of explosives on that country, with London as the main target. For Londoners the air-raid siren and the shelter became a way of life. Thousands of persons were killed and vast sections of the city destroyed by bombs and raging fires. It was terror bombing at its worst.

The raids, the devastation and the grim will and courage of the British people were reported by a corps of American newsmen who lived through it all at the risk of their lives. Their names read like a roster of a modern journalism hall of fame: Quentin Reynolds, Raymond Daniell, Edward R. Murrow, Larry Rue, Drew Middleton, Wallace Carroll, Robert J. Casey, William H. Stoneman, James B. Reston, Robert Brunnelle, H. R. Knickerbocker, Vincent Sheean and others.

Daniell, of *The New York Times,* was bombed out of his home and office in London but often drove through the ruined streets to check damage from the raids. One of his rivals was winsome Tania Long, of the *Herald Tribune.* But love won over competition and they were married during the war. They are both *Times* reporters today.

Larry Rue, a seasoned *Chicago Tribune* correspondent, was known for his icy calm during the worst of the London attacks. During one blitz he was playing chess in the Savoy Hotel bar with a British friend. Stanley Johnson, another *Tribune* reporter, was about to leave when a huge land mine exploded outside the door, knocking him several feet back into the room. As he lay dazed in the darkness and rubble, Johnson heard the composed voice of Rue accusing his opponent of wrongfully moving a pawn in the sudden blackout.

A native of Fosston, Minnesota, Rue broke into newspaper work on the *Duluth News Tribune* in 1913. He was an Air Corps pilot in World War I and later flew his own plane to cover stories all over the world. He was a genial companion, but tireless and creative in his job. When the Nazis overran Holland, Rue and other American correspondents were trapped with no way to communicate the story. This was only a temporary setback for Rue. He got some expensive paper, red ribbon and sealing wax to make an official looking document on which he described himself as a very important person. He then hired a car and roared down the road, waving the phony pass in the face of every guard he met. The paper enabled him to drive through half of Europe until he got back to his base in London. Rue died in 1965 at the age of seventy-two. Forty-six of those years had been spent as a newspaperman.

Dan Campbell, of United Press, was another correspondent bombed out of his London home. He stumbled into the UP office that night, his face blackened, wearing one shoe and carrying a kitten he had grabbed up while tearing out of the apartment. In the office it was standard practice for UP men to dive under their desks during a raid and then resume working when the danger was past.

There was more than just straight reporting from London. Many correspondents felt deeply about the cruel destruction of the famed city and hammered out their feelings on the typewriter. Here is a story filed by Wallace Carroll of United Press:

LONDON, December 30 (UP) Some of the London that Americans learned about in school or read about in books met death tonight in the flaming fury of a German fire raid.

Some of the London of Shakespeare and Dickens, of Oliver Goldsmith and Dr. Johnson, I have seen crashing around me. . . . I wish I could ask Americans to put on their tin hats and go with me as I went through the City of London. . . . Beyond the fire we could see St. Paul's cathedral. I had never seen it looking so serenely beautiful. As the smoke and flames whirled around its dome it seemed to rise higher above them. So far as we could tell no military objective was destroyed, but what the Germans destroyed during the night can never be restored—beauty, serenity, grandeur, history in stone.

One group of American correspondents set up a watch station on the famed cliffs of Dover, over which the German planes flew each night. The reporters, who dubbed their perch "Shakespeare Cliff," included Vincent Sheean, who wrote:

. . . In general we lived in expectation of a full German attack any night, and the nerves of some of our friends grew so exacerbated by suspense that they actually said they would welcome it. . . . The daily spectacle was out of all ordinary experience or easy credibility. In color alone it defied description. Sometimes the Messerschmitts would attack our barrage balloons with green or yellow tracer bullets; the silver balloons would explode in flame and sink gracefully to earth; our Bofors guns around the port would attack the Messerschmitts with balls of fire . . ."

The American press corps suffered a crushing casualty in the Battle of Britain. Webb Miller, the superb UP correspondent, was killed when he was either pushed or fell from a train during a London blackout. He was covering his eleventh war.

The number of American war correspondents involved in World War II shot up sharply after Japanese bombs smashed down on Pearl Harbor. We were at war and the communications media were aware that the demand for news would be greater than ever. American men would be fighting and dying and no one here could any longer think of the war as a remote event involving "foreigners."

Earlier, I described the excited reaction of the wire services and newspapers here to the Pearl Harbor attack. In Honolulu, newsmen on that fateful Sunday flung on their clothes and raced to telephones, where they poured out the story as it was happening. Joe Alex Morris tells how Frank Tremaine, the United Press bureau manager in Honolulu, was awakened by the sound of falling bombs, looked out his window at the Japanese planes, confirmed the raid with the Navy and then went to work. He dictated cable flashes to San Francisco and Manila and then rushed out of the house, telling his wife to stand by the phone for a call from San Francisco's UP office. "Tell them everything you see," he shouted as he jumped into his car and sped off to Fort Shafter.

At 8:30 A.M., Jim Sullivan, UP San Francisco, rang the Tremaine home and Mrs. Tremaine stood at the window and delivered an eye-witness account of the second wave of enemy planes coming over the island, the warships being hit and the efforts of anti-aircraft batteries. As she talked, bombs dropped near her home and one fell so close that Sullivan heard it on the other end. Even while she was on the phone, UP rewrite men were pounding out the story in San Francisco.

Also shaken out of bed was Dick Haller of International News Service. He climbed to the roof of the Honolulu *Advertiser* building and watched the spectacle for several minutes before scurrying for a phone.

The Pearl Harbor episode provided Larry Nakatsuka, *Honolulu Star-Bulletin* reporter, with an interview that was as fantastic as it was exclusive. Nakatsuka, a native Hawaiian of Japanese ancestry, was sent to get a reaction to the bombing from the Japanese consul general in Honolulu, Nagao Kita. The official refused to believe his country's planes were attacking Pearl Harbor, insisting that it was all part of an American training exercise. He stuck to this view even when Nakatsuka showed him the *Star-Bulletin*'s first edition, which announced the bombing in big, black headlines. Kita probably thought there was something to the story when FBI agents came later and took him away.

Like many civilians in Honolulu, some newsmen couldn't believe there was a war on. Joseph C. Harsch, of the *Christian Science Monitor,* awakened by the thud of bombs, turned to his wife and remarked that what they were hearing was a "good imitation" of a European air raid. The Harsches then proceeded to take their usual morning swim, convinced the Navy was engaging in another maneuver.

It was evident from the correspondents' accounts that the United States was caught tragically by surprise. The December 15, 1941, issue of *Time* magazine reported to a stunned nation:

. . . The clock on the Aloha tower read 7:55.
The Japs came in from the southeast over Diamond Head. They could have been U.S. planes shuttling west from San Diego. Civilians' estimates of their numbers ranged from fifty to 150. They whined over Waikiki, over the candy-pink bulk of the Royal Hawaiian Hotel. Some were (it was reported) big four-motored jobs, some dive bombers, some pursuits. All that they met as they came in was a tiny private plane in which lawyer Ray Budwick was out for a Sunday-morning ride. They riddled the lawyer's plane with machine-gun bullets, but the lawyer succeeded in making a safe landing. By the time he did, bombs were thudding all around the city. The first reported casualty was Robert Tyce, operator of a civilian airport near Honolulu, who was machine-gunned as he started to spin the propeller of a plane.
Torpedoes launched from bombers tore at the dreadnoughts in Pearl Harbor. Dive bombers swooped down on the Army's Hickam and Wheeler Fields. Shortly after the attack began, radio warnings were broadcast. But people who heard them were skeptical until explosions wrenched the guts of Honolulu. All the way from Pacific Heights down to the center of town the planes roared, leaving a wake of destruction . . .

Honolulu was the hottest news spot in the world that day and thousands of words were filed by reporters who gathered the details even as the bombs fell. But on Monday the navy censorship apparatus was in full operation and the correspondents had to adjust to a new set of rules.

When the marines sloshed ashore on a steamy, Japanese-held island called Guadalcanal in 1942, there was one civilian among them. He was a gangling, twenty-six-year-old INS reporter named Richard Tregaskis, who would vividly portray for the reader in Sioux City the horrors of jungle warfare. He was among the first of a swarm of American correspondents who reported from the far off places that are now part of our history—Guadalcanal, Tarawa, Iwo Jima, Okinawa, the Philippines. The South Pacific war was different from that in Europe, and newsmen had to adapt to conditions of which they had never dreamed.

Tregaskis, who had been told before the landing that Guadalcanal was one of the most heavily fortified Japanese bases in the Solomons, got the information confirmed on the beach.

He wrote in his diary:

> . . . The worst time in a bombing is the short moment when you can hear the bombs coming. Then you feel helpless, and you think very intensely of the fact that it is purely a matter of chance whether or not you will be hit . . . and while your mind is racing through these thoughts, your ears, without any conscious effort on your part, are straining to gauge the closeness of the bombs from the swishing and the rattling of them. . . . After the sticks have hit, you wait a few more minutes, suffering from a disinclination to get up immediately; you watch the ground, close in front of your eyes, very patiently, and wait to see if there will be another stick . . .

Tregaskis was hospitalized with a stomach ailment but returned shortly to the fighting. One of his reasons for leaving Guadalcanal after seven weeks was that he had worn out his last pair of shoes and the marines had none to fit him. The six-foot, seven-inch reporter wore size fourteen. He was later wounded in Italy.

A few months earlier, several American correspondents had escaped from the Philippines when they fell to the Japanese. Frank Hewlett, United Press, and Nat Floyd, *New York Times,* fled in an automobile minutes before key bridges were dynamited by retreating American forces. The Associated Press's Clark Lee, Melville Jacoby, of *Time,* and his bride of one month, slipped out on a small island freighter, dodging Japanese ships for twenty days before reaching Australia.

Not all the journalists were so fortunate. The Japanese captured *Life* photographers Carl and Shelley Mydans and the UP's Frank Weisblatt, who was wounded on Bataan. Two months later, Jacoby, a twenty-five-year-old former Stanford University student, was killed in an airplane crash in Australia. Another air casualty was Kansas-born Raymond Clapper, a well-known Scripps-Howard columnist. The fifty-two-year-old Clapper was killed when the plane in which he was riding collided with another in February, 1944, during the Marshall Islands invasion.

American newsmen went out of their way to find trouble in the South Pacific. Bob Cromie, *Chicago Tribune,* rode in a Liberator bomber on an historic raid on the Japanese stronghold of Rabaul right after recovering from malaria. Vern Haugland, a slim, thirty-four-year-old AP correspondent, lived through one of the most extraordinary adventures of the war after he bailed out at 13,000 feet from a stricken plane over the wild Owen Stanley Mountains in New Guinea in August, 1942. For forty-three terrible days the Minnesota-born reporter wandered sick and half starving through uninhabited jungle, living on berries, grass and weeds. Through most of this period he kept a diary, parts of which follow:

Aug. 19—Second day lying on rocks, chewing grass and reeds, praying a great deal. Getting so weak. Hardly any hope now. Lost life preserver. Watched vainly all day for a plane. Only hope is a plane dropping food or ground aid arriving—both extremely unlikely. Looks like I shall die here soon.
Aug. 20—Worst rainy nite since Mike [co-pilot who bailed out with Haugland] and I spent two terrible ones. I was just

lying in the mud, soaked and stinking, all night. Somehow stronger today. Foot healing, too. If could get real food think could hike around mountain. Seems too bad to die when maybe could struggle to a village. If only the mountains didn't stretch on, sharper and sharper. If only knew shortest way to go to sea.

Aug. 22—Worst rainy nite yet—didn't think I could stand that torture. Rain today—dread tonite.

Aug. 24—Hard warm dry nite. Two and one-half weeks with nothing to eat—my body looks terrible. If some one comes today I can still live—but I need food. Head clear—position good otherwise.

Aug. 26—Rained early last night, drenching me. Found dirty hole for head under rotten log—rest exposed. Awful nite. Awoke a bit delirious for first time. Looks equally bad tonite —I'm still wet from last nite.

Sept. 4—After tough day, worst wettest cold nite. Hand so numb can't write. Terrible struggle through jungle today.

Half crazed, his emaciated body blotched by hundreds of insect bites, Haugland was found by missionaries in a native village into which he had wandered. The co-pilot was never found.

The reporter was recovering in an army hospital when a nurse announced one day that he had a visitor. In strode General Douglas MacArthur, who took a small blue box from his pocket, removed a medal and pinned it on the startled Haugland. The general had awarded him the Silver Star, declaring that it was an "outward symbol of the devotion and fortitude with which you have done your duty." Then, MacArthur added:

"I can't tell you how much we have been inspired by your getting back after such trials and hardships."

It was the first time the Silver Star, which denotes heroism, had ever been awarded to a civilian.

Another AP man, Clark Lee, was trapped with United States troops on the island fortress of Corregidor in the Philippines. The Americans lived in tunnels which were bombed constantly by the Japanese. Lee wrote later:

. . . The bombs didn't screech, whistle or whine. They sounded like a pile of planks being whirled around in the air by a terrific wind and driven straight down to the ground. The bombs took 30 years to hit. While they were falling they changed the dimensions of the world. The noise stripped the eagles from the colonel's shoulder and left him a little boy, naked and afraid. It drove all the intelligence from the nurse's eyes and left them vacant and staring. It wrapped a steel tourniquet of fear around your head, until your skull felt like bursting . . .

There was air-tight censorship on Corregidor, but Lee later was able to slip over to Bataan on an island boat and file his stories. Before the surrender to the Japanese, General MacArthur ordered Lee and other correspondents to destroy their notes and diaries lest they fall into enemy hands. When the fortress fell, Lee managed to escape through the Japanese blockade.

About eleven months later, eight American correspondents took part in one of the bloodiest actions of the entire war—the landing on Tarawa in the Central Pacific. Hundreds of American troops were killed and wounded in the seventy-six terrible hours it took to capture the island. The reporters, like the infantrymen, dug in on the beachhead and waited for a Japanese counterattack. Robert Sherrod of the *Saturday Evening Post* remembers saying to William Hipple, AP, as they shoveled out holes:

"Well, Bill, it hasn't been such a bad life."

"Yeah," replied Hipple, "but I'm so damned young to die."

Sherrod, in recalling the incident, noted that the AP newsman was not making a flip remark. "He had scant hope that we would survive the night," Sherrod said.

That morning Hipple was pushing his way through the surf when a battalion commander next to him was shot through the head.

Gilbert Bundy, a Hearst Newspapers artist, was on a landing boat that got a direct mortar hit. Everybody on board except Bundy was killed or hurled into the water. He remained on the craft for several hours with the bodies and then swam to another boat only to find that it too was full of dead marines.

In the South Pacific war American forces seized about one hundred islands.

"For the war correspondent island-hopping had a lot to be said for it," Sherrod wrote. "Between battles he could ride the aircraft carriers, retreat to Pearl Harbor and rewrite communiqués or go home and rest for the next show."

Some correspondents paid with their lives for their stories. William Chickering, *Time-Life,* died on the battleship *New Mexico* when it was struck by a Japanese kamikaze (suicide) plane. Byron Darnton, *The New York Times,* was killed when American fighter planes mistakenly fired on a landing craft taking him and soldiers onto the Buna beachhead. Darnton had applied for war duty at the age of forty-five. A twenty-seven-year-old INS correspondent, Jack Singer, lost his life when a torpedo struck the aircraft carrier *Wasp.* Ship's officers wrote Singer's last dispatch and sent it to his wire service "to maintain the traditions of the fourth estate." A former New York sports writer, Singer was the first American correspondent to go on a navy torpedo plane mission. Asahel Bush, AP, Stanley Gunn, *Fort Worth Star Telegram,* and John B. Terry, *Chicago Daily News,* were killed in a Japanese attack on the island of Leyte. The Associated Press's Charles McMurtry was burned in the torpedoing of the aircraft carrier *Hornet.* It was the second ship sunk under him. Also wounded in the Pacific was big Howard Handelman, INS.

War often has no logical pattern, and newsmen sometimes found their greatest story where and when they least expected it. Ira Wolfert, thirty-two, a New Yorker, hitched a ride on a Flying Fortress bomber to get an air view of the 3,700-mile battle front in the Solomon Islands. He was doing a rather routine "over-all picture" story for the North American Newspaper Alliance.

Once he was aloft, however, the story became anything but routine. The American crew spotted a four-motored Japanese bomber at about the same time it saw them. These two lumbering monsters then engaged in of all things an aerial dog fight, wheeling in and out of cloud banks and blasting away at each other with cannon and machine guns. Here is how Wolfert described the action:

> . . . we hurtled clear through the cloud and into blinding sunlight and there the Jap was, right along side of us, maybe 50 feet away. . . . Every trigger on every gun on both planes was pressed at once and held. Thousands of bullets criss-crossed through the narrow spread of air. The planes rocked along side by side. . . . Our plane shuddered under the impact of bullet after bullet and teetered and buckled under the blasts of its own guns. . . . The thousands of explosions seemed one vast unending blast. I could see the Japs clearly, four or five, something like that, small, shrunken-seeming figures huddled up over their guns. I could see a cannon firing at us, smoke blowing from its open mouth, and I could see our red tracer bullets pelt like darts into the Jap . . . This was kill or be killed all the way through . . .

The American bomber shot down the enemy craft and Wolfert, who had worked his way through Columbia University's School of Journalism by driving a taxi, went on to win the Pulitzer Prize for his reporting of the Solomon Islands campaign.

7

World War II—
From North Africa
to Berlin

ON THE OTHER SIDE OF THE WORLD AMERICAN CORRESPONDENTS were having their first experience at covering United States troops in combat. They reported from the time our green G.I.s in North Africa received their first baptism of fire to the final days when our toughened, battle-weary forces defeated the German army on its own soil and ended Hitler's dream of world conquest.

The Americans landed in Africa in 1942 to assist the British Eighth Army, which had fought bitterly across the desert sands against General Rommel's Afrika Korps. Among the American correspondents there were Don Whitehead and Hal Boyle, Associated Press; Ernie Pyle, Scripps-Howard Newspapers; Robert J. Casey, *Chicago Daily News;* and Leo Disher, United Press, who suffered twenty-four wounds, including two broken legs on a United States Coast Guard cutter in the battle for Oran. The ship was raked so heavily by fire from defending French Vichy forces that Disher was the only man left alive on the bridge. He still managed to swing himself over the side and swim to shore.

The AP's Don Whitehead, a slim Kentuckian, had been with General Montgomery's British Eighth Army before we entered the war. He later made five amphibious assault landings in Italy and Europe. He won the Pulitzer Prize twice, once in World War II and the second time in Korea.

Most of the reporters in North Africa followed the Allied offensive through Sicily, Italy and France. Jack Belden, an experienced and first-rate *Time* magazine man, went ashore with the American landing unit at Salerno, Italy, and stopped a German rifle bullet which fractured his thigh bone. From his hospital bed he sent this cable to *Time:*

"Your burly, silent, broody correspondent got slugged in the leg at Salerno. . . . Doctors estimate it will be six months before I can use crutches, so you had better send another correspondent."

Belden had come through North Africa and Sicily without a scratch, although in the first Sicily landing his boat was machine-gunned, bombed and strafed. Before he was taken out of Italy on a hospital ship, Belden filed this dispatch on the Salerno assault, which had gone badly for our forces:

> The Germans knew we were coming and waited for us. All they had to do was study the map and see that the obvious place for us to strike was south of Naples. The day before our landing our LST's were bombed continuously. Probably the German air force had us under observation at all times. The enemy knew not only approximately where we were going to land, but when.

The *Chicago Tribune*'s John Hall Thompson became the world's first paratrooper-reporter when he jumped into combat near Tebessa, Algeria, during the North African invasion in November, 1942.

Thompson, who sported a neatly trimmed Van Dyke beard, later dropped behind enemy lines in Sicily and was with one of the first assault waves on D-Day in Normandy. He was awarded the Purple Heart for jump injuries and the first Medal of Freedom given a war correspondent.

A native of Chicago and graduate of Williams College, Thompson was credited with being the first Allied correspondent to meet the Russian army at its historic contact with the American forces on the Elbe River in Germany.

The Sicily landings in 1943 also drew a number of other American correspondents, since they represented the first Allied invasion of Europe. Among them were John Gunther, famous for his "Inside" books; Drew Middleton, *The New York Times;* and Richard Mowrer, *Chicago Daily News.* Gunther, writing for North American Newspaper Alliance (NANA) and broadcasting for the old Blue Network, was caught between a British and German artillery exchange. He described exploding shells as "huge firecrackers angrily snapping."

Another "specialist" in Italy was novelist John Steinbeck, who said he got his best war reporting advice from Robert Capa, the famous photographer, who told him: "Stay where you are. If they haven't hit you, they haven't seen you." Steinbeck also had a fatalistic philosophy about combat correspondence.

"If you stayed a correspondent long enough," he wrote, "and went to the things that were happening, the chances were that you would get it."

This gloomy prediction proved true for his friend Capa and for another great correspondent, Ernie Pyle.

He weighed only about 111 pounds, even with a steel helmet, which he usually refused to wear. He balked at wearing an officer's uniform like other combat correspondents because "I'd feel silly in one." Lined up against other World War II reporters, he was not the best writer, and many of his colleagues had a better grasp of the big picture. He was not concerned with scoops and seldom, if ever, tried to get one. At forty-two he was older than most war correspondents and he was subject to frequent illnesses.

Yet Ernest Taylor Pyle was one of the outstanding combat reporters of all time, known to millions of both soldiers and civilians. The enlisted man thought of him as their friend, generals were proud to shake his hand and his fellow correspondents admired and respected him. At the height of his career his column was syndicated in more than two hundred daily newspapers, and when he returned to the United States on leave he was treated as a celebrity.

All this began modestly enough for Ernie Pyle. He was born in 1900 on a farm in Dana, Indiana. An only child, he enrolled as a journalism student at Indiana University but dropped out to take a job as a reporter on the *La Porte Herald* in his home state at twenty-five dollars a week. His work was considered "unimpressive" by the paper's editor.

The slight, restless newsman drifted through a series of newspaper jobs in the following years. He went to the *Washington Daily News,* then to the *New York Evening World* as a copyreader, from there to the *New York Post* and then back to the *News,* where he eventually became the managing editor. But inside work irritated him and he wangled a roving assignment which took him all over the United States. When America entered World War II, Pyle was eligible for the draft, but the selective service board gave him a six-month extension, which he used to ship off to Europe as a correspondent for the Scripps-Howard newspapers.

At first he had no thought of front-line duty, planning only to come in after the fighting to chronicle the less spectacular activities of the troops. Ernie Pyle had little ego and in 1942 never imagined that he would become one of the most famous combat correspondents in history.

After spending a few weeks with troops in Ireland, Ernie Pyle embarked for North Africa, where American G.I.s, under General Dwight D. Eisenhower's command, were battling the Germans and Italians. Soldiers and sailors held their breaths as the wizened little newsman staggered down the gangplank in Algiers, loaded down with a stuffed barracks bag, bedroll, gas mask, helmet, canteen, pack sack and typewriter. But he made it and he made it through a lot tougher conditions in the next two years before he died from a Japanese sniper's bullet in the South Pacific.

Pyle was a great war correspondent because he could put himself in the place of the common soldier. He had a deep feeling of respect and admiration for the mud-slogging infantryman who does the dirty work in any war. Once he wrote:

> . . . Now to the infantry . . . the God-damned infantry as they like to call themselves. . . . I love the infantry because they are the underdogs. They are the mud-rain-frost-and-wind boys. They have no comforts, and they even learn to live without the necessities. And in the end they are the guys that wars can't be won without.

Hal Boyle, another top correspondent and Pyle's friend, said of him: "He was able to write about war in terms of the men who fought it. He had a down-to-earth quality that gave him a deep understanding of the G.I."

Pyle shared many foxholes with his friends in the infantry, often writing his column with a pencil while a soldier stood guard with a rifle or machine gun. His frailty made him prone to every cold germ kicking around and he was frequently laid up with flu or some other virus infection. Lee G. Miller, in his biography of Pyle, noted that he once took a break from the front line to do a series of articles on General Omar Bradley. So identified was he with the enlisted men that other correspondents kidded him about "hobnobbing with the brass."

"There goes that social-climbing columnist," Hal Boyle chortled when he saw Pyle one day.

Ernie Pyle marched with the infantry through North Africa, Sicily and Italy and in the invasion of France. "I had lived with the army so long I actually felt like a soldier," he wrote. He chronicled the bone-wracked weariness of the G.I. after days and weeks on the line, his grim sense of humor and his constant flirtation with death. In one memorable column, Pyle told the people back home:

> The front-line soldier I knew lived for months like an animal, and was a veteran in the cruel, fierce world of death. Everything was abnormal and unstable in his life. He was filthy, dirty, ate if and when, slept on hard ground without cover. His clothes were greasy and he lived in a constant haze of dust, pestered by flies and heat, moving constantly, deprived of all the things that once meant stability—things such as walls, chairs, floors, windows, faucets, shelves, Coca-Colas, and the little matter of knowing that he would go to bed at night in the same place he had left in the morning. . . . The front-line soldier has to harden his inside as well as his outside or he would crack under the strain.

Of the war correspondent, Pyle wrote:

> . . . Writing is an exhausting and tearing thing. Most of the correspondents actually worked like slaves. Especially was this true of the press association men. . . . The result was that all of us who had been with the thing for more than a year finally grew befogged. We were grimy, mentally as well as physically. We'd drained our emotions until they cringed from being called out from hiding. We looked at bravery and death and battlefield waste and new countries almost as blind men, seeing only faintly and not really wanting to see at all. . . . I am not writing this to make heroes of the correspondents, because only a few look upon themselves in any dramatic light whatever. I am writing it merely to let you know that correspondents, too, can get sick of war—and deadly tired.

But still another ordeal was to come—the Allied invasion of fortress Europe. Ernie Pyle and many other "tired" correspondents reported that titanic clash.

Walter Cronkite, United Press reporter, was getting ready for bed in his London apartment on the night of June 5, 1944, when there was a knock on his door. It was an Air Corps public relations officer, who suggested that he get dressed quickly. "There's a good story breaking," he confided.

Other reporters in England also vanished quietly from their usual haunts that night. The "good story" was the historic "D" Day landing on the Normandy beaches, the great turning point in the war and the prelude to victory for the Allied forces. The invasion brought together the biggest armada of ships and men in history. This was the moment for which the world had been waiting. The Allied forces numbered nearly 3,000,000 soldiers, sailors and fliers. Piled up on British docks were 2,500,000 tons of supplies. The strike across the English Channel under the code name "Overlord" would involve thirty-nine divisions and 11,000 aircraft. The fleet assembled to transport men and materiel included 600 warships and 4,000 supporting vessels. Early the next morning, June 6, 1944, this huge juggernaut moved toward the coast of France. With it went seventy-eight news correspondents who wrote a new chapter in the history of journalism.

Before the invasion, the correspondents accredited to United States forces were summoned to headquarters and given instructions. They were told that their gear for the assault would be limited to 125 pounds of baggage plus their typewriters, musette bags and what they could carry on their person. They were advised to take enough paper and carbon sheets to last at least ten days. (Because of censorship requirements reporters made four copies of every story.)

The reporters also were told to get necessary medical shots, have their blood type marked on their identification tags and have their money converted into travelers checks.

Later, correspondents attached to Supreme Headquarters were told by General Eisenhower:

"I believe that the old saw—'Public opinion wins wars'—is true. Our countries fight best when our people are best informed.

"You will be allowed to report everything possible, consistent, of course, with military security.

"I will never tell you anything false."

The AP's Don Whitehead, who had survived four other beach landings under fire, was given an even more succinct send-off by the commander of an assault unit to which he had been assigned. The officer said:

"We are ready to help you. . . . The people at home won't know what is happening unless you are given information and I want them to know. . . . If you're wounded, we'll take care of you. If you're killed we'll bury you."

The chances of getting killed on D-Day were excellent, but remarkably only one civilian correspondent died in that action. He was Arthur Thorpe, veteran newsman for the British Telegraph Exchange, who was hit by shrapnel as he observed the landing from a coastal craft.

A number of other reporters had close brushes with death. The first American press casualty was the AP's Henry B. Jameson, whose boat was offshore for fourteen hours under intense fire before it landed after four attempts. One shell burst slammed young Jameson against a truck, wrenching his shoulder and spraining his knee. Then fragments from another blast got him in the leg. He was removed to a navy flagship, where he sent his dispatch on the invasion. The newsman included a note to his office, explaining that his injuries, although not serious, "will prevent me from carrying out my assignment at the present time."

Another Associated Press man, Roger Greene, straining under a sixty-pound pack, waded ashore as several soldiers fell dead beside him. When he hit the beach he found his knapsack soaked with the blood of a fatally wounded man next to him. Robert Miller, United Press, spent two bone-chilling hours in the English channel after his vessel was torpedoed and sunk by a German U-boat. He lost his life belt but managed to grab hold of a raft, to which he clung until rescued by a British corvette. Miller was blocked by censorship from filing a story from a British port, but the AP's Tom Yarbrough relayed it to London for him.

The old campaigner Robert J. Casey, *Chicago Daily News,* trudged into the beach on D-Day and endured what he described as an "uncomfortable hour in a wild storm of machine-gun bullets."

"Probably the most amazing feature of our life on the beach was that we seemed to have solved the problem of getting along with no sleep at all," he added. "For the first couple of days we were so tired that we could hardly lift a teacup. Then we were just numb."

Some newsmen covered the invasion from the air. Wright Bryan, lanky associate editor of the *Atlanta Journal,* squeezed his six-foot, five-inch frame into the forward "blister" of a troop-carrying plane that was among the first to cross the channel. He was the first war correspondent from the invasion front to broadcast an eyewitness account of the fighting.

After Walter Cronkite was awakened in his London apartment, he was invited to fly with a B-17 bomber group over the French coast at low altitude as a spearhead to the invasion.

"Of course," said an officer, "you don't have to go if you don't want to." Cronkite quickly accepted and had a grandstand seat for the Normandy assault. Later Cronkite switched to broadcast journalism and became a well-known newsman for the Columbia Broadcasting System.

Collie Small, another United Press correspondent, was a D-Day guest on a Marauder plane that snaked through a wall of German flak to dump fragmentation bombs on German gun emplacements along the Normandy coast.

In cases where the military can only take one correspondent on a particular mission, it usually selects a wire service reporter because of the number of newspapers and other media he serves.

Despite the number of invasion correspondents, several reports directly from the beaches arrived in the United States from twenty-eight hours to four days late. *Time* magazine reported that special radio transmitters for the press "had been washed out in the landings." Another plan for sending copy to London by courier did not materialize, *Time* said. Some correspondents used carrier pigeons to file their dispatches.

Among the first American newsmen to file from France were William Stoneman, rugged *Chicago Daily News* veteran; the UP's Henry T. Gorrell and Richard D. McMillan; and Joseph Driscoll, *New York Herald Tribune,* who wrote this story from a small French town:

> The smoke of flaming Isigny is still in my eyes. When we entered that picturesque provincial town yesterday in the wake of our conquering troops, the main street was a long row of crackling, collapsing buildings. Nearly everything along the cobblestoned Rue de Cherbourg was on fire except the enamel highway sign which proclaimed Cherbourg to be 61 kilometers . . . ahead.
>
> . . . it's appleblossom time in Normandy right now, and on the outskirts of Isigny we found a formation command where they had pitched their tents and dug their foxholes. It was a beautiful setting for a deadly business.

Ernie Pyle's first invasion dispatch, written aboard a landing craft, described vividly his feelings when notified by the military to prepare for the channel crossing. He wrote:

> . . . I began having terrible periods of depression, and often would dream hideous dreams about it. All the time fear lay blackly deep upon your consciousness. It bore down on your heart like an all-consuming weight. People would talk to you and you wouldn't hear what they were saying . . .
>
> . . . you see, we had all been living comfortably in hotels or apartments for the last few weeks. We had got a little soft, and here we were again starting back to the old horrible life we had known for so long—sleeping on the ground, only cold water, rations, foxholes and dirt. We were off to war again.

The invasion was page-one news all over the United States. The first report of it came from the German radio, which was followed by an Allied announcement. The military and civilian correspondents who accompanied the first landing forces filed about two hundred stories to London by press wireless, courier and pigeon. They were funneled through a single censorship system and then passed to a pool desk, where the best were picked by a British-American correspondents' committee for distribution around the world. On the day before D-Day, a twenty-two-year-old AP telegrapher in London mistakenly filed a false invasion flash, causing a momentary panic in the wire service office. But the message was killed before it could be printed anywhere. The first official news of the Normandy landing was given by radio to the three major United States press associations, Associated Press, United Press and International News Service.

Despite first-day communication problems, the Normandy assault was a journalistic triumph. Within a week dispatches were flowing smoothly to the United States, delayed only by normal wartime censorship. Elmer Davis, director of the Office of War Information, declared that the story received the "widest and best news coverage of any military operation in all history."

Other newsmen who went in with advance Allied units on D-Day were Clark Lee, INS; John H. Thompson, *Chicago Tribune;* Joseph Willicombe, INS; Hanson Baldwin, *The New York Times;* Jack Tait and John O'Reilly, *New York Herald Tribune;* W. C. Heinz and Gault MacGowan, *New York Sun;* Kenneth Crawford, *Newsweek;* Ira Wolfert, North American Newspaper Alliance; John McVane, National Broadcasting Company; Larry Lesueur, Columbia Broadcasting System; Gladwin Hill, AP; and several others.

The UP's Henry Gorrell was credited with filing the first story from French soil after the dateline: "With U.S. Assault Troops in North Central France."

The advancing Allied forces in Europe and in the South Pacific were equally well covered by American correspondents, many of whom kept right on going from the beachheads.

One of them was Hal Boyle, a stocky, likable AP man, who began his brilliant journalistic career as a campus correspondent for the wire service while attending the University of Missouri. He joined AP full-time after his graduation in 1935, moving from Kansas City to St. Louis to New York, where he became night city editor. When

World War II erupted he volunteered for correspondent's duty and was sent to North Africa in 1942. He quickly sought the front line and remained there throughout the rest of the war. His adventures were many and varied.

As he was riding into a Tunisian town one day, Boyle was startled to hear natives chanting along the roadside: "Vote for Hal, the Arab's pal." They had been coached by Boyle's prankish news colleagues as a respite from what usually is a grim business.

In Sicily, Boyle and Don Whitehead walked into the port city of Messina just ahead of British General Montgomery's main forces. Crossing over to Italy with Allied troops, Boyle was under almost daily fire. He recalls once lying in a ditch as bullets from a German Messerschmitt plane "ripped along the road by my head." Sharing the same ditch was Ernie Pyle, Boyle's friend, who, the AP man remembered, held a trench shovel over his head.

"Pyle rarely wore a helmet," said Boyle, "and this was his way of protecting himself during an air attack."

Like Pyle, Hal Boyle had a talent for plucking out human interest material from the daily brutality that is war. He wrote the hard news battle stories, but he also found time to dig up vignettes about the men in the foxholes—material that didn't fit into the "big picture" in Europe but that would tell the reader that the G.I. was not a faceless, impersonal statistic, a symbol to be used only for recruiting advertisements and war bond rallies. Boyle collected anecdotes, offbeat experiences and other feature material into a column he called "Leaves From a War Correspondent's Notebook," which soon became familiar to millions of American readers.

Already a veteran of beach assaults in North Africa and Italy, Boyle also splashed ashore at Normandy and stayed with Allied forces until the end of the war. In the dark winter of 1944 he scored a notable scoop on a German atrocity that came to be known as the Malmédy Massacre. Near the little Belgian town of Malmédy, Nazi troops cut off and captured an American artillery observation battery. The entire unit was then lined up on a snowy field and cut down by machine gun fire. It was an execution.

Meanwhile, in a nearby town, Boyle and other correspondents had received news of a battle a few miles away. The others left for the spot but Boyle headed in another direction.

"I knew how fast the German army could travel," he said, "and I had a hunch the important action was elsewhere. Along a road near Malmédy I ran into a jeep carrying wounded men and some of them were crying. They told me about the massacre. They had either played dead or ran for the woods when the Germans began shooting. They were the survivors."

Boyle hurried to the site and confirmed the slaughter. Sprawled in the snow were the bodies of 144 American soldiers. The AP newsman dashed back to headquarters and filed the story. Later he informed other correspondents of the facts—but the Malmédy Massacre was his beat.

Hal Boyle also was one of the first American correspondents to cross the famed Remagen Bridge over the Rhine River in Germany. By a lucky stroke of fate the Nazis had left the bridge intact, but it was under intense shell fire.

"I had to guess when there would be a break in the firing," Boyle said. "Then the moment came and I figured it was now or never." He made it across the bridge successfully, but just ahead of him an American infantryman was killed by a piece of shrapnel.

Boyle's other stories included the historic meeting at the Elbe River in Germany between victorious American and Russian troops. For his general excellence as a war correspondent, Hal Boyle was awarded the Pulitzer Prize for 1944. As a post-war AP columnist, he won a number of other journalistic honors, including those from the Overseas Press Club of America and his alma mater, the University of Missouri School of Journalism.

Many other fine newsmen contributed to the massive flow of World War II information to the American public. Another book would be required to list all of them and their individual exploits. A few others should be mentioned here, however.

The *Chicago Tribune*'s Robert Cromie, a veteran of South Pacific action, resumed in England his old habit of hitching rides on bombing missions. On one raid over Germany his plane was damaged so badly by flak that the pilot suggested that he had better bail out. Cromie declined, later giving this reason:

"It wouldn't have looked good if a *Tribune* man bailed out and the others got killed."

With the tail assembly half shot away, the plane limped back over the channel as Cromie gave first aid to the wounded tail gunner. The bomber crash-landed in England and Cromie walked away from the wreckage without a scratch. That afternoon he hopped another bomber for a new raid over enemy territory.

Lowell Bennett, INS, had an equally horrendous ride in a British Lancaster bomber which was attacked by German fighters over Berlin. The newsman related:

> . . . Disaster struck with a terrifying abruptness. Our world burst into an inferno of flame. The plane shuddered, then heaved and rocked violently. A long burst of cannon fire had slashed into our right wing and both engines had exploded into a furious fire . . .
>
> . . . One of the fighters was near us, closing for the kill, his target a flaming beacon. . . . Searchlights swung onto us and coned the stricken bomber with blinding brilliance. . . . I snatched up my parachute. . . . I knew without being an airman that this Lancaster would never carry us home . . .

Bennett jumped from four miles up while flak zipped by him. From that point he lived through a series of hair-raising adventures, including capture by the Gestapo and three daring escapes from prison camps. He was caught each time, but in one attempt he somehow filed a story to INS from occupied Prague, datelined INSIDE NAZI EUROPE! And at his last prison he and other inmates published an underground newspaper, *Pow Wow,* which ran a story of the Normandy invasion twenty minutes before it was carried by New York dailies! The illicit paper's news sources were newly arrived prisoners, German newspapers and magazines and a hidden radio over which they heard BBC reports.

Also flying bombing runs was middle-aged battle veteran Ernest Hemingway, who covered the British Royal Air Force for *Collier's* magazine. The novelist-journalist later attached himself to the American Fourth Infantry Division, staying with it all across France and Belgium and up to the Battle of the Bulge.

AP correspondent Daniel DeLuce got into Yugoslavia for exclusive stories about the partisan fighters opposing the Nazis, a coup which earned him a Pulitzer Prize. Stoyan Pribichevich, *Time* writer, was one of four Allied correspondents captured in a German paratroop raid on Marshal Tito's headquarters. He was threatened with death before a firing squad, but the Nazis gave him a reprieve at the last moment. Instead he was ordered to carry wounded German soldiers through a no-man's land under murderous fire by Yugoslav partisans. "We were merely to be offered another way of dying," Pribichevich wrote. A German with a machine gun stayed behind the correspondent to make sure he wouldn't run away. But he escaped during an exchange of fire that killed most of his captors.

The Associated Press's A. I. Goldberg got an exclusive interview with Nazi bigwig Hermann Goering when he surrendered to American 36th Division troops. Goldberg also got a beat on the rescue of King Leopold of Belgium by United States soldiers.

Mark S. Watson, of the *Baltimore Sun,* a World War I veteran, uncovered the brutal slaying of seven Belgian villagers by the Gestapo. His story of the incident was one of a series that rated a Pulitzer Prize.

Gault MacGowan, *New York Sun,* was captured by the Germans in 1944 but escaped when American troops attacked the town in which he was being held. Another captured correspondent, Joseph Morton, Associated Press, was executed by the Nazis in an Austrian prison camp in January, 1945.

Big, hard-driving Wes Gallagher today heads the Associated Press. During World War II, he was one of the AP's star reporters. He was in Athens when the city fell to the Germans on April 27, 1941, and flashed the first news of the seizure to the outside world. Gallagher was later arrested by the Gestapo in Vienna but managed to make his way across Europe to Lisbon. When the British and Americans invaded North Africa, Wes Gallagher led an AP field crew which covered every phase of the fighting there. He was out of action twice, once with yellow jaundice and again after he fractured his spine when his jeep overturned in Africa. Even in bed he was not idle. While confined in plaster casts, he wrote a book about his war experiences, *Back Door to Berlin.*

Among the correspondents sickened by the Nazi death camps was Gene Currivan, *The New York Times,* who toured the infamous Buchenwald after its liberation by American troops.

Look magazine's Donald Grant, a former Des Moines, Iowa, reporter, flew with Flying Fortresses over Germany, sailed with British gunboats on night raids on the German-held coast and was the first correspondent to cover the Greek guerrilla fighters.

James E. Roper, United Press, was awakened in his Milan hotel room by the shouts of "Mussolini, Mussolini" outside his window. He flung on his clothes and raced out to a public square where the Italian dictator and his mistress lay dead, killed by partisans. Roper dashed for a telegraph office to file a story that electrified the world. Another eyewitness to Mussolini's end was Milton Bracker of *The New York Times.* A day later, April 30, 1945, Adolph Hitler shot himself to death in a Berlin bunker. The story of his final days was written by a number of correspondents, notably Pierre J. Huss of INS, who interviewed the German dictator's secretary for the details.

By 1945 a number of "hometown" correspondents were in Europe, backing up the wire services with stories of local boys in action. Among them were Duke Shoop, *Kansas City Star;* Gordon Gammack, *Des Moines Register and Tribune;* Lee McCardell, *Baltimore Sun;* Reelif Loveland, *Cleveland Plain Dealer;* Jack Carlisle, *Detroit Free Press;* and Tom Treanor, *Los Angeles Times,* who was killed when his jeep was crushed by a tank just before the liberation of Paris.

Several correspondents entered Paris with the Allied troops, including James McGlincy, United Press; Paul Manning, Mutual radio network; and Larry Lesueur, CBS. The three were suspended for thirty days because they broadcast news of the liberation from a Paris radio station without clearance by the censor. But the big story had been told and the reporters took their sentence lightly by celebrating in Paris.

In World War II history was to repeat itself with another disputed surrender scoop—but with a major difference. In the First World War, Roy Howard of United Press filed an armistice story on November 7, four days before the fighting actually ceased. He claimed (and it was substantiated) that he had been given incorrect information by an official source.

On May 7, 1945, Edward Kennedy, chief Associated Press correspondent at General Eisenhower's headquarters, filed a bulletin to the London AP office announcing that Germany had surrendered unconditionally. The story was *true* but it set off a journalistic controversy that is still discussed today.

Kennedy, a seasoned and respected war correspondent, was among the seventeen reporters selected to witness Germany's signing of the surrender at the red schoolhouse in Reims, France. En route in an Air Corps plane, the newsmen were told by Brigadier General Frank Allen that he was putting them on their honor not to release the peace story until it had been announced officially by the Supreme Headquarters of the Allied Expeditionary Force (SHAEF). Kennedy said he phoned the bulletin to London only after returning to Paris and hearing the surrender reported on the Office of War Information's American broadcasting station in Europe. He also pointed out that the Germans had broadcast a cease-fire to their troops on the same day as the formal signing ceremony in Reims.

Kennedy's beat touched off wild celebrations in the United States, but in Europe the press and the military unleashed a torrent of recriminations against the AP reporter. SHAEF stopped all Associated Press filings for more than six hours. Kennedy himself remained under the ban until July, 1946.

But this was mild compared to the reaction of many of Kennedy's fellow correspondents. Fifty-four of them accredited to SHAEF

Editors, as well as reporters, often earn positions in the annals of war correspondence. The flamboyant abolitionist editor Horace Greeley, of the *New York Tribune,* urged Lincoln to move the ill-prepared Union forces into Virginia. His critics blamed him for the Northern defeat at Bull Run. The Civil War also saw the emergence of American war photography. The pioneering combat photographer Mathew Brady developed his pictures of this conflict in traveling darkrooms like the one below, which were dubbed "Whatizzit Wagons" by soldiers.   *New York Times Photos*

Two of America's most fam
World War I corresponde
were Richard Harding Davis (
low) and Frazier Hunt (left). 7
handsome and high-living Da
a veteran of four wars, was
foremost correspondent of
day. Davis enjoyed luxury,
would go anywhere for a sto
He rode with the Rough Rio
in the Spanish-American V
and was arrested as a spy by
Germans during World War
Hunt, like Davis, filed dispatc
from south of the border dur
the Mexican Revolution, a
later reported World War I a
the Russian Revolution. His
ports from Russia were influ
tial in bringing about the w
drawal of U.S. troops.

Wide World Photos Inc.

The famed correspondent Ernie Pyle identified with the common soldier, sharing his hardships and telling his story. Most correspondents wore officers uniforms, but Pyle refused to do so. He was a small man, but never shirked his job, even under fire, until the day he was killed by a Japanese sniper's bullet in the South Pacific. One of Pyle's outstanding colleagues in World War II was *Times* correspondent Walter Duranty (below), who covered the French armies.

Bob Bryant and Frank Hewlet were the only two civilian war correspondents to accompany Merrill's Marauders behind the Japanese lines in Burma. Although most correspondents did not carry arms, Bryant and Hewlet had to defend themselves against enemy ambushes in the jungle through which they traveled.

Margaret Bourke-White, shown here on the Italian front, photographed the action for *Time and Life* in World War II. This outstanding woman photographer is also famous for her pictures of guerrilla warfare in Korea.

Margaret Bourke-White, LIFE Magazine © Time Inc.

Among the many American correspondents covering World War II was Edwin L. James (above right), shown here with a number of his colleagues interviewing General Joseph L. Dickman in France in 1918. The dashing Edward R. Murrow brought World War II into American livingrooms. During the London blitz, he broadcast night after night from the roof of the BBC building.

George Rodger, LIFE Magazine © Time Inc.

The plane in which the daring *Chicago Tribune* correspondent Floyd Gibbons is seated crashed en route to Warsaw, where he was to cover the Polish retreat and the advance of the Russian forces. Gibbons was unhurt, and continued his journey on another plane dispatched from Paris. The veteran war photographer Robert Capa(above), was admired by the troops for his bravery under fire. The Israeli-Arab War of 1948 was his last—while on patrol he stepped on a land mine and was killed instantly.

Many of the correspondents reporting for the various branches of the armed forces during World War II were not professional newspapermen; but they got their stories under fire, concentrating on human interest materials. The Marine correspondents pictured here did not have their own publication. Their dispatches were released to publications at home.

Official U.S. Marine Corps Photos

Photographer Joe Rosenthal's shot of the flag-raising on Iwo Jima won him a Pulitzer Prize.

Marguerite Higgins interviews Brigadier General John S. Bradley near the front in Korea in 1951. She covered the fall of Hitler's war machine as a 23-year-old and six years later won a Pulitzer Prize for front line reporting in Korea. She was determined to earn her right to carry a press card at the front, often working 20 hours a day under hazardous conditions, and died at the age of 45 from a tropical disease contracted in Vietnam. *Associated Press*

Many of the correspondents in Vietnam are young but others, like Nobel Prize-winning author John Steinbeck, are veterans of World War II. At 64, Steinbeck came to Vietnam to "go up the rivers and into the mountains" to see it for himself. *Associated Press*

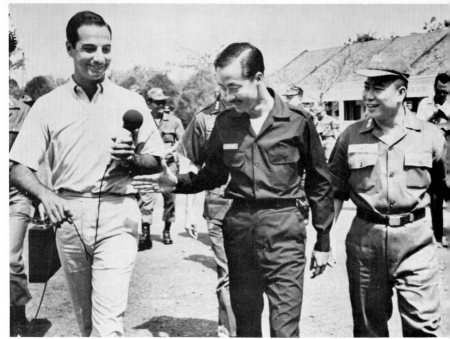

NBC-TV reporter Ron Nessen, shown here interviewing Premier Ky, was wounded while filming an operation in the central highlands of Vietnam. Veteran reporter Hal Boyle, who won the Pulitzer Prize for his human interest stories of World War II, continued his work in Korea and (below right) Vietnam.

ABC

Newsday correspondent John Van Doorn won the Ernie Pyle Memorial Award for his human interest stories from Vietnam. ABC-TV and radio newswoman Marlene Sanders is one of several women to file stories datelined Vietnam. Here, she is shown preparing for her trip to Southeast Asia.

Newsday

Associated Press

Conditions at the front for American correspondents in Vietnam are, as these pictures show, anything but luxurious. Rain is no hindrance to AP's Peter Arnett, whose reporting from Vietnam has placed him in the front rank of American journalists. Horst Faas (right), who was awarded the Pulitzer Prize for his Vietnam pictures, will go anywhere for a good picture. The same is true of award-winning TV reporter Morley Safer (top right). Vietnam is Safer's third war; he was also in the Congo and Cyprus.

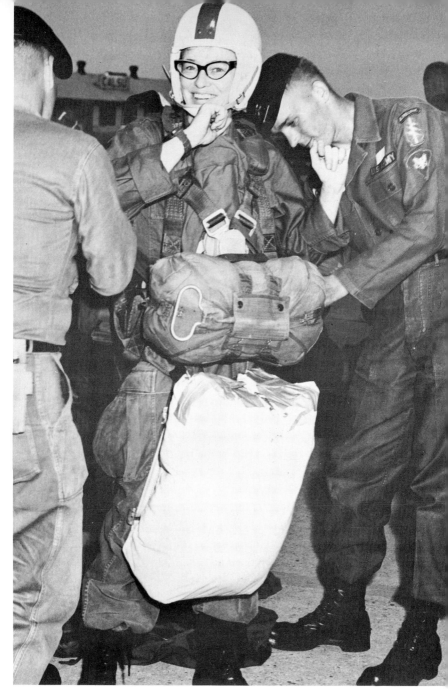

Dickey Chapelle, one of America's best-known newspaperwomen, was killed in action in Vietnam. Both photographer and writer, she consistently hunted the dangerous, difficult, hard-to-get stories. Here, she receives last-minute instructions for one of the thirty parachute jumps she made during her lifetime.

Nancy Palmer Photo Agency

signed a stinging letter to General Eisenhower, declaring:

"We have respected the confidence placed in us by SHAEF and as a result have suffered the most disgraceful, deliberate, and unethical double-cross in the history of journalism."

The debate raged in the United States as well, with some newspapers and newspapermen taking Kennedy's side. A. J. Liebling, also a World War II correspondent, intimated that the objections were based not so much on ethics as on regrets by the other correspondents that they had not done the same thing.

Kennedy, who was showered with personal abuse by his colleagues, was later fired by the AP. He stoutly defended his action and said he would do the same again under similar circumstances. The newsman claimed also that the SHAEF news embargo was political in that it was designed to allow the Russians to hold a surrender ceremony of their own in Berlin. Supporters of Kennedy add that the AP release probably saved many lives by forcing an early SHAEF armistice announcement.

Editor & Publisher, the newspaper trade magazine, defended Kennedy editorially, saying, ". . . Had we been in Kennedy's position we are inclined to believe we would have attempted to do just as he did."

To the general public, the issue mattered little. Its concern was only that the war in Europe was over.

One footnote should be added here on the general reputation of war correspondents in the eyes of military leaders. General Dwight D. Eisenhower, in his book *Crusade in Europe,* declared:

> In World War II the great body of the American and British press representatives comprised an intelligent, patriotic and energetic group of individuals. They could, with complete safety and mutual advantage, be taken into the confidence of the commander. When this was done the press body itself became the best possible instrument for the disciplining of an individual who violated any confidence or code under which the group was operating. Throughout the campaigns in the Mediterranean and Europe, I found that corre-

spondents habitually responded to candor, frankness and understanding.

General Omar N. Bradley, First Army commander, said of newsmen:

> . . . But though they were privy to many of our secrets, not once during the war did a newspaperman accredited to my command willfully violate a confidence of mine.

While people in New York danced in the streets to celebrate victory in Europe, American soldiers on a Pacific island called Okinawa listened to the screaming shells and whining bullets and wondered what all the fuss was about back home. Their war was not over and it seemed on that May day in 1945 that it would be months before it was. American forces were pushing to victory in a series of bloody island campaigns, but the Japanese mainland stood virtually intact. Gordon Cobbledick, *Cleveland Plain Dealer* correspondent, wrote from Okinawa:

> . . . So this was V-E Day. It was V-E Day in the United States and Great Britain and Russia, but on Okinawa the ambulances skidded through the sticky red mud and bounced over rutted, rocky coral roads. Some of the men who rode them gritted their teeth behind bloodless lips and let no cry escape them. . . . Some screamed with pain that morphine couldn't still. And some lay very quiet under ponchos that covered their faces.

But the end came. It came after United States planes dropped atomic bombs on the Japanese cities of Hiroshima and Nagasaki, wreaking terrible death and destruction and changing the face of war for all time. William L. Laurence, *New York Times* science writer, rode on one of the two bombers that shepherded the B-29 that unloaded the A-bomb on Nagasaki. He wrote:

> Out of the belly of the Great Artiste [the bomb plane] what looked like a black object went downward. . . . A giant flash broke through the dark barrier of our arc welder's lenses

and flooded our cabin with intense light. . . . A tremendous blast wave struck our ship and made it tremble from nose to tail.

Later in the story, Laurence described the "giant pillar of purple fire" from which issued a "giant mushroom."

It was not mere chance that Laurence was picked as the only correspondent on the historic atomic bomb flight. A highly respected reporter and Pulitzer Prize-holder for science writing, Laurence, then fifty-seven, was the official historian of the atom bomb project and as such was privileged to share secrets that no other reporter was given. His account of the Nagasaki raid and his work generally on the bomb resulted in a second Pulitzer award.

What Laurence did not see from the air, the horrifying devastation of the two Japanese cities, was reported by other war correspondents. One of them, Homer Bigart, *New York Herald Tribune,* went into Hiroshima and saw ". . . flat appalling desolation, the starkness accentuated by bare, blackened tree trunks and the occasional shell of a reinforced concrete building . . ."

There was one last big story to cover—the formal surrender by the Japanese aboard the U.S.S. *Missouri* in Tokyo Bay. More than two hundred Allied correspondents were on hand for the ceremony. There would be more wars to cover but for most of the newsmen World War II would be one of the high points in their careers. For some it would be the highest point. One fact stands out. Never had a war been reported so thoroughly by so many first-rate and dedicated journalists. In many cases they gambled with their lives to get the story. Thirty-seven lost the gamble.

Marquis Childs, the columnist, paid the World War II correspondents this well-earned tribute in a 1945 *Look* magazine article:

> If there is anything a fighting man has done in this war that a war correspondent has failed to do, I do not know what it is. . . . The number of war correspondents killed is far greater in proportion than the number of deaths among combat troops. That is because their own zeal to see it themselves,

to be there when it happens, drives them into the face of danger. . . . Battle reporters on the job have the hardboiled nonchalance of the fighting man. Outwardly they take themselves and their work with the utmost casualness. That, however, is largely a facade. They are adventure-loving, deeply sentimental and insatiably curious. If they weren't, of course, they would be writing about something a lot quieter and safer than war.

8

Korea:
The Shattered Calm

IN 1950, AMERICANS BECAME FAMILIAR WITH A NEW TERM: THE 38th parallel. On June 25 of that year 150,000 Communist North Korean troops crossed that dividing line into South Korea, igniting a war that was to last three years and cost thousands of lives.

The history of the conflict went back to September, 1945, when American occupation forces landed at Inchon, Korea, following the Japanese surrender in World War II. In January, the United Nations ordered elections in South Korea, which became an independent republic under American protection and guidance. North Korea took no part in the election and remained in the Communist sphere. Three days after the invasion of South Korea, President Harry Truman

committed United States military forces in support of that country.
Red China came to the aid of North Korea.

Coverage of the war came quickly. The wire services and major
newspapers rushed men from the States and from their Tokyo bureaus to Korea. The fighting produced some of the best reporting
and writing in the annals of journalism.

Keyes Beech, of the *Chicago Daily News,* was one of the first
correspondents on the scene. Here is part of his description of the
fierce battle of the Changjin reservoir:

> . . . Thousands of Chinese troops—the marines identified
> at least six divisions totaling 60,000 men—boiled from every
> canyon and rained fire from every ridge.
>
> Sometimes they came close enough to throw grenades into
> trucks, jeeps and ambulances.
>
> Whistles sounded and Chinese ran up to throw grenades
> into marine foxholes. Another whistle and the Chinese ran
> back.
>
> Then mortar shells began to fall. The 3rd Battalion of the
> 5th Marine Regiment was reduced to less than two compa-
> nies, but still was ordered to "attack regardless of cost."
>
> "We had to do it," said Lt. Col. Joe Stewart, Montgomery,
> Ala. "It was the only way out."
>
> Fox Company, 7th Regiment, was isolated for three or
> four days—nobody seems to remember dates or days—but
> held at terrible cost.
>
> One company killed so many Chinese the marines used
> their frozen bodies as a parapet. But for every Chinese they
> killed there were 5, 10, or 20 to take his place . . .
>
> If there was an occasional respite from the enemy there
> was none from the cold. It numbed fingers, froze feet, sifted
> through layers of clothing and crept into the marrow of your
> bones. . . . Feet sweated by day and froze in their socks by
> night.
>
> Men peeled off their socks—and the soles of their feet with
> them.

The United Press's Gene Symonds filed this account of Christmas eve on the Korean front:

> SOMEWHERE NORTH OF SEOUL—It's a quiet Christmas eve up here in the foxholes—quiet and frightening and bitter cold.
>
> There are no Christmas trees, no presents, no laughing friends shouting "Merry Christmas," no tousled-haired kids to creep downstairs before dawn to see what Santa Claus brought them.
>
> Christmas eve here is a machine gun sitting on the edge of your foxhole with the bolt back ready to go. It's a pale full moon casting grotesque shadows among the fierce, rugged mountain peaks around you. It's your buddy crouching in the bottom of a freezing dugout with a blanket around his shoulders to smoke a cigaret . . .

Five years later Symonds was beaten to death by a rioting mob he was photographing in Singapore. Before he left on the assignment, other newspapermen asked him why he was risking his life to take pictures of rioters who already had killed several persons.

"That's where the story is," Symonds replied.

Some of America's top newsmen and women were dispatched to Korea as the war grew in size and intensity. Among them were Hal Boyle, Don Whitehead and Stan Swinton, Associated Press; Homer Bigart, *New York Herald Tribune;* Hal Levine, *Newsweek;* Bob Considine, Hearst Newspapers; Carl Mydans, *Life;* Edward R. Murrow, *CBS;* Phillip Potter, *Baltimore Sun;* Jack Foise, *San Francisco Chronicle;* Marguerite Higgins, *Herald Tribune;* Jim G. Lucas, Scripps-Howard Newspapers; and many others. About 270 accredited correspondents were in Korea in the early months of the war and hundreds more came later. As in all wars, some reported at safe distances from the front line—but scores of others exposed themselves to danger time after time to get the news. Veteran observers considered it the most hazardous assignment a war correspondent could get. Six American newsmen were killed in the month of July,

1950. By the end of the hostilities seventeen correspondents, including ten Americans, had lost their lives.

Walter Simmons, the *Chicago Tribune*'s Tokyo bureau chief, took time out from his coverage of the raging battle of the Naktong River to write home this appraisal of the Korea press corps:

> The newspapermen now covering the war in Korea are doubtless the hardest working, dirtiest, and most flea bitten gang of press correspondents assembled anywhere in recorded history. . . . Swarms of flies in the daytime and mosquitoes at night are usual. Like morning and afternoon papers, they split the day, one taking over when the other leaves off. Fleas are everywhere. In general they seem to prefer the plump, pink-cheeked newsmen who have recently arrived from New York with Abercrombie and Fitch sleeping bags. The regular Far East correspondents are commonly thin, emaciated individuals who do not contain much in the way of nourishing juices. Veteran correspondents agree that the Korean war is the most dangerous they have covered.

Once Simmons went to an advanced regimental command post of the South Korean army to get an eyewitness report of a Communist drive across the 38th parallel. The post came under fire from three directions and Simmons got out twenty minutes before it was captured.

The war correspondent's two main problems, communications and censorship, were in abundance in Korea—in addition, of course, to the ever-present problem of staying alive. Ansel Talbert, *New York Herald Tribune,* wrote later:

> Time after time you found yourself with a Page One eye witness story and no way to get it back to the U.S. Some of the best war stories never got filed or had grown stale by the time of arrival.
>
> A story filed at Radio Tokyo, if sent "Urgent Rate" would be in Los Angeles or New York within an hour, sometimes within minutes. But a story given to the U.S. Army in Korea

might take 24 hours or even a week by Army teletype. It might never show up or it might show up without a lead and several adds.

If you had a good story, you always tried to thumb a flight back to Tokyo and filed from there.

Eventually Press Wireless opened an office in Seoul, and correspondents were able to file directly to the States.

Up front, newsmen constantly ran the risk of being trapped with the troops by Communist infiltrators who sneaked behind American lines and attacked. Said Talbert:

"You knew the enemy was brutal and if you were caught you were not to be treated hospitably."

Communications were especially bad in the first weeks of the war, when Communist armies were on the offensive. Seventy correspondents at the 24th Division command post at Taejon had to share one military telephone to Japan—and then only if the army wasn't using it. They stood in line to use the phone, each hoping that the man ahead of him wouldn't take too long. Joe Alex Morris wrote:

"There were no secrets and no exclusives over that communications route and there were times when a correspondent went through a special kind of torture—hearing a competitor dictate a hot bulletin to Tokyo with a dozen long-winded reporters still in line in front of him."

Peter Kalischer, United Press, endured unbelievable danger and hardship to file his eyewitness story of a crushing defeat of green American troops. He watched the battle from a foxhole only yards from where twenty tanks poured fire on United States' positions. The reporter scrambled out of his hole as waves of green-clad enemy troops advanced on the crumbling American lines. Machine gun bullets cut down G.I.s all around him as the rout became complete. He joined a group of American survivors who had become separated from the main body. They all sought shelter in a farmhouse as a torrential rainstorm hit.

The next day an enemy broadcast announced that Kalischer was a prisoner. This was a gross inaccuracy. The newsman, bone-weary and filthy, was tramping through rice paddies, his mind on one objective—getting his remarkable story to the outside world. The chances of this seemed dim since the small column was in no-man's land and likely to be encircled by Communist forces at any moment.

But luck was with them. An American artillery observer directed them to Taejon, where he filed his account of how the North Koreans had battered the first American battalion to see action.

Another United Press correspondent, Rutherford Poats, tried to beat the communications snag by using carrier pigeons borrowed from a Tokyo newspaper. One of the birds took a leisurely eleven days to fly copy from Korea to Tokyo. The UP put the story on the wire anyway.

Censorship, particularly in the first months of the war, created bitterness between correspondents and military authorities.

One of the first correspondents to be penalized was Bill Shinn, Korea-born Associated Press staffer. He attended a Korean general's press conference at which the famed Inchon landing was announced. Shinn telephoned the news to his Tokyo bureau, which shot it to the world in minutes. American headquarters called the bulletin "premature" and revoked Shinn's accreditation, forcing him to leave the front.

Kalischer and the AP's Tom Lambert were banished to Tokyo for "reorientation" after they filed stories based on interviews with wounded and dazed soldiers in the July, 1950, retreat. A public information officer termed the accounts "lousy" and criticized correspondents for irresponsible reporting.

The newsmen fought back as censorship tightened by order of General Douglas MacArthur. There were strong press complaints to the Army high command. Some reporters resorted to various tricks to slip copy past the censors. Peter Webb, United Press, sent an exclusive story of the death of General Walton Walker, commander of the United Nations Eighth Army, in a jeep accident. When the news broke, Webb was arrested and held for eighteen hours until it was determined he had not violated censorship rules.

During the 1951 UN negotiations at Kaesong, newsmen were

barred from the area by armed guards and barbed wire fences, although the Communist press was admitted inside. It was explained to the Americans that Kaesong was a Communist-held city and thus the Red correspondents had special privileges.

"But," warned an American censor, "you can't say that Kaesong is in Communist hands."

Fred Sparks, *Chicago Daily News,* snapped back:

"I regard this information as so important that I will not abide by your censorship." The order was reversed. Later, General Matthew Ridgway relented and allowed twenty American correspondents to cover the Kaesong meeting.

A number of the correspondents in Korea were "retreads" from World War II—experienced men who knew their way around a battle zone. One was Jim G. Lucas, Scripps-Howard Newspapers, a Marine Corps combat reporter at Guadalcanal and other South Pacific hotspots. In Korea, Lucas, following his usual custom, got his news the hard way—in the bunkers and foxholes with the front-line troops. His stories rang with realism in their harsh portrayal of men in war. Like this one:

ALONG THE IMJIN RIVER, NORTH KOREA, JAN. 7—This is such a miserable country to die in.

It's not just that it's Korea. It would be miserable country if it were Ohio, Texas, Indiana or Pennsylvania. War is universal and battlefields are the same.

Three of our men got it last night. Old timers say it was their own fault. They say it gruffly—because they know it could have been themselves as if that explains everything. It was their own fault, they say, because the guys let themselves get trapped. One enemy patrol deliberately exposed itself and the kids chased it up a draw where another was waiting in ambush. Our people heard the shooting, saw the flashes and, after the survivors got home, went out and recovered the bodies.

One foul out here and you're through. Every man here remembers at least once when he almost fouled out. They sit around bunkers at night and talk about it. It is pitiless self-examination and it isn't pretty to hear. The patrols they talk about are those which didn't come off. Those are the ones they remember. Each man blames himself for something he didn't do—some oversight he fears cost some buddy his life . . .

Another news veteran of the Second World War was Relman "Pat" Morin, Associated Press, a two-time Pulitzer Prize winner. Recalling his assignment to Korea, Morin noted:

"Now only five years later, we were in business again at the same old stand, reporting a war, trying to put on paper the essentially untranslatable emotions of the soldier in combat."

The United Press's Bob Vermillion broke his leg in a parachute jump behind enemy lines but managed to dictate his story from an aid station. Ray Richardson, International News Service, was the first correspondent to die in action. His last story was a vivid account of how a "Lost Battalion" of American troops had smashed through Communist lines to rejoin its regiment.

One of the most celebrated rivalries in Korea was that between Pulitzer Prize-winning Homer Bigart and Marguerite Higgins, both of the *New York Herald Tribune*. Bigart, a tough, enterprising World War II correspondent, reportedly resented having to share his "beat" with a woman from his own paper. Maggie Higgins, on the other hand, was a fighter for women's rights to carry a press card and she was determined to earn *her* right to be in Korea.

Both took incredible risks. In one story Bigart reported:

"This correspondent was one of the three reporters who saw the action and . . . the only newsman to get out alive."

Not to be outdone, Miss Higgins filed this dispatch:

"A reinforced American patrol, accompanied by this correspondent, this afternoon barreled eight miles deep through enemy territory. . . . Snipers picked at the road, but the jeep flew faster than the bullets which nicked just in back of our right rear tire."

Miss Higgins got the Pulitzer Prize for her work in Korea and Bigart got a second one. They may not have emerged from the conflict with affection for each other, but there was mutual professional respect.

"She certainly made me work like hell," Bigart said.

Before the Inchon invasion, Hal Levine, *Newsweek,* cabled his office:

"There's outside chance that outfit here may do something. Joining up with them in hope they do . . . will be helluva story but you may not hear from me for a little while."

When Levine came up with his story it was a dandy. He was the first newsman ashore with the marines at Inchon, from which he cabled this dispatch:

> . . . Just past the [sea] wall is a trench which the Reds have dug but from which planes and ships have driven them. I jump over it and fling myself behind a mound of earth where two or three marines have already taken cover. Off to our left a Red machine gun is chattering. Dirt spurts around us. But the machine gun is firing at the group to our left. We don't bother with it.
>
> [Lt.] Hershey yells: "For God's sake, don't sit there all night; get going." Half crouching, we dash across the beach. My spine tingles. I am certain that in a split second machine guns will start hammering, mines will start exploding, and mortar shells will start bursting. Nothing happens. I just can't believe it.

Levine also reported the Naktong River battle, in which the marines ran into much stronger opposition.

"The marines kept on and on," Levine wrote. "They reached the base of the hill and started crawling up. There was a tiny plateau there and the Reds raked it with machine gun fire. Marines fell by the scores but the survivors kept going. . . . When they reached the point at which the hill bulged out, the Reds leaped from their foxholes and started rolling grenades down on top of them."

In the press corps there also was time for humor and a kind of gallows camaraderie in tight situations. Frank Holeman, a lanky

North Carolinian who represented the *New York Daily News,* remembers the time when he and a group of other correspondents were flying from Japan to Kimpo Airport near Seoul in an Air Force cargo plane carrying rocket ammunition and drums of high-test gasoline.

The plane made a pass at the landing field but then zoomed up and began circling.

"What's wrong?" Holeman asked the crew chief.

"Landing gear won't go down," was the answer.

The reporters looked at each other in silent understanding of what a crash would mean. "We had enough explosive on board to blow up half of Seoul," Holeman said.

But the newsmen, including Bigart, Hanson Baldwin, *The New York Times,* and Keyes Beech, *Chicago Daily News,* decided to ride it out in style. Someone produced a bottle of whiskey, another man a package of fried chicken. Still another came up with a bag of sweets. Forty minutes later, with the craft still in trouble over the field, the hungry reporters were down to army "C" rations. A can of this food was passed to Beech, who snubbed it, declaring firmly: "No one will ever say that Keyes Beech's last meal was a can of beans."

At last the pilot announced that he was flying back to Japan, where he would attempt a belly landing at the Ashyi airport.

"Why not try it here?" Holeman inquired.

"Because," the pilot retorted, "the Ashyi runway is longer and there's a good hospital close by."

The hospital was not needed. Somehow, the landing gear locked in the normal position and the plane made a safe touchdown. The next day the correspondents went back to the war.

By the end of the war in 1953, more than six hundred news reporters, magazine writers and photographers had covered the Korea story.

E. J. Kahn, who was there for the *New Yorker* magazine, probably expressed the feelings of many Korea correspondents when he wrote:

> . . . From the point of view of practically anybody else who has recently traveled to the troubled peninsula once

known as the Land of the Morning Calm, I was luckiest of all, undoubtedly, in that after what by local standards was a relatively brief stay there, I was able to leave the place and go home.

In the period after Korea there was enough shooting to keep a number of combat correspondents in business. Strife broke out in the Middle East, the Congo, Hungary, Cuba, Cyprus, the Dominican Republic and Vietnam.

Among those assigned to the Dominican fracas was the late Jules Dubois, of the *Chicago Tribune,* an old Latin America hand. In his career he had been survived machine gun fire, a mob attempt to lynch him, a beating with rifle butts, a challenge to a duel and an attempt by Fidel Castro to starve him out of Cuba.

Dubois was the first English-speaking reporter to get into the Dominican Republic. He did it by chartering a small, single-engine plane and persuading the pilot to fly 100 miles over the sea from Puerto Rico. In Santo Domingo he was almost killed by sniper fire.

Jules Dubois was used to violence. During fighting in Bogotá, Colombia, in 1948, he missed being shot on the streets by reaching the presidential palace in an exhibition of broken-field running that would have made a college halfback burn with envy. But the president ordered him out of the palace, saying he didn't want to have a dead American on his hands if the rebels stormed the building.

9

Vietnam:
Terror in the Jungle

EACH AFTERNOON WAR CORRESPONDENTS IN VIETNAM GATHER FOR a press briefing at the Saigon headquarters of the United States Information Agency. Newsmen dub the meeting the "Five O'Clock Follies," a phrase which reflects their bitterness at the lack of information in the Army's handouts. American officials, on the other hand, complain often of biased or slanted reporting by various reporters.

The sensitivity of the officials is understandable. The Vietnam war, still raging at this writing, is not a popular one. In the United States millions of people are opposed to our role in that little Southeast Asian country. Many more millions are uneasy about the prolonged conflict which has cost thousands of American lives. In addition, there is the great tragedy of the growing number of civilian deaths in both South and North Vietnam. The current debate over the war is between the so-called doves and hawks. The former want a cessation of American air bombing and a peace table settlement with North Vietnam. The Hawks believe the war can be ended only if we press hard for a military victory, even if it means escalating the conflict.

In some ways, of course, this is an oversimplification. There are degrees of feeling and there is a fairly large segment of the population that has no firm convictions on the issue.

The background of the Vietnam war is tangled and controversial. Since this is a book about correspondents, I shall not attempt to unravel or explain it in detail. In the 1950s and early 1960s, the United States commitment in that country consisted only of military and economic support to South Vietnam. American soldiers were not sent into battle against the dissident Viet Cong and the Communist troops from North Vietnam. In the years that followed the relatively small conflict expanded to a large-scale war with more than 500,000 American soldiers and marines fighting in the steaming jungles and large-scale bombing of enemy targets in both South and North Vietnam by United States planes. President Lyndon B. Johnson and other administration officials say that this action is aimed at halting Communist aggression. Opponents claim our interests are not involved in Vietnam and that we should make peace and pull out.

Right or wrong, the war is front-page news all over the United States. The more than three hundred correspondents in Vietnam are concerned less with its causes than with its effects. Many are risking their lives daily to report the conflict. They slog through the jungles with combat units and ride helicopters over rice paddies infested with Viet Cong who shoot at anything in the sky. Even their headquarters at Saigon, the South Vietnamese capital, is not safe. Terrorists may lob a grenade into an American compound or civilian restaurant at any moment.

At this date ten correspondents have met death in Vietnam and several others have been injured. There are different ways to die in that ravaged land. Sam Casten, thirty-one, lean senior editor of *Look* magazine, was killed by mortar fire while covering the First Cavalry Division's "Operation Crazy Horse." A veteran of the fighting in Cyprus and the Dominican Republic, Casten called his last assignment "the dirty little war in Viet Nam."

Once an army major wrote to *Look:*

> The purpose of this letter is to relate to you the gallant bravery of Mr. Casten when under mortar, automatic weapons and small arms fire delivered from close range. Based on demonstrated courage, he would qualify as an excellent soldier in any army. He exposed himself to hostile fire repeatedly in an effort to record the action accurately and I was personally proud to observe this reporter in action.

Jack Rose, a free-lance writer and former *Time* correspondent, died in an airplane crash. Bernard Fall, French author of several books and magazine articles on Vietnam, died when he stepped on a booby trap on a road named "Street Without Joy." Ronald D. Gallagher, a twenty-nine-year-old free-lance photographer from Fort Scott, Kansas, was killed by artillery shells accidentally dropped on our troops by an American battery.

Some of the problems faced by correspondents in Vietnam are unique. There are no clearly marked battle lines and much of the ground operation consists of looking for the enemy. Said Charles Mohr of *The New York Times:*

> If military intelligence officers always knew where to find the Viet Cong, the war would have been over long ago. Because they do not, reporters must to some extent gamble on which operations they will cover, and sometimes they get a long, hot walk in the sun instead of a story (which is one reason there are so many long, hot walks in the sun stories filed from Vietnam).

Mohr noted that "this is not a jeep war. A correspondent must be able to walk, and especially when going uphill, you pay dearly for a misspent life of martinis and cigarettes."

There also are advantages for the reporter in Vietnam. The country is small and a newsman can fly into a fighting zone and fly out in time to be in Saigon for dinner. Military transportation is available to them most of the time and one helicopter is permanently assigned to the Saigon press corps on a stand-by basis.

"The reporter can go anywhere," said George Esper, Associated Press, who spent fourteen months in Vietnam. "But we couldn't report troop movements or operations until they had taken place. Otherwise the Viet Cong monitor radio would pick up the information and endanger our men."

According to Esper, the Army's daily information briefing is a poor substitute for getting the news where it's made.

"Most newsmen get the best stories by going out in the field," he explained. "You have to see for yourself what is happening."

He added that G.I. troops "take good care of newsmen in the jungle."

"The fighting men want their story to be told," Esper continued. "They will even share their water and rations with newsmen."

Reporting in Vietnam differs from previous wars. There are few large-scale engagements or significant battles, such as those of Verdun in World War I, the Normandy invasion and the Ardennes in World War II and the Changjin Reservoir in Korea. Vietnam is a jungle war on the Asian mainland, fought most of the time against an unseen enemy. There is seldom any "front line," and even the terms victory and defeat take on different meanings. This has meant, among other things, that correspondents in the field are closer to the action and to the troops than was generally the case in other wars. The Vietnam struggle is being reported in intensely human terms. The agony of both the soldier and the civilian is being told as perhaps it never has been told before.

"The only way you can tell about the real war is to write about the real men caught in the battle," said Jack Foise, *Los Angeles Times* correspondent in Vietnam and a reporter in both World War II and Korea.

Here is how Foise described one action:

American troops are coming to grips with one of the most difficult problems of the war—how to clean out Viet Cong villages without shooting the innocent.

Marines in their small but aggressive operations to push the Viet Cong back from around the Da Nang airfield have entered villages under sniper fire and felt forced twice during this week to employ tough counter measures.

In one village that meant grenading all tunnels not knowing whether there were armed guerillas in them or terrified women and children taking refuge.

The sad result was that while the American communiqué reported 25 Viet Cong dead, it did not say five of them were women and children.

Foise, a balding, bespectacled man who drives to the heart of a story, sums up his feelings about war correspondence this way:

> . . . I know that good solid men are not only to be found in battle. But I can never feel the kinship back in everyday life that I sense from being with men whose loyalty and respect for one another is so profound—because it has been tested under battle. Some people call it "comradeship." It is a relatively exclusive society, and a correspondent can, at best, become only an associate member.

The good correspondent and his editor know that the reader is better able to understand the war when it is told in terms of the individuals who fight it, the young men from all the towns in America who are thrust into a situation that is brutal and terrifying. Thus, many newspapers send special reporters to Vietnam. Their job is not to get the over-all picture (although sometimes they do) but to pick out human interest stories. Such a writer is John Van Doorn, thirty-two, of *Newsday,* a Long Island, New York, newspaper, who spent three months in Vietnam and won the Ernie Pyle Memorial Award in journalism for his work. One of Van Doorn's dispatches is typical of his intimacy with his subjects:

BIEN HOA—What most of the guys remember is that God! it was dark that night. The heat? Well, it's always hot and filthy in that equatorial way, but sometimes it is not so dark as it was that night, when the mortars came through the roof.

They came with their painfully inadequate announcement —a distant popping that only the most alert translate, then with the whoosh that is unmistakable and which precedes the terror in the night: the mortar's ugly blam.

From pop to blam is 10 seconds on the outside, and if a special darkness gets in the way, someone's going to get hurt. That's what happened at Bien Hoa, an airbase only twelve miles north of Saigon: the mortars came in and the American airmen ran for their bunkers, but some were stumbling for just a few seconds and they caught pieces of shell . . .

[Oliver] Heckendorn, of Newville, Pa. . . . found the bunker and stayed put. [Jon D.] Nutzman was not so lucky, for as they reconstruct the events, just as Meares and Heckendorn got inside the bunker, a mortar shell hit the roof of the cottage and tore a dirty hole. The explosion shredded the top bunk immediately beneath the hole and sent jagged pieces of metal spraying through the cottage. Nutzman was still in there, stumbling in a night gone mad. His injuries were not serious but they were bloody. Nutzman is a tough guy, too, from Fremont, Neb., and he went to work on his next shift . . .

For some newsmen the Vietnam war put them in the front rank of American journalists. David Halberstam, of *The New York Times,* and Malcolm W. Browne, of AP and now a *Times* reporter, won Pulitzer Prizes and other writing awards for their war coverage. Also noted for their brilliant on-the-spot reporting were Neil Sheehan, United Press; Jack Raymond, *New York Times;* Peter Arnett, Associated Press; and Francois Sully, *Newsweek.*

Halberstam, a New Yorker who graduated from Harvard, was frequently critical of the United States actions in Vietnam and of some Vietnamese leaders. He and other newsmen also complained often about army information practices. In his book *The Making of a Quagmire,* Halberstam wrote:

> . . . The traditional right of American journalists to report what they see was at stake here, even though the situation was a particularly sensitive one: ambiguous involvement in a wretched war with a ruthless enemy. Because the news was bad, there were many people who for varying reasons did not want it exposed. Yet an American reporter must believe, if he believes nothing else, that the United States has never survived in times of crisis by playing ostrich. Too much policy and too deep a commitment had already been made in Vietnam on the basis of too little factual information . . .

But Halberstam, who volunteered for Vietnam and stayed there fifteen months, was in the thick of the action. In one instance he rode a helicopter that took part in a bitter gunfight with Viet Cong guerrillas on the ground.

> We bore down on one fleeing Viet Cong. The paddy's surface was rough and his run was staggered, like that of a good but drunken broken-field runner against imaginary tacklers. We came closer and closer; inside the helicopter I could almost hear him gasping for breath, and as we bore down I could see the heaving of his body. It was like watching a film of one of your own nightmares, but in this case we were the pursuers rather than the pursued. . . . Then there was a flash of orange and a blast of heat inside the ship, and the helicopter heaved from the recoil of its rockets. When they exploded the man fell . . .

Malcolm Browne has been in Vietnam since 1961. A slender reporter of great integrity, he qualifies as an expert in both the political and military sides of the conflict. In 1963 he shocked the world with his story and exclusive pictures of the Buddhist monk Quang Duc burning himself alive in a Saigon public square.

Browne has accompanied many American and South Vietnamese

patrols into villages where he saw the horrible mutilation of soldiers and peasants by Viet Cong terrorists. He also witnessed the torture and killing of guerrilla suspects by the South Vietnamese soldiers. He learned to be careful of booby traps, a common weapon in Vietnam. In one village he hugged the ground as government troops pulled down a Viet Cong flag. The move saved his life. As the pole came down it triggered an explosion that sent hundreds of grenade fragments flying through the area.

"Vietnam is a highly personal war, in which specific terror against specific people or groups of people is a principal weapon," Browne wrote. "Part of the new face of war here, as I see it, is the use of terror for terror's sake."

Michael Mok, a *Life* associate editor and a marine veteran of Korea with five battle stars and the Purple Heart, left the comforts of his New York office to see what the war was like in Vietnam. He and photographer Paul Schutzer made a beach assault with a marine detachment, an action that Mok found "eerily familiar."

"We are aboard ship in a task force, heading for an amphibious landing, and it is as if time had been turned backward to World War II or Korea," he wrote.

The actual landing also was familiar to Mok. The marines were in a fire fight minutes after hitting the shore. Here is part of the *Life* reporter's first-hand account:

> Bravo [company] starts to move through a stand of pine trees and the marine on the point spots five figures sitting on the ground, their backs to the tree trunks on the edge of a clearing. They appear so relaxed and unconcerned that he thinks they are marines. "Are you people lost?" he hollers. "This is Bravo's sector . . ." His answer is a burst of machine-gun fire. The marines zero in on the group and let them have it.

In that same skirmish, Mok saw a woman running with her bleeding baby to a navy corpsman. The child had been wounded during the earlier strafing by jet planes.

Peter Behr, a young reporter for the *Rochester* (New York) *Times-Union,* took a Sunday walk with an American and Vietnamese patrol seeking three Viet Cong leaders supposedly holed up in a small village. The newsman snapped pictures of the brief but vicious fighting as snipers' bullets sang by his head. His description follows:

> A half dozen soldiers were running on our left, firing into a tangle of brush nearby, non-coms were yelling orders, all in Vietnamese, but luckily no one was getting hit.
>
> It was a little chilling, watching, but not knowing what was going on. The experience was akin to sitting in a Saigon movie where the actors speak Vietnamese with subtitles in French and Chinese.

Frequently the Viet Cong have carried the war to the streets of Saigon, and American newsmen found death and destruction only minutes from their offices. American billets, restaurants and other public places have been the target of terrorist bombs. Once shells landed very near the American embassy.

One night the United Press International office in Saigon got a report that the city's airport was under enemy fire from recoilless rifles. That meant the Viet Cong were close in. Bureau manager Bryce Miller quickly sent reporters and photographers to the scene. For cameraman Maury Wilmott it almost was his last assignment. As his car neared the airport the aging battery gave out and the vehicle stalled. Wilmott and a helpful Saigon newsboy started to push the car toward the American barracks at the airfield.

Suddenly, the pair were caught in the blaze of a searchlight. The guards raised their rifles and other soldiers dashed from the barracks, their guns at the ready. More guns poked out of sandbagged walls. The boy dashed off but Wilmott froze by the auto.

He recovered from the shock in time to yell out his identity. The sentries let him through. Later, Wilmott learned that airport units had been warned that a car loaded with plastique explosives was going to blow up the place.

Phil Newsom, UPI foreign news analyst, labeled Wilmott's experience "one of the risks of the correspondent's trade."

Another UPI correspondent, Thomas Cheatam, twenty-five, was seriously wounded when his bunker took a direct mortar hit. Before he was evacuated by helicopter he dictated by field telephone one final dispatch—a personal report on the action in which he was hurt. The newsman, whose wife was in Saigon at the time, suffered head, chest and back wounds.

Arnaud de Borchgrave, *Newsweek* senior editor, was nicked by shrapnel in the bitterly fought battle between United States marines and North Vietnamese regulars along the Demilitarized Zone between North and South Vietnam. The *Newsweek* office in New York received this message from its Saigon bureau:

ARNAUD BACK WITH FANTASTIC STUFF. HE HAS BEEN WITH UNIT THAT WAS FIGHTING FOR 100 YARDS FOR TWO DAYS. . . . HE OKAY.

De Borchgrave was no stranger to Vietnam or war. In 1954 he parachuted into Dienbienphu with French forces in that historic siege. He also covered the Congo rebellion in 1960.

Tom Tiede, Newspaper Enterprise Association, somehow found time to be a mailman for more than one thousand servicemen in Vietnam. The Christmas project was dreamed up by the *Cleveland Press,* which distributed cards to the soldiers' parents. Tiede, a crewcut midwesterner who started out as a sportswriter, traveled 450 miles by plane and jeep, a fourteen-hour trip, to deliver one letter to a jungle-based corporal. At one point, he revealed in a dispatch to the *Press,* his jeep was held up for "a water buffalo which was in labor pains in the middle of the road."

Tiede also had a word for Cleveland mailmen: "If you are lamenting the sleet, snow and dark-of-night burdens of your appointed rounds this Christmas, I say buck up—you never had it so good."

Like Tiede, many of the Vietnam correspondents are young—in

their twenties and thirties. One of the youngest, Barry Cunningham, twenty-five, left his journalism studies at New York University to report the war for the *New York Post*. One of his stories was a grimly etched picture of a battle-shocked infantryman after twenty-four hours of bloody fighting. A sample:

> . . . This morning as the sun slanted over piles of enemy carcasses strewn through the Michelin rubber plantation, Taylor quietly tried to explain what it's like to fight for survival in Vietnam.
>
> "This place does something to your mind," he began. "People at home don't realize what Vietnam is like. You can't explain it in a letter. People wouldn't believe a human being could go through this kind of torture.
>
> "For four hours we were carrying guys bleeding to death on stretchers. In the dark we were holding hands with the next guy in front. My best friend, Thomas Cartonia, just dropped in front of me. I was still holding his hand. . . . One of our people got half his head chopped off. We didn't have a stretcher. It took us two hours to carry him out on a poncho. I couldn't stand it. We'd slip in the mud and drop him. The weeds were brushing against his head. All you could hear were guys around us screaming for medics."

Barry Cunningham, after living through four mortar attacks and two major battles, developed a philosophy about war correspondence.

"I always felt that my assignment was to stay alive to report the war," he told me. "There are risks that no correspondent can be casual about considering. During Operation Attleboro, I hitched a chopper ride out to a jungle area where a company was being evacuated after being pinned down for twelve hours. The pilot warned me at the outset that he had room for exactly seven troops aboard. I would have to get off to make room. This was a familiar warning. I had had to make way for casualties several times riding Medevac [medical evacuation] helicopters. This time I got stranded. I had to lay low in a bomb crater, watching the troops move out seven at a time. It was a sick feeling. Finally I attached myself to a sergeant who was taking a patrol out of the danger area. We made it back to Dau Tieng, about a five-mile distance, in four hours."

The Vietnam press contingent is constantly being salted by older veterans of other wars. Among these have been S. L. A. Marshall, Homer Bigart, Robert Sherrod and John Steinbeck.

Marshall, *Los Angeles Times-Washington Post* News Service military writer, respected historian and a retired army brigadier general, took his younger colleagues to task for going after off-beat yarns instead of reporting large combat operations, which he claims are more significant in terms of news value. In a *New Leader* magazine article, the outspoken general charged that the "overwhelming majority of reporters evince a cynical faddishness."

"Today's average correspondent prefers a piece that will make people squirm and agonize," he continued.

It's true that many reporters in Vietnam are turning out highly personalized accounts of men under stress, but it's equally true that the broad military picture is being fed to readers by the wire services and major news organizations. Correspondents like Barry Cunningham and Peter Behr were assigned to Vietnam not to provide a sweeping appraisal of the over-all military effort but to write about the personal side of the war. That is also of interest to readers, as was proved by Ernie Pyle in World War II.

Robert Sherrod, another distinguished World War II correspondent twice decorated by the navy for bravery, went to Vietnam for *Life* magazine. He went on his first air combat mission since 1945 and his first ever in a jet. His description of it follows:

> Half a mile from the designated area Anderson [the pilot] started our dive from 5,500 feet. . . . When we reached 2,600 feet, a dull klunk under the right wing told us that Anderson had released a bomb. Going down was fun, like riding in a roller coaster, but the pull-out at 5½ Gs—five and one-half times gravity—was a new, unearthly sensation for me. The upsweep tied my stomach into a hard knot and my legs felt as if they had been transformed into iron. In World

War II we used to make one dive, drop our bombs and head for home. But I soon realized we were dropping our bombs one at a time, which meant that we would repeat the process until we had laid all four of our eggs. It was quite a morning for an over-age war correspondent.

Another "over-age" correspondent in Vietnam was novelist John Steinbeck, sixty-four. He performed like a twenty-year-old, however, trudging through the rice fields with infantry units and going on armed helicopter missions. In his columns for *Newsday,* Steinbeck aligned himself with the hawks in the Vietnam debate, telling his readers in one dispatch: "If you hear someone celebrating the misunderstood and mistreated Viet Cong, just punch him in the nose."

Sometimes newsmen themselves make news. A striking example of this was Harrison E. Salisbury, of *The New York Times,* whose stories bore a Hanoi, North Vietnam, dateline. Salisbury, a veteran foreign correspondent, was the first United States reporter granted a visa by the North Vietnamese, enabling him to score the biggest beat of the war. His stories from behind enemy lines also touched off one of the most heated flaps in journalism history. The trip created headlines throughout the world and made him a controversial figure. The Pentagon made no secret of its irritation over Salisbury's reports of civilian casualties and damage resulting from American bombing. Army information officials charged that Salisbury's casualty figures came from Communist sources, a fact which he failed to note in his initial dispatches. The *Times* man acknowledged this was an oversight and in later stories he listed the North Vietnamese as the source for his statistics.

Salisbury, a *Times* assistant managing editor, had had years of experience in Communist countries. In 1955, the tall, distinguished-looking journalist received a Pulitzer Prize for his reporting from Soviet Russia. He also has had extensive assignments in Asia.

His visit to Hanoi came after eighteen months of trying to obtain a visa for North Vietnam. A week before Christmas, 1966, he got a cable telling him that the visa could be picked up in Paris. Salisbury flew into Hanoi on a creaky, aging plane operated out of Cambodia by the International Control Commission. This is the truce supervisory agency created by the 1954 Geneva agreement that ended the French-Indochina war, the forerunner of the present conflict in Vietnam.

"It was a strange feeling," Salisbury said, "to step off that plane in Hanoi and realize that the men waiting to greet you were the enemy. I had never reported before from behind enemy lines."

In one of his cables, he wrote:

"To a correspondent with years of work in communist countries, reporting from Hanoi has many familiar aspects. But the fact that the reporter is behind enemy lines in a very real if undeclared war gives the experience special atmosphere. . . . Interviews, trips, visits are arranged by the press department of the North Vietnam foreign office."

For the most part, Salisbury said, he was allowed to roam freely and neither his copy nor pictures appeared to have been censored. At first his hosts fixed his stay at one week but finally allowed him to remain two weeks. During that time Salisbury was taken to bomb damage sites and he also talked to Communist officials.

The *Times* correspondent provided an interesting sidelight to the way a reporter obtains news in a foreign country. He said the bar of his hotel in Hanoi was a meeting place for most of the visitors to the city, including newsmen from Communist and neutral countries, diplomatic representatives and an assortment of other guests.

"Of course," Salisbury explained, "you couldn't believe everything you heard but it was a good listening post and sometimes I got some usable information."

Although controversy surrounded Salisbury's trip, there seems to be no doubt that his dispatches disproved repeated Pentagon statements that American planes were hitting only military targets. That civilian dwellings and other nonmilitary establishments were struck was acknowledged fully by Washington after Salisbury's stories appeared.

Part of Salisbury's first dispatch read:

. . . Christmas Eve found parts of Hanoi still picking over the wreckage of homes said to have been damaged in the United States raids of Dec. 13 and 14. United States officials have contended that no attacks in built-up or residential Hanoi have been authorized or carried out. They have also suggested that Hanoi residential damage in the two raids could have been caused by defensive surface-to-air that misfired or fell short . . .

This correspondent is no ballistics specialist but inspection of several damaged sites and talks with witnesses make it clear that Hanoi residents certainly believe they were bombed by the United States, that they certainly observed United States planes overhead and that damage certainly occurred right in the center of town . . .

Other American newsmen were admitted into North Vietnam after Salisbury's trip. Lee Lockwood, a free-lance photographer-writer, spent twenty-eight days and traveled about one thousand miles, always with a government functionary at his side. His pictures and story appeared in *Life* magazine, which said: "What he [Lockwood] was allowed to see and photograph was circumscribed by the foreign ministry." In his account, Lockwood wrote:

. . . Of the four weeks I stayed in North Vietnam, as it turned out, about two were wasted to bureaucracy and ceremony—delays in planning my itinerary and in providing interpreters, interminable formal briefings and greetings, and always that three-hour recess for lunch. I was not unique in this torment; the same thing happens to all foreign journalists, Communists included. Considering I was an American behind enemy lines, the strictures on my operations were not surprising . . .

Lockwood reported seeing heavy damage on the outskirts of Hanoi and elsewhere. Damage also had been reported by William Baggs, of the *Miami News,* another newsman admitted into North Vietnam.

There is no American censorship in South Vietnam, but many war correspondents chafe under what they feel is news manipulation—withholding of certain facts and unnecessary delay in feeding information to the press. Newsmen have disputed casualty figures announced by the military. Others have complained that briefing officers and other American officials in Saigon tend to favor representatives of news media which take a favorable stand on United States policies in Vietnam. Correspondents also accuse Army officers and other sources of dodging embarrassing questions in press conferences. One Vietnam reporter told me:

"A lot of correspondents in Vietnam believe the Public Information Office credo, 'Maximum information, minimum delay' should read: 'Minimum information, maximum delay.'"

Naked censorship is practiced by the South Vietnam government, according to correspondents. One newsman said that during President Johnson's visit to Cam Ranh Bay, the government threw the main power switch on its overseas cable, causing an eight-hour transmission blackout that continued two hours after the president arrived safely back in Manila. The Association of Foreign Correspondents in Vietnam has charged the government with "outrageous interference" with members trying to cover the war.

On the other hand, Arthur Sylvester, former Assistant Secretary of Defense for Public Affairs, said the United States government is putting out more news on the Vietnam war than any government has done at any time in any war.

In a public speech, Sylvester acknowledged that coverage of the early stages of the conflict was spotty, adding: "We had good operational people there, but we didn't have good informational people." The official also said he doesn't believe "a government has a right to lie to the people." But he asserted that there are times in wars when printing the whole truth isn't in the best interests of the nation.

The information battle goes on as new correspondents arrive periodically while others leave after their tours of duty. Among the temporaries have been columnist Joseph Alsop, cutting a stylish figure in his white suit, Panama hat and cane; NBC newscaster Chet Huntley; and James Reston, *New York Times* political pundit and associate editor.

Some reporters in Vietnam can be called the regulars. Robert Shaplen, of the *New Yorker* magazine, has spent many years in Asia and is regarded as one of the most knowledgeable men of the Vietnam press group. Another "old Asia hand" is New Zealand-born Peter Arnett, who has been with the Associated Press Saigon bureau since 1962. He has gone into the field many times with the troops, packing a Mauser machine pistol or a .38 caliber revolver. Most newsmen do not wear arms, however.

There are political as well as military aspects of the Vietnam war, and a number of the reporters concentrate more heavily in this area. This is the news that will be reported long after the war is over in that unhappy country. Even the most hawkish observers realize that the United States must rely on more than a military victory or settlement to win the hearts of the people.

10

War in the Desert

AS THIS BOOK WAS BEING WRITTEN WAR BROKE OUT IN THE MIDDLE East. It started June 5, 1967, and was over six days later, with Israel victorious over the United Arab Republic (Egypt), Jordan and Syria. It was the third time since 1948 that hostilities had erupted between Israel and her Arab neighbors.

The latest outbreak found the press ready for instant coverage. Hostilities had been expected momentarily in view of the tense situation existing between the two sides. Two weeks earlier, President Gamal Abdel Nasser of Egypt had closed off the southern sea route to Israel by a naval blockade in the Strait of Tiran. Armies of the two nations had been massed on their borders.

Several newsmen reported the war from front-line Israeli units. Three were killed in the line of duty.

Ted Yates, an NBC television producer-director, was fatally wounded by machine gun bullets while leading a film crew in the Jordanian sector of Jerusalem. The thirty-six-year-old ex-bronco buster had covered combat in Vietnam and the Congo and had been stoned by rioting Communists in Sumatra. He once had said:

"Covering combat zones is spooky work. You have to stick your neck out a mile."

He was shot when bullets raked the walls of a hotel lobby in which he and his crew were filming the action. Everyone hit the floor except Yates, who scanned the streets for the gun.

"He was too brave," said CBS commentator Eric Sevareid.

Brooklyn-born Paul Schutzer, thirty-six, a *Life* magazine photographer, was killed as he was shooting pictures from an Israeli half-track that was hit by an anti-tank shell and burst into flames. Riding with Schutzer was another *Life* correspondent, Michael Mok, who was unhurt. They had covered the Vietnam fighting together. Schutzer, who had filmed the Algerian war and other hot spots, had insisted on going to the Middle East, telling his editors that he would fly there whether assigned or not.

Killed in a land-mine explosion was Ben Oyserman, forty, a freelancer for the Canadian Broadcasting System. Serge Fliegers, forty-six, reporting for the Hearst Newspapers and the Mutual Broadcasting System, was injured in the same blast.

A number of American newsmen were able to report the conflict —despite the lightning-like thrust of the Israeli armies over the desert, the problems of censorship on both sides and a confused political situation in the Arab countries. Americans generally got a comprehensive and reliable account of the fighting.

The news media moved fast to provide this coverage. *The New York Times* dispatched Vietnam veteran Charles Mohr from Hong Kong to Israel. The wire services pumped up their Middle East staffs by rapid shifting of personnel. The highly experienced Hugh Mulligan, of AP, hurriedly left New York and was filing from the war zone the next day. More than two hundred newsmen reported the war from the Israeli side.

James Reston, *New York Times* columnist and associate editor, filed a daily story out of Tel Aviv. On the first day of the war he wrote:

> . . . Thus in a single day all the symbols of a country at war were in place; the wildly contradictory and uncheckable official reports from the different warring capitals, the charges of aggression and claims of victory on both sides, the censors eliminating things the enemy obviously knows—all so reminiscent of past wars—and the darkness and—one saving grace—the thoughtfulness of simple people caught in a common predicament . . .

Newsweek magazine reported:

> . . . Many correspondents in Israel were forced to go to war in slacks and sport shirts, riding taxis and looking for the "front." They were quickly turned back at roadblocks. A few lucky ones, usually dressed in Vietnam combat fatigues, managed to bluff their way through, link up with Israeli units and see what was happening behind the communiqués and briefings in Tel Aviv.

Most correspondents considered Israeli censorship tough but acknowledged that its censors operated swiftly to clear stories for filing.

Covering the war was much harder from the Arab side, according to the correspondents who were there. The Syrians jailed several newsmen, including the AP's David Lancashire, who was then forced out of the country. Dana Adams Schmidt, respected *New York Times* man, was arrested by the Jordanians on a charge of sending messages on his transistor radio receiver. When Louis Rukeyser, ABC broadcaster, began taping a spot broadcast from the top of a hotel in Jordan's capital of Amman, he was hustled down and questioned for several hours on suspicion that he was giving signals to the Israelis.

But correspondents got the harshest treatment in Egypt. Twenty-five of them were herded into Cairo's Nile Hilton Hotel and locked up. Others were subjected to mauling by angry mobs, imprisonment, confiscation of their film and other equipment and further humiliations. A number of American newsmen were expelled as Arab propaganda accusing the United States of intervention on the Israeli side intensified. ABC correspondent Charles P. Arnot escaped from Alexandria on an Italian ship by pretending to be a European. Garven Hudgins, AP bureau chief in Cairo, was ordered out of Egypt with several other correspondents. He told *Editor & Publisher* magazine:

"Believe me, this was the kind of experience I could have done without. The situation was ridiculous; everything during the crisis time was comic opera, a kind of crazy orchestration of managed news, staged demonstrations, all provided under direct orders from Nasser . . ."

Hudgins said that the first "objective, uncensored" copy he filed during the brief war went on the wire via a radio link from a Greek ship to the AP office in Athens, which relayed it to the United States.

The newsman said that "the final departure scene was in line with all the other happenings. We got to the docks, about 16 United States newsmen, then the customs went to work on us. . . . They took away film and cameras, they took our money, they even took personal snapshots, dumping them into a heap on the ground. . . . The customs authorities, on direct orders from Nasser, were told to give the press a hard time it appeared."

Tom Streithorst, NBC, was beaten by the Nile Hilton staff when they caught him filming from the roof of the hotel. He said that newsmen were not allowed anywhere near the front and that the Egyptian people considered the United States the enemy. "That included correspondents," he added.

New York Times staffer Eric Pace was one of the last American newsmen to leave Cairo. He managed to telephone his dispatches to *Times* bureaus in European cities, circumventing censorship. How he did it was "top secret," a *Times* executive said.

Other American correspondents covering the Middle Eastern war were Joseph W. Grigg, United Press International, who rode with

Israeli armor in the Sinai desert, and Flora Lewis, *Newsday* columnist, who reported from Jerusalem in the midst of the battle for that city.

When the shooting stopped, the issues that created the conflict were argued in the United Nations. But an uneasy truce prevailed in the Middle East and many American correspondents stayed on the spot or were prepared for a quick return. The situation remained explosive as sporadic clashes between Arabs and Jews continued for months afterward. At this moment the conflict is far from resolved and men are dying on both sides.

11

War in Pictures

DOCK WORKERS GAPED AT AN UNUSUAL PIECE OF CARGO THEY unloaded at the Russian Crimean port of Balaklava in the winter of 1855. The object was called a "Photographic Van" by its owner Roger Fenton, who had arrived on the ship *Hecla* to cover the Crimean War for the *Illustrated London News*.

Fenton was probably the world's first combat photographer. He shot pictures of the Crimean battlegrounds under fire, taking his wagon wherever he went. The van was fitted out as a darkroom and also contained five cameras, seven hundred glass plates, chemicals, rations, harnesses and tools. The rig was pulled by four horses. Cannon fire once tore away part of the wagon but Fenton pushed on with the troops. Several months later he returned to London with more than three hundred negatives. Fenton held picture exhibitions in London and Paris, and wood engravings of the best scenes were printed in the *Illustrated London News*. The subjects were battle-grounds, fortifications and officers and men. The camera had not been developed sufficiently to record action.

Seven years later Fenton went into the practice of law, but the tradition of the camera reporter was carried on. Photographers have clicked their shutters on battlefields over the world, often taking the same risks as the front-line soldier. We know something of the horror of the Civil War through the stark photos of Mathew Brady. Loaded down with bulky equipment, cameramen waded ashore amid the terrible fire of the Normandy and Tarawa beaches in World War II. Some took their last pictures on those sands.

American war photography first came to the public attention largely through the efforts of Brady, an ambitious, hard-working man who dramatized the Civil War on film. Brady was born in New York State of poor parents in 1823. As a young man he studied the daguerreotype photographic process invented by a Frenchman, Louis Daguerre. The process involves fixing a photo image on a copper plate with the help of chemicals.

Just before the Civil War Brady was a fashionable portrait photographer in Washington, D.C., and New York. His distinguished clients included Abraham Lincoln, who once remarked, "Brady and the Cooper Union speech made me president." When the war broke out, Brady turned over his business to assistants and headed for the sound of the guns. Dressed in a long linen duster coat and floppy straw hat, he lugged his bulky camera from battlefield to battlefield— Bull Run, Petersburg and Fredericksburg, where he was almost killed by Confederate fire. He usually made his pictures after the heavy firing ceased, but sometimes they were shot while the guns still roared.

Not all of the pictures credited to Brady were taken by him. A superb organizer, he employed twenty field operators who snapped war photographs under his direction. He had two photographic wagons especially built for him. These traveling darkrooms and equipment carriers were dubbed "Whatizzit Wagons" by soldiers. At Bull Run, panicky Union soldiers spread rumors that Brady's camera was a new Confederate "steam gun" that could discharge 500 balls a minute.

Brady was lost at Bull Run for three days, finally appearing in Washington bone-tired and grim-faced. A sword given to him by a Zouave soldier poked out of his duster. He quickly bought new equipment, rounded up his assistants and hurried back to the fighting. By 1862, Brady had thirty-five bases of operations in various Civil War theaters. After completing a portfolio of pictures, he would return to Washington. The plates were printed on albumen paper and given a platinum-sepia tint. They were then mounted on cards with printed titles. Bookstores and galleries sold them for 75 cents to $1.00. By this time Brady had won the grudging approval of the Army, which began to like the idea of having its achievements recorded on film. But the master also had his problems. It wasn't easy to find photographers willing to expose themselves to gunfire—but those he recruited were nearly as good as their boss. Among Brady's top assistants were George Cook, J. B. Gibson and D. B. Woodbury. Their cameras were box-like instruments, mostly 16″ x 20″ and 4″ x 4″ types, mounted on tripods. Each shot was a time exposure, which ruled out any action scenes. Camera development was a long way from the split-second shutter speeds of today.

Brady insisted that his men take care of their photo gear before stretching out to sleep, even if they were achingly tired after a grueling day on the battlefield. Brady himself worked harder than any of his staff.

Brady received permission to cover the Civil War after unwinding government red tape, but he had to pay his own expenses. Photography was not considered important enough to merit government support. The result was that he made his name in history but ruined himself financially. In 1866, right after the war, the stockhouse that had supplied him with photographic material seized many of his negatives in default of payment. Brady also was in debt to a warehouse that had stored his equipment. To raise the money, he prepared a collection of "War Views" which he hoped to sell to the government, a plan endorsed by several newspapers. Washington said it was not interested, despite the fact that buyers in London and Paris were making attractive offers. Although broke and discouraged, Brady declined them. In 1869 he tried again to sell the collection to the government without success. Then, in desperation, he put the pictures up for public auction. Finally, the War Department bought them. They are now in the National Archives in Washington.

Brady was struck by a runaway horse car and died in 1896. He did virtually no work in his last years. But he had made a lasting contribution to the art of photography and to history. His pictures are remarkable even by today's standards. They were sharp and clear with fine definition and composition. Brady had an eye for the dramatic and the poignant. His shot of a dead Confederate sniper summed up the horror of war as few pictures have. *Humphrey's Journal,* a Northern newspaper, editorialized: "The correspondents of the rebel newspapers are sheer falsifiers, the correspondents of Northern journals are not to be depended upon, and the correspondents of English newspapers are altogether more than either. The public is indebted to Brady of Broadway for his excellent views of grim visaged war."

While Brady and his assistants were training their cameras on the Civil War fronts, another group of pictorial correspondents was on the march. These were the sketch artists who worked for the illustrated periodicals. By 1860 there were three leading graphic journals: *Frank Leslie's Illustrated Newspaper, Harper's Weekly* and the *New York Illustrated News.* They fielded about thirty correspondent-artists, who were paid from five to twenty-five dollars per sketch. They were a colorful lot, sporting a variety of uniforms, no two the same. These special artists were under the same strict rules governing the some three hundred other Northern reporters in the war and the rules were harshly applied. The *Harper's Weekly* artist was banned for carrying maps of the Union's siege works between the York and James rivers in Virginia. Some of these men drew faster than the camera, with its ten- to thirty-second exposure time, could put an impression on film. Two of the most noted artists were Alfred Waud, of *Harper's,* and Edwin Forbes, of *Leslie's,* which also made engravings from some of Brady's pictures.

At this time it was not known how to reproduce photographs directly on paper. News photos, however, had been taken as early as 1842 and were models for wood engravings in the illustrated journals. The breakthrough in news photography came with the invention of a process called halftone.

Photojournalism was solidly established in the American press when World War II broke out in 1939. Tabloids and standard-size newspapers went in heavily for pictures, and photo staffs were commonplace. *Life* magazine was born in 1936, giving further impetus to photojournalism. Trailing after it were a rash of imitators, most of which are no longer publishing.

The Second World War was the most photographed conflict in history. It also produced some of the most skillful and daring cameramen of our time. They scrambled ashore with invasion forces, marched with the troops and shot pictures under fire.

In the summer of 1942, Robert Capa was down to his last nickel and living in a studio apartment in New York City's Greenwich Village. To add to his troubles, the government had classed him as an enemy alien because he was a native of Hungary, a nation at war with the United States. Capa was informed that he would have to surrender his cameras, binoculars and firearms and obtain a permit to travel more than ten miles from New York. The possible loss of his cameras worried him most, since he needed those to make his living. Not yet thirty, Capa was already an established news photographer. In 1936, at the age of twenty-two, he had covered the Spanish Civil War for *Life.* It was there that he first displayed his icy calm under fire. One of his most famous pictures is that of a Loyalist soldier falling dead from a sniper's bullet. From Spain he went to China for its war with Japan. The year 1941 found him in London filming the horrors of the German blitz attack.

As he paced his tiny apartment, Capa knew he must get another assignment—fast. He flew to Washington, got his immigration problem temporarily ironed out and then managed to get a job from *Collier's* magazine. Forty-eight hours later he sailed for Europe in a convoy that encountered German submarines and an enemy plane that tried to sink his ship. In London, his next assignment was waiting for him —the North African invasion. The *Collier's* bureau manager, famed correspondent Quentin Reynolds, asked Capa if he were accredited. "Not only had I not been accredited," Capa recalled, "but my chances of being accredited to the U. S. Army—indeed to any Army but the Hungarian—were practically nil. I pretended to be just as surprised as he that *Collier's* didn't know I was Hungarian." Capa registered in England as an alien while his office sought to get him accredited. Meanwhile, he took pictures of American bombers on their way to Germany. One of the planes returned badly shot up with some of its crew members killed or wounded. Seeing Capa on the runway, the pilot yelled bitterly: "Are these the pictures you were waiting for, photographer?" Capa, in his book *Slightly Out of Focus,* remembered that "I hated myself and my profession. . . . I held a conversation with myself about the incompatibility of being a reporter and hanging on to a tender soul at the same time."

The accreditation finally came through and Capa hopped a troopship to North Africa. He landed in Algiers to learn that the fighting was hundreds of miles away in the Tunisian hills. Capa and Will Lang, of *Time* magazine, rounded up a jeep and driver and chased after the American First Armored Division. After shooting several ground actions, Capa flew five bombing missions and was recommended for the Air Medal. But a few months later employment problems again plagued this great photographer. *Collier's* learned to its dismay that his pictures, under military regulations, were being pooled with those of other photojournalists. Thus, his prints were appearing in newspapers before *Collier's* even got them. The upshot was that the magazine decided to drop Capa, who had to get a job or lose his precious accreditation. Unable to connect with an American publication, Capa, in desperation, went to the Army's public information office in Algiers, hoping to grab some kind of assignment. The only newsman there was a combat photographer sick with diarrhea. The man had been accredited to cover the imminent invasion of Sicily.

"Why don't you take my place?" he suggested to Capa, who needed no urging. He approached General Matthew Ridgway, 82nd Airborne Division commander, who snapped: "I don't care whether you're Hungarian, Chinese or anything else as long as you're willing to jump and take pictures of my division in combat." The indisposed photographer had had several months of parachute training but Capa had never jumped. He flew in the lead plane, taking pictures of the paratroopers as they leaped into space. The last one out turned to Capa and commented, "I don't like your job, pal. It's too dangerous."

When he returned to Tunis to develop his pictures, the official word had arrived that he had been fired by *Collier's*. He was ordered to return to Algiers immediately. A friend had a solution. There was another mission that night over Sicily. If Capa jumped in, the army wouldn't be able to get to him for weeks. He strapped on a parachute, climbed aboard a plane and tried not to think of the jump ahead.

Here is how Capa described his first jump:

> I stepped out with my left foot forward into the darkness. I was still groggy, and instead of counting my thousands [standard method for timing of opening emergency chute], I recited: "Fired photographer jumps." Less than a minute later, I landed in a tree in the middle of a forest. For the rest of the night I hung from the tree. . . . There was a lot of shooting going on around me. I didn't dare yell for help. With my Hungarian accent, I stood an equal chance of being shot by either side.

American paratroopers found him the next morning.

The G.I.s liked the relaxed, wisecracking Capa. They also admired him for his calm bravery under fire. The brass respected him for his knowledge of military tactics and strategy. The late Brigadier General Theodore Roosevelt said: "Bob knows more about the art of war than many four-star generals."

Capa was picked as one of four photographers to make the "D" Day landing in Normandy. He went in with the first wave of troops. "I just stayed behind my tank," wrote Capa, "repeating a sentence from my Spanish Civil War days—'Es una cosa muy seria'—This is very serious business." Draped over one arm was an expensive Burberry raincoat. "I was the most elegant invader of them all," he added. But Capa also carried two Contax cameras. He shot frame after frame as the shells exploded around him. Then his camera jammed. He wrote:

> I reached into my bag for a new roll, and my wet, shaking hands ruined the roll before I could insert it into my camera. I paused for a moment . . . and then I had it bad. The empty camera trembled in my hands. The men around me lay motionless. Only the dead on the water line rolled with the waves. . . . I just stood up and ran toward the boat. . . . I held my cameras high above my head and suddenly I knew that I was running away. I tried to turn but couldn't face the beach, and told myself, "I am just going to dry my hands on that boat." . . . I saw that the superstructure had been shot away . . . the skipper was crying. . . . His assistant had been blown up all over him and he was a mess.

Capa took more pictures from the ship and then blacked out. He awoke in a bunk, his naked body covered with a rough blanket. Attached to his neck was a piece of paper which read: "Exhaustion case. No dog tags." His camera case was safe.

Robert Capa had gone ashore at Omaha beach, the bloodiest of all the landings in Normandy. The invasion was his greatest triumph and, at the same time, his greatest professional tragedy. Seven days later he learned that the pictures he had taken on "Easy Red" beach were the best of the landing. But an excited darkroom assistant in London had turned on too much heat while drying the negatives, destroying all but eight of the 106 pictures Capa had made.

Heartbreaking as this error was, it did not stop Capa. He continued filming the war, always in the thick of action. He was at Bastogne and he parachuted into Germany. After VE Day, Capa marked time until the next war. He had to wait only three years. He was among the first photographers on hand for the Israeli-Arab war in 1948. In 1954 he flew into Indochina to report the French-Viet Minh conflict. It was Capa's last war. While on routine patrol he stepped on a land mine and was killed. *Life* magazine, for whom he was working at the time, called him "the most famous war photographer of his generation."

Bert Brandt, of Acme Newspictures, was also one of the first cameramen to hit the beach at Normandy. He hitchhiked aboard three boats in the rough channel before he got his negatives back to England. His invasion pictures were the first to reach the United States.

On the front line, photographers often had to develop their own film, sometimes using a steel helmet to mix developing solutions and covering it with a raincoat to keep out the light. A group of Marine Corps cameramen improvised an entire photo laboratory, using an old airplane fuel tank for a sink.

Another brilliant World War II photographer was W. Eugene Smith, also of *Life*, who was badly wounded in the South Pacific. Smith frequently attached himself to combat units headed for battle. A product of a school *Life* ran for army photographers, he produced some of the finest pictures of the war.

Before he was hit in the face by a Japanese bullet, Smith had refused the offer of a rifleman to protect him because he wanted to "be in the same spot as the guy I was photographing."

Earlier in the war he had made this comment about his job:

"The trouble with taking photographs when the air is full of lead is that you have to stand up when anyone with any sense is lying down and trying to disappear right into the earth."

A veteran of thirteen Pacific actions and twenty-three bombing missions, "Wonderful" Smith, as he was known to other correspondents, shot ground action by going ahead of his subject so he could get him advancing under fire or ducking into foxholes.

Carl Mydans, another *Life* photographer, was taken prisoner by the Japanese in Manila. His captors offered to free him if he would take propaganda pictures for them. Mydans refused and was transported to Shanghai, where he spent several months in a prison camp. He was later freed in an exchange of prisoners. During the process a State Department man handed Mydans a camera and he went back to work. A native of Boston, Mydans later covered the Italian campaign, frequently under fire. He once had a close call without realizing it. After the capture of Velletri, Mydans spotted a huge bottle of wine with a German helmet perched on top. He thought it would make a good picture but the bottle had to be moved into better light. A soldier helped him push it about six inches. Later, two G.I.s picked up the bottle, which blew up and seriously injured them. It had been booby-trapped.

Another *Life* photographer, George Silk, and reporter Will Lang also were at Velletri, where they were pinned down for half an hour by rifle-like German artillery shelling. Said Lang:

"Having just seen what one American shell had done to ten Germans, we were so nervous that Silk spent five futile minutes trying to change his film before he noticed he was jamming a roll of Life Savers into his camera."

Perhaps the most famous World War II photo was the flag-raising scene atop Mount Suribachi on Iwo Jima. It was shot by Joe Rosenthal, of the Associated Press. The picture achieved such popularity that it was used as the official poster of a United States War Loan Drive. It has been reproduced thousands of times in newspapers and magazines and was chosen for the design of a commemorative postage stamp. For Rosenthal, it won the Pulitzer Prize and numerous other honors.

After Pearl Harbor, Rosenthal, already a top civilian lensman, tried to enlist in the army, navy and marines. All of them turned him down because of his poor eyesight. Even so, he managed eventually to become a warrant officer in the United States Maritime Service. But the AP offered him a chance for more action and he resigned to go to the Pacific for the wire service. To get the flag picture, the stocky but diminutive Rosenthal scrambled up the sandy, volcanic slope, narrowly avoiding Japanese mines while snipers' bullets whizzed past him. On the summit, he made a perch of rocks and Japanese sandbags to get a wider field for his Speed Graphic camera. He made three shots, the first one being the one that stirred the world.

Following the war, Rosenthal became a cameraman for the *San Francisco Chronicle*.

Another fine AP war photographer was Frank E. "Pappy" Noel, who was awarded the Pulitzer Prize in 1943 for a picture he took while awaiting rescue at sea. Noel was in Singapore when Pearl Harbor was attacked in 1941. He got aboard a United States-bound Indian ship, but it was bombed and sunk by Japanese planes a few miles out. Noel was among the twenty-eight crewmen and passengers who survived and escaped in lifeboats. While his boat drifted toward Sumatra, another lifeboat floated by. In it an Indian pleaded with Noel and his companions for water. The cameraman snapped a picture of the pitiful figure, and the shot became one of the great illustrations of the war.

Noel also covered Korea and was captured by the Chinese near the Changjin Reservoir in 1950. Even in prison camp "Pappy" Noel managed to get exclusive pictures. AP correspondents at the Korean truce meeting site relayed to Noel a camera, film and flash bulbs. A few days later he sent back photos of captured United Nations forces, a world scoop. He was freed in 1953.

The Pulitzer Prize for news photography was also given to Associated Press staffer Frank Filan for his stark picture of the battle for Tarawa in the South Pacific. Filan was landing with an assault boat when it sank. He seized his heavy pack and fought his way toward shore through shoulder-high surf. He turned back to assist a wounded marine, slipping under several times. The two made the 600 yards to the beach but Filan's cameras were ruined. He borrowed a Coast Guard photographer's camera for his historic shot. Admiral Chester Nimitz commended Filan for "inspiring devotion to duty."

Combat photographers usually picked their own assignments, often those which carried the greatest risk. For example, Bob Bryant of INS was one of only two correspondents to sneak behind Japanese lines in Burma with the famed Merrill's Marauders. After getting the permission of General "Vinegar" Joe Stillwell to join the unit, Bryant parachuted into the jungle and then hiked for miles to catch up with Merrill's force. Although officially a noncombatant, the cameraman said, "I carried a rifle and had to shoot my way out when we were ambushed on the trail several times. In that outfit, everyone had to fight since we were surrounded by the enemy all the time."

Often he tried to develop his film in the jungle.

"There were times," he recounted, "when I would hire Chinese runners to bring water from a stream or have them wash the films in a river by swishing them back and forth."

Drying negatives was an even greater problem because fungi would form on the emulsions, he said.

Later, Bryant was honored by being picked by the Navy as the number-one camera for the peace signing on the battleship *Missouri*. When the war ended he joined the *San Francisco Examiner*.

The armed services produced a number of great photographers who often risked their lives to shoot some of the finest pictures in World War II. One of these was David Douglas Duncan, who took his first news picture while a freshman at the University of Arizona. A fire swept through the Congress Hotel in Tucson and young Duncan raced to his room to get the thirty-nine-cent camera his sister had given him. He shot a picture of a "frantic little guy" trying to rescue his suitcase. The man turned out to be the notorious outlaw John Dillinger, and the suitcase was stuffed with stolen cash. Duncan, however, was too shy to take his print to the local newspapers.

In World War II, as a marine combat correspondent, he once squeezed in a pod under the wing of a P-38 fighter plane to snap pictures of the strafing of a Japanese-held hill. In another incident the pilot of a bomber was killed by anti-aircraft fire as Duncan was leaning on his shoulder, shooting pictures from the window. After the war Duncan joined *Life* and was one of the first combat photographers in Korea. Ever ready for the usual, offbeat shot, he once entered a fighter jet squad room where a young pilot sat silently. Something in the man's face prompted Duncan to take his picture.

Later, the photographer learned the pilot had shot down the first enemy plane in the Korean War. Duncan usually carried two Leica cameras, one on each side hanging by leather straps crossed like ammunition bandoliers in front of his chest. Film rolls were tucked in a back-pack with his toothbrush, soap and bottle of insect repellent. The Leica, Contax and Rolleiflex were the cameras most preferred by combat photographers in World War II and Korea. The first two are 35-millimeter types and the last is a reflex model.

Marine photographers were often shooting pictures under murderous enemy fire. On Peleliu, a marine sergeant and a cameraman worked side by side while flame throwers and demolition men flushed Japanese from a concrete pillbox. Suddenly an enemy soldier rushed out and headed straight for the photographer, bayonet first. The sergeant stopped him with one shot from his carbine and then turned and yelled at the photographer: "Did you get that?"

"Get what?" the correspondent replied.

"I just shot a Jap right in front of you. Did you get the picture?"

"Well, I didn't see him," the cameraman admitted. "Do it over again."

The Army Signal Corps and the Navy also had combat photographers, most of them enlisted men. One Army lensman was Lewis J. Merrim, who had been a New York City free-lancer before the war. He was attached to the famed First Special Service Force and stuck with it through fighting in Italy, France and Germany. Once in southern France the Army high command decided it needed aerial photographs of enemy positions. The only plane available for the job was a light spotter plane belonging to the artillery. Merrim thought about the problem and then fastened a makeshift rack to the craft's side and attached a Speed Graphic camera to it. Aerial photos are usually taken at 10,000 feet with special lenses, but Merrim had only standard equipment so his pilot flew at 1,000 feet.

"The first time we passed over," Merrim recollected, "the Germans looked at us dumbfounded. It was obvious they thought we were absolutely mad. The second time we flew over they weren't so unbelieving. They began firing at us. We were so low that they didn't waste their big guns on us but pecked away with small arms. We made 13 passes and it was a miracle we weren't killed."

Sgt. Merrim, who was wounded later, got dozens of prints from the flight. Lt. Col. Robert D. Burhans, in his book *The First Special Service Force,* said of Merrim's pictures: "Excellent coverage was gained of enemy terrain. . . . In most cases the enlargements were superior in clarity to the regular Air Corps photos." Today, Lew Merrim has his own successful photography business in New York.

World War II cameramen, both civilian and military, were killed in action. Frank Prist, of Acme Newspictures, died from a sniper's bullet on Leyte Island in the South Pacific. Bede Irvin, of the Associated Press, was fatally hit by a bomb fragment from an American B-26 "Marauder" which dropped its load short of the target. Martin Barnett, of Paramount News, was wounded while filming the first assault on Lae in New Guinea. Three Japanese bombs hit near his boat and he was hurled to the deck by the concussion. He suffered an injured spine and was shipped home.

World War II also was recorded with paint, pen and pencil. In 1943, General Dwight D. Eisenhower approved a plan to send forty-two artists to create a pictorial history of the great conflict. One of these was George Biddle, who slogged through North Africa, Sicily and Italy with the infantry, sketching as he went. Later the War Department withdrew funds for the artists' project but the contract was taken up by *Life* magazine. Biddle wrote in his book *Artist at War:*

> . . . In Italy after Naples, we were to slug it out with the enemy in rain, mud and foxholes. . . . All this made for a slower rhythm and therefore a more intimate contact with our troops. To all purposes I was part of the fighting forces. I spoke German and Italian and so I could be useful to the staff. I carried my own equipment and pack. I was neither an officer nor an enlisted man, and so I could share the confidence of both.

The artist most familiar to the foot soldier was a slightly built G.I. named Bill Mauldin. He became famous through his "Willie and Joe" cartoons which appeared in the Army newspaper *Stars & Stripes*. There was nothing glamorous or heroic about Willie and Joe. They were a couple of cynical, battle-scarred dogfaces whose principal aim was survival. They were dirty, bearded and hollow-eyed and their uniforms hung on them like sacks. Their humor was usually grim but it was of a special kind with which the line soldier could identify. Willie and Joe were an extension of himself. The pair, like him, suffered through enemy shells, Army red tape, C-rations and civilians and rear-echelon brass who tried but could not understand the way it really was in combat. The G.I. could laugh knowingly when Willie, confronted by an irate Italian woman whose home had been destroyed by American bombers, shrugs his shoulders and replies: "Don't blame me, lady." Mauldin also spoofed the army's special privilege policy for officers. One cartoon showed a general and other brass gazing out from a mountain clearing. "A magnificent view!" the general exclaims. "Is there one for the enlisted men?"

Mauldin accurately portrayed the common soldier because he marched, slept, ate and fought with them. His cartoon ideas were born of front-line experience. He spent time with more than fifteen infantry divisions and was wounded in action. He said of his work: "I draw pictures for and about the dogfaces because I know what their life is like and I understand their gripes."

Other *Stars & Stripes* cartoonists were Sergeant George Baker, who drew "Sad Sack," a hapless draftee, and Sergeant David Breger whose soldier creation was named after himself. Mauldin became a successful political cartoonist after the war and the other two continued their drawings in civilian newspapers.

Photographers since World War II have covered the action in Korea, Vietnam, the Dominican Republic and wherever else there has been fighting—Cyprus, the Congo and the Middle East.

Max Desfor, long one of the mainstays of the AP camera staff, carried off a Pulitzer Prize in 1951 for his dramatic shot of Korean refugees fleeing across a bombed-out bridge. Desfor, who began his career as a messenger boy in the AP photo department, also had covered World War II.

Two of the most outstanding new photographers are Horst Faas, of the Associated Press, and Kyoichi Sawada, of United Press International. Both have won Pulitzer Prizes for their Vietnam pictures. Faas, 32-year-old native of Germany, met his first war in the Congo, where Katanga troops forced him to eat his UN pass. Tough and tenacious, he will go anywhere for a good shot. He commented in a *Popular Photography* magazine piece:

> War, like anything else one photographs, is human and war is more human than anything else. A good war photo shows human beings in a situation that is described as war. I think the best war photos I have taken have always been made when a battle was actually taking place—then people were confused and scared and courageous and stupid and showed all of these things. When you look at people right at the very moment of truth, everything is quite human. You take a picture at this moment with all the mistakes in it, with everything that might be confusing to the reader, but that's the RIGHT combat photo.

Faas, who spends from twenty to twenty-five days a month with various military units, also teaches AP reporters basic photography so they can grab a picture if need be. He carries two Leica cameras and a Nikonos in the field. One Leica is for color work.

The Vietnam war has attracted a number of free-lance photographers. One of the best is James Pickerell, a bespectacled, crew-cut lensman who has been there since 1963. This is how he describes his working habits:

"I cover the war from the level of the foot soldier, as all photographers must, because this is where the pictures are. My sources are almost exclusively men at the lowest level—captains, lieutenants, sergeants . . ."

Vietnam is a dangerous place for photographers. Bernard J. Kolenberg, of the *Albany Times-Union,* and Huynh Thanh My, a Vietnamese working for AP, were killed within ten days of each other. Tim Page, twenty-two, of *Life,* was wounded for the second time in 1966 by a Viet Cong grenade which exploded in mid-air.

All correspondents' pictures must be taken to Saigon and then radioed to Tokyo or Manila, where they are relayed by cable or radio to the United States.

Faas readily admits that he has been terrified by some of his experiences in Vietnam. In a talk before editors and publishers in New York he told of one reaction under Viet Cong mortar fire:

> I pressed my helmet and face into the dust. The rounds kept coming and coming. I glanced to my left and saw a soldier. Shrapnel had cut off his face.
>
> Then my knees and shoulders started trembling. I could not take any pictures. When the last round had exploded, it took me five minutes to steady my trembling hands. Then I took pictures again.

How does a war photographer work? Faas explained:

> I always go in the area that seems most promising, and stay with the troops until they are through. Often pictures develop only after a couple of days of walking and crawling— and much frustration. But sometimes patience pays off. When troops get into a fight I go with them but since I carry no weapon and do not take part in the fighting, I keep my head down—the privilege of a noncombatant.
>
> One way of staying relatively safe: never take pictures when the odds are against you. The most graphic picture I have ever seen was one I decided not to take because of a little added danger that might kill the careless. There were three dead American soldiers lying 200 yards away—but I never got there because the area between them was under sniper fire.

But even luck and caution run out. After five years in Vietnam, Faas was wounded by rocket fire in late 1967.

The civil war in the Dominican Republic was another hotspot for combat cameramen. Douglas Kennedy, a *Miami Herald* man, was mistakenly wounded by United States marines who fired on a Dominican taxicab in which he was riding. Douglas Downs, an NBC cameraman, rode through rebel sniper fire atop a marine armored personnel carrier. An NBC crew knocked over a $4,000 television camera in the scramble to flatten themselves on the roof of an office building when an artillery shell screamed over their heads during an interview.

As do all wars, the Dominican struggle produced its own brand of humor. According to *Newsweek* magazine, when NBC staffers entered the marine compound in Santo Domingo, their credentials were examined by a guard who then passed them on with a smart salute and a "Goodnight, David," a reference of course to NBC's popular commentator, David Brinkley.

12

The Soldier Reporters

TOM HOGE, A WORLD WAR II COMBAT CORRESPONDENT, HAD A HARD time convincing the Germans he was not a spy after his capture in Holland. They were suspicious of his black tie and low shoes.

But Hoge was indeed a bona-fide reporter. He also was a soldier, despite the personal touches of his uniform. The young man was on an assignment for *Stars and Stripes,* the army newspaper, when the C-47 in which he was riding was shot down, forcing him to parachute out.

At the same time dozens of other *Stars and Stripes* correspondents were covering front-line action in Europe and the Pacific. The Marine Corps had its own correspondents, who also risked their lives daily with the fighting troops.

From the time of the Mexican War, the soldier reporter has had an honorable place in journalism. The service newspapers and news bureaus produced some top-grade writing and writers, some of whom —like Jim Lucas of the Scripps-Howard Newspapers—went on to civilian prominence. The work of the Army and Marine correspondents was also a valuable contribution to history.

When United States troops invaded Mexico in 1846, newspapers were printed in General Scott's and General Taylor's armies by soldiers. They were distributed in the camps and sent home to friends and relatives. Type, presses, ink and paper were hauled by the troops with other provisions.

The first edition of *Stars and Stripes* was published in Bloomfield, Missouri, on November 9, 1861, by four Union soldiers on a captured Rebel press. Then, as now, the paper was printed for Army troops.

It went out of business the next day when the Northern troops took up the pursuit of the fleeing Confederates. However, other *Stripes* editions were printed throughout the Civil War in Boston; Jacksonport, Arkansas; New Orleans; and Thibodaux, Louisiana, where it was run off on wallpaper, the only paper available. The Southern armies also put out troop newspapers.

Stars and Stripes was revived in World War I but no longer on a hit or miss basis. It came into its own as a full-fledged newspaper serving the thousands of "doughboys" of the American Expeditionary Force. General John J. Pershing, AEF commander, decreed that the weekly paper was to be strictly "for and by the soldiers." It began publishing with six people under the direction of Lt. Guy T. Viskniskki, a news syndicate man in civilian life. The first editions were run off in a hall bedroom of the Hotel St. Anne in Paris, with an initial printing of 20,000 to 30,000 copies. This jumped to a half million by the end of the war. By February, 1919, the staff numbered 200 and occupied an entire floor above the American Chamber of Commerce office in Paris.

Several *Stripes* staffers became famous journalists after the war. Among them were Harold Ross, editor of the *New Yorker* magazine;

Grantland Rice, sportswriter; Alexander Woollcott, drama critic; and Franklin P. Adams, columnist. One contributor was Sgt. Joyce Kilmer, the poet who wrote "Trees." He was killed in action.

The World War I *Stars and Stripes* was a lively paper, featuring cartoons by Charles Dana Gibson and Rollin Kirby and promoting such causes as the adoption of French war orphans by AEF units. There were a number of features about front-line riflemen, new uniform styles and the arrival in France of a unit of the "Women's Overseas Corps," the forerunner of today's WACs.

Stars and Stripes was the largest of the World War I troop publications, but it was not the only one. The marine's magazine *Leatherneck* made its debut then, and individual army outfits published their own newspapers. The ambulance service, for example, had one called *Radiator,* and the air corps printed its *Plane News.*

The Second World War saw the rebirth of *Stars and Stripes,* whose circulation went over a million before the end of the conflict. It was a weekly at first but turned daily on November 2, 1942, with editions printed in at least twenty-five locations in Europe, North Africa, the Middle East and the Pacific. General George C. Marshall, the army's chief of staff, said that the new *Stripes* would again be strictly by and for the soldier. The policy was so firmly upheld that it was not uncommon to see lieutenant reporters working for private-first-class editors. Rank was not as important as meeting deadlines. In some areas the paper was printed in captured newspaper offices or from mobile units within earshot of the front lines, where *Stripes* staffers were getting the news. Reporters like Sergeant Jack Foise, a former machine gunner, were under fire for days on end. Foise, who marched with the troops in the Italian campaign, was praised by Ernie Pyle as one of the great war correspondents.

A thin, balding man, Foise sought the action. In one battle he got an exclusive on an invasion because of the army's brass-bound rule that enlisted *Stripes* reporters must bunk with the G.I.s. When the press corps got to the staging area for an amphibious assault in Italy, the civilian newsmen were assigned to the officers' quarters. Foise mingled with the enlisted men on the beach as night drew near. In the dawn hours the order was given to attack and Sergeant Foise went in with the first wave. The other correspondents were awakened the next morning and learned to their dismay that the invasion had been launched without them.

Later, Foise got another exclusive story of a tragic error in which American planes carrying paratroopers were shot down by Allied anti-aircraft guns. Jack Foise went on to a brilliant career as a civilian newsman and at this writing is Southeast Asia bureau chief for the *Los Angeles Times*.

Big Phil Bucknell, another *S&S* reporter, collected a Purple Heart to go with his journalistic laurels. Dropped in a parachute over France on D-Day, he drifted to earth as tracer bullets sped around him. When he hit the ground his shinbone snapped and he lay helplessly through the night as German patrols searched for paratroopers. American soldiers found him at daybreak but he insisted on dictating his story before being removed to an aid station. A lieutenant grabbed a motorcycle and roared off to file the dispatch to the *Stripes* London news office.

A number of other *S&S* reporters made airborne invasions. Ed Clark landed in a glider with Seventh Army troops in southern France. When he saw that he and the other men were surrounded by Germans he snatched a machine gun and joined the fighting. So did another *Stripes* correspondent, Bud Hutton, who parachuted down on a German command post. Many of the Americans were dead before they hit the ground. Somehow Clark and Hutton survived twenty-four hours of bloody fighting. They stayed on the line for five days, sending out pictures and stories of the momentous battle. After the war Hutton and another *S&S* reporter, Andy Rooney, teamed up to write a book, *The Story of the Stars and Stripes*.

Greg Duncan, of the Naples *Stripes* staff, was killed when a German shell hit his jeep after the Allies broke through the Anzio beachhead.

Stars and Stripes was sometimes published under fire. In the French city of Strasbourg the staff was overjoyed to find excellent printing facilities shortly after Allied troops moved in. But suddenly the American and French troops received orders to pull back. Someone forgot to notify the *S&S* staffers, who happily continued working, unaware that a German counterattack was imminent. When they finally learned of their situation they decided to stick it out. One of the *Stripes* crew, Vic Dallaire, recalled:

> There we were with two typewriters, two Colt .45s and a jeep to defend the town of Strasbourg. We were damned if we were going to leave if we could help it, because that plant was a sweetheart, and we knew there was nothing as good back at Nancy or Besançon, the only printing towns to which we could retreat . . .

Dallaire and Ed Clark went along the streets, urging the French citizens to "stand fast" because everything was going to be all right. They figured the sight of United States uniforms would boost morale in the beleaguered community. Somehow, the *S&S* staff got out a paper and delivered copies to the front-line troops—behind them.

The sight of the Americans calmly putting out a newspaper averted a panic among the populace. When the Allied forces re-entered the city there was talk of court-martialing Dallaire and Clark, but instead they were decorated with the Bronze Star and the French *Croix de Guerre* for their heroism.

Another *Stars and Stripes* staff wasn't so fortunate. It went into Liège, Belgium, with the first American columns and located a suitable printing press, but was forced out a few hours later when Nazi planes bombed the plant.

G. K. Hodenfield, who came to *Stripes* by way of Iowa and United Press, had a chilling D-Day experience. He attached himself to a Ranger outfit assigned to scale a steep Normandy cliff and silence a German naval battery. As he neared the top the fire became intense and he jumped into a convenient foxhole to find himself face to face with an enemy soldier. Hodenfield shot first.

Occasionally, *Stripes* reporters were able to help civilian correspondents gather news. When the Ludendorff Bridge crashed after First Army troops had crossed the Rhine on it, Lindsey Nelson, an

S&S newsman, was an eyewitness to the heroism of engineers who dived into the river to save their buddies. He and two assistants spent five hours getting the complete story, including the names of hundreds of rescuers and victims and their home towns. After hammering out the article, the soldier-reporters mimeographed it and gave it to fifty correspondents who arrived on the scene long after the disaster. Said Rooney and Hutton in their book:

"All these men wrote stories, and the pieces appeared under their by-lines at home, but it was Lindsey Nelson who was actually responsible for every one of the thousands of words they wrote."

Stars and Stripes correspondents covered virtually every big American battle and were on hand for the final surrender ceremonies in Europe and the Pacific. Some *S&S* staffers had had years of experience on civilian newspapers, but many, like Andy Rooney, learned their craft on the job.

One of the former stateside newsmen was Howard Taubman, who worked in the *Stripes* Rome office as a reporter and rewrite man. One night in 1945 he was assigned to cover a performance of the reactivated Rome Opera Company which was featuring the renowned tenor, Beniamino Gigli. The singer was appearing after a long absence from the stage, due largely to his support of the Italian dictator Mussolini.

Taubman thought Gigli's artistry was on the hammy side and said so in his review the next day. *Stars and Stripes* was immediately flooded with indignant letters demanding to know by what authority a mere army corporal criticized the great Gigli. The newspaper printed most of the letters and at the end of them ran a one-line editor's note disclosing the fact that Corporal Taubman had been music editor of *The New York Times*.

But despite his civilian specialization, Taubman rarely wrote about concerts. Like other *S&S* staffers, he handled hard news. One of his notable stories was an exclusive interview with the Italian partisans who had fought with American troops. Today Howard Taubman is *The New York Times* critic-at-large.

Stripes was in business in Rome the same day the city was captured, taking over the plant of *Il Messagero*. That afternoon the Army newspaper ran off an edition with the banner: WE'RE IN ROME.

One of the notable stories in Italy was covered by *Stripes* reporter Stanley M. Swinton, a young man not long out of the University of Michigan. He and Rita Hume, an INS correspondent, were taken by Italian partisans to Milan, where they saw the hanging bodies of Benito Mussolini and his mistress, Claretta Petacci, at a filling station. The two reporters jeeped back to the press camp, wrote their copy and filed it. Miss Hume, a former Seattle newswoman who got overseas by joining the Red Cross, received congratulations from her office in New York for her great job. Swinton was not as fortunate. He recounted ruefully:

> My story won unusual distinction, too. The Signal Corps lost it somewhere between the press camp and the *Stars and Stripes* office in Rome. It showed up a day or two later. Journalistic historians will be able to say mine was the only eyewitness account of Mussolini's hanging by his heels first to see print in the following Sunday's "Review of the Week" in the *Stars and Stripes* magazine section.

The tabloid daily was not always held in esteem by Army bigwigs. Crusty General George S. Patton once threatened to bar *Stars and Stripes* from his command because of his objections to cartoonist Bill Mauldin's cartoon characters, "Willie and Joe." Patton felt that the two dogfaces set a poor military example by their unshaven faces and generally sloppy dress. The matter came to the attention of Supreme Commander Dwight D. Eisenhower, who resolved it in favor of the newspaper. Ike wrote Patton:

> A great deal of pressure has been brought on me in the past to abolish such things as Mauldin's cartoons, the B Bag, etc. You will make sure that the responsible officer knows he is not to interfere in matters of this kind. If he believes that

a specific violation of good sense or good judgment has occurred, he may bring it to my personal attention.

The "B Bag" column by Charles White gave G.I.s a chance to air their gripes. The title derived from a canvas sack issued soldiers to carry their gear on long trips. "Blow it out your B Bag" was the answer a man often got from his fellow sufferers when he complained too often. The idea for a column was born after an infantryman wrote to *Stripes* of his desperate need for a pair of shoes, size 13 EEEE. White's story of the plea brought in a huge pile of brogans which the reporter was stuck with when the letter-writer disappeared. But by this time White began receiving requests for other odd-size shoes and advice for other problems. The column, which proved to be highly popular, was on its way.

Stars and Stripes still serves our troops today on three continents. The European edition in Darmstadt, Germany, prints over 150,000 copies a day and is a $10-million-a-year business. Now, however, many of its editors and reporters are experienced civilians.

Stars and Stripes' sister publication was *Yank,* a *Life*-like weekly magazine, which also had a soldier staff of correspondents, photographers and artists. It was not primarily a news magazine and frequently published fiction as well as articles. Its by-liners included writers well known today. Among them are William Saroyan, Irwin Shaw, Marion Hargrove, Merle Miller and Bill Davidson.

Yank's main editorial office was in New York and, unlike *Stars and Stripes,* it published stateside as well as twenty-two overseas editions around the world. The Paris edition began in September, 1944, on a rotogravure press on which a few weeks before was published *Wehrmacht,* the German army's equivalent of *Yank.*

Under the capable direction of managing editor Joe McCarthy, writers and cameramen frequently rotated from desk to combat assignments. Sergeant Dave Richardson was awarded the Legion of Merit for his front-line reporting of the New Guinea campaign.

Later he took part in the famed 500-mile jungle march with Merrill's Marauders, who were behind Japanese lines for three months. Describing this grueling experience, Richardson noted:

> Besides the regular 60 pound horseshoe-type pack which every Marauder carried (containing a blanket, poncho, kukri knife, 3-5 days rations, entrenching shovel, water wings for swimming rivers and an extra pair of shoes) I lugged two cameras, film, notebooks, maps, pencils and my carbine. And I brought along a typewriter. But the only chance I had to use it was during a two-day rest and after our first battle. I spent the first day repairing the damage that had been done to it by the incessant rain and by its being carried on a mule over bumpy ground . . .

Richardson, who had suffered a shrapnel wound in his eye in New Guinea, earned his keep with the Marauders as a working gunner on a tank.

Yank correspondent Walter Bernstein trekked through Yugoslavia for several days, crossing enemy lines to interview Marshal Tito, the resistance leader.

Yank also had its combat deaths. Sergeant John Bushemi was killed by enemy mortar fire in the Eniwetok invasion and Sergeant Peter Paris, one of the magazine's first staff members, died on D-Day in Normandy, going in with the first assault wave.

Corporal Bob Krell, a curly-haired *Yank* combat correspondent from Brooklyn, jumped with American paratroopers in a super-secret strike in Germany. They were fighting as soon as they hit the ground and young Krell joined three soldiers blasting away at a Nazi tank holding up the advance. German troops surrounded the four Americans and killed them shortly before help arrived.

Sergeant Barrett McGurn, another New Yorker, was wounded by mortar fire in the second battle of Bougainville in the Pacific. McGurn, after the war, became an oustanding foreign correspondent for the *New York Herald Tribune*.

Two *Yank* correspondents, Sergeants George Aarons and Burgess

Scott, set what was believed to be a record for long-distance jeep travel. Starting from Cairo, they drove to Aleppo, Syria, where they did a superb picture story of the execution of two Nazi spies. They then turned around and motored all the way across Africa to Algiers. There, they loaded their jeep on a transport plane for Italy, where they used it for frequent trips to the Cassino battle front. And finally, they wheeled the battered vehicle into Rome with conquering Allied troops.

Yank and *Stars and Stripes* had many things in common but millions of G.I.s would have agreed that their main virtue was that they spoke for the enlisted man and mirrored his needs and interests. *Yank* regularly furloughed reporters back to the states so they could tell the overseas troops what was happening on the home front. The magazine also ran a "What's Your Problem" column and a comic strip that completely captured the hearts of the common soldiers. It was called "Sad Sack" and was written by Sergeant George Baker, who embodied in his little character all the frustrations of the man in uniform. Yet it was funny. The G.I. was able to release a lot of his own tensions and annoyances while laughing at Sad Sack muddling his way through army situations which were not of his making —being last in the chow line, for example, and getting not only cold soup but a bawling out from an officer as well.

Yank was not afraid to snipe at the pomposity of army brass if it felt it could help enlisted men. In one issue the magazine printed the following item:

> When the chicken [Army slang for excessive rank privileges] was setting in on the island [Iwo Jima] this past summer, the officers in the AAF station posted a big sign in their area. "Officers Country," it read. "Restricted." The area was between the EM [enlisted men] living area and the place where the EM worked, and the restriction meant that GIs had to make a circle around it four times a day to get to and from their work—an extra half mile every morning, noon and night. The EM thought things over and came up with a big sign of their own. It said, "God's Country—No Restrictions."

The officers got PO'd and made the GIs take the sign down. But the feeling lingers.

Before it suspended publication in December, 1945, *Yank* had reached a circulation of 2,500,000 and was on the "best-seller" list for troops of all ranks throughout the world. General Eisenhower recognized *Yank*'s contribution by giving it an "Honorable Discharge," an exact duplicate of the one given to millions of servicemen after the war.

In December, 1941, a tiny marine garrison held Wake Island for fifteen days against an entire Japanese task force, a feat which Americans did not learn about fully until months later.

Brigadier General Robert L. Denig, Marine Corps public relations director, was convinced the story would have been better told if there had been a newspaperman, particularly a marine newspaperman, on the besieged island. Thus was hatched in his mind the idea of a special unit of marine combat correspondents. After getting approval for the plan, General Denig recruited many of the reporters himself, visiting newspaper offices and outlining his plan to editorial staffers, most of whom were going to be drafted anyway.

The general's sales talk was brief but effective. "We'll send you where the news is being made," he promised them. More than 150 newspapermen signed up.

The fighter-writers underwent the same rigorous training as other marines before they were assigned to combat units. If necessary, they could operate a rifle or machine gun as well as a typewriter—and they frequently did. Unlike *Stars and Stripes* or *Yank* staff writers, the marine correspondents did not have their own publication. Their material was distributed by the Marine Corps public relations branch to hometown newspapers throughout the United States. The marine newsman rarely tried to paint the big war picture but instead concentrated on the heroism or post-war aspirations of Private John Jones of Battle Creek, Michigan. He was after human interest. In getting it the combat correspondent waded ashore on virtually every bloody beach in the South Pacific.

Staff Sergeant Don A. Hallman, a former *New York Daily News* staffer, was one of the first to hit the shore on Cape Gloucester. His story read:

> A communications line is strung across a dugout. Three hours later two dead Japs and two live ones are dragged out of the emplacement. A Jap is hiding under a smashed barge. Communications men pass within a few yards. Cleanup men get the Jap a few minutes later.

Hallman failed to name the "cleanup men," but his commanding officer took care of this matter in a note penciled at the bottom of the story: " 'Clean-up men' consisted of Staff Sergeant Hallman."

Sergeant Jim Hurlbut stowed away in a landing barge to become the first marine correspondent on Guadalcanal. Another CC, Lieutenant Jim Lucas, was with a marine patrol that was fired upon by a Japanese force. The marines returned the fire, killing all the enemy but one who played possum. Suddenly he popped up and made a dash for it. Lucas and the others let go with their rifles and the correspondent was credited with one seventh of the kill. Lucas, a Tulsa newspaperman before the war, became a Scripps-Howard by-liner after the conflict.

On Tarawa, marine correspondent Pete Zurlinden, of Dayton, Ohio, came under Japanese sniper fire. He dived for protection in the only spot available—behind a pile of enemy bodies. The tough, crew-cut sergeant-reporter unlimbered his carbine and aimed carefully at where he figured the sniper was hiding. The gun responded with only a click. Three days of exposure to salt water had damaged the mechanism. Zurlinden picked up a dead marine's rifle and opened up on the Japanese marksman, who let loose with a volley of his own. The duel continued for more than an hour before a marine machine gun squad came up and wiped out the sniper. Later, his head sizzling with a dozen good stories, the marine correspondent got out his typewriter and prepared to peck away. "TARAWA, Nov. 22" his piece began. Then the machine went haywire, producing a line that wobbled all over the page. Pete Zurlinden soon found the reason. A bullet had gone through the casing, shattering the shift key!

Some marine combat correspondents were recruited in the field. On the third day of the fighting on Okinawa, DeWitt G. "Dick" Phelan, a rugged young rifleman from the Bronx, was pressed into service as a photographer and reporter.

"It seemed to be a better job than the one I had," Phelan recalled. Wounded twice, Phelan finished out the war as a CC and years later served in the same capacity in Korea. He also was elected president of the Marine Corps Combat Correspondents and Photographers Association.

One of Phelan's fondest memories is of the marine landing on Lebanon during the 1958 crisis in the Middle East. "As the assault boats were being lowered," he said, "the voice on the ship's public address system yelled, 'Away landing party and watch for the kids on the beach.'" This was one of the few landings where the marines did not have to fight for the beachhead. Instead, they encountered astonished sun bathers and swimmers.

Several marine combat correspondents were killed in action in World War II.

Staff Sergeant Richard J. Murphy, a graduate of Georgetown University and a pre-war reporter for the *Washington Star,* died while covering the landing on Saipan in June, 1944.

A young correspondent from Mamaroneck, New York, Staff Sergeant Solomon I. Blechman, was fatally wounded on the Guam beachhead and was posthumously awarded the Bronze Star. The citation read:

> . . . Staff Sergeant Blechman voluntarily joined those units engaged in the heaviest fighting to observe assault operations at first hand. Fearlessly making his way forward among the forces who were blasting the enemy's formidable defenses in an advance over the perilously rugged terrain, he repeatedly

exposed himself to the devastating Japanese machine-gun, mortar and small-arms fire as he gathered authentic material for his news reports. . . . [He] rendered gallant service to his division throughout a period of fierce hostilities . . .

In Blechman's memory, the Marine Corps Reserve established a journalism trophy to be presented annually to the Reserve ground unit publishing the best newspaper.

Sergeant Robert W. S. Stinson, a native of Flint, Michigan, and a former *Philadelphia Inquirer* reporter, was the first marine combat correspondent killed on active duty in the Second World War. He died in an airplane crash at sea off the Ellice Islands in 1943.

Marine correspondents filed more than forty thousand stories during World War II, ranging from accounts of titanic battles to a paragraph or two telling of a promotion from private first class to corporal of some marine from a small Iowa town. A CC sergeant told his fellow reporters in uniform:

"Though it is the war headlines that people will read first, your story is the one some family will clip and save. You'll be in the scrapbooks of the nation long after the headlines are in the ash can."

13

Ladies on the Front Lines

"JOURNALISM IS NOT A GAME, AND IN JOURNALISM THERE ARE NO excuses."

Arnold Bennett, the famed English writer, offered this advice in his book *Journalism for Women, A Practical Guide,* published in 1898.

Of the thousands of women who have taken up journalism careers since that time, few have taken their responsibilities lightly or asked for special favors because of their sex. In modern times women have covered virtually every kind of assignment, including wars and revolutions. One lady correspondent, Dickey Chapelle, was killed in action in Vietnam. Another, Marguerite Higgins, died of an illness contracted there.

Women worked as foreign correspondents as far back as 1866,

when Laura Catherine Redden reported from Europe to *The New York Times*. It was significant that she wrote under the pen name of Howard Glyndon. Journalism was not then considered a respectable occupation for women. The twentieth century was something else, however, and it saw the emergence of several female war correspondents who not only wrote under their own names, but had by-lines recognized by millions of readers.

No women reporters covered combat in World War I but several were in Europe during the conflict. Sigrid Schultz, considered one of the best foreign correspondents in the business—male or female— reported from Germany for the *Chicago Tribune* right after World War I. A native of Chicago and the daughter of a well-known portrait painter, she was educated in Paris and in Germany, where she studied international law. When World War I broke out Miss Schultz was living in her father's Berlin studio. In 1917, with America's entry into the war, she and her father and mother were ordered to register as enemy aliens. After the war she covered the Berlin riots, often at great danger to herself. Miss Schultz remained a newspaperwoman between wars, becoming a legend in her own time. In World War II she suffered shrapnel wounds in the first British air raid over Berlin and later almost died from typhus. Miss Schultz covered central Europe for the *Chicago Tribune* from 1926 to 1941, and later was Berlin correspondent for the Mutual Broadcasting System and *McCall's* magazine. Her experiences included a harrowing interview with Adolph Hitler in which he shouted at the top of his voice: "My will shall be done."

In the early 1930s, Miss Schultz recalls, she wrote "very nasty stories" about the Germans, who threatened her several times with expulsion.

"I told them to go ahead," Miss Schultz continued. "I said to them that if I were tossed out I would finally get a little rest and that I would make a wonderful martyr." The Nazis let her stay, but she never felt completely safe. She said she was afraid to drive a car in Berlin because of one particular Gestapo device used to keep "unfriendly" reporters in line.

"The Gestapo cars," she related, "were equipped with a specially built front which was used as a ramming device. When they wanted to frighten, threaten or kill someone, they would wait on a road until the victim came driving by, and then ram his car or simply push it over a bridge or into a river. Some of my friends had this experience. Even walking, I was careful in getting to my office since my stories had to be filed at one in the morning."

When the Second World War came the Germans refused to let Miss Schultz visit the front because she was a woman and because she had written anti-Nazi stories. But later she covered the Battle of the Ruhr with the First American Army and was with the first group of Americans to enter Berlin.

Anne O'Hare McCormick, another fine reporter of that era, grew up in Cleveland with a yen to make her mark in journalism. Small and red-haired, she got into the field in a way that is almost impossible today. With no reporting experience in the United States, she sailed to Europe with her husband, hoping to connect as a free-lance writer for an American newspaper. In a few months she was contributing pieces to *The New York Times* from Italy, where she chronicled the rise of dictator Benito Mussolini. In 1937 she won the Pulitzer Prize for distinguished foreign correspondence.

The career of Alice Rohe reads like exciting fiction. Unlike Mrs. McCormick, she had had extensive newspaper experience before she became Rome correspondent for the United Press in 1914. She was stoned in Ravenna as a spy and later imprisoned in Rimini for the same reason. After World War I she smuggled a story out of Greece concerning the king's love for an American girl.

The only woman to get an accredited pass from the United States War Department in World War I was Peggy Hull, a *Cleveland Plain Dealer* reporter, who first attracted her editor's eye by allowing herself to be held up by a bank bandit as a newspaper stunt. Miss Hull wanted desperately to get to France but she had trouble getting a paper or news agency to hire her. Finally she signed with the Newspaper Enterprise Association, which sent her overseas. She became friends with such famous reporters as Ring Lardner and Floyd Gibbons, who helped her find her way among America's fighting troops. She visited United States troop camps, spending two months with an infantry brigade. After the war she joined the American expeditionary force to Siberia, reporting its activities for NEA.

Other intrepid women were finding adventure and journalistic fulfillment in this era. Rheta Childe Dorr covered the Russian Revolution of 1917 for the *New York Mail,* as did Bessie Beatty of the *San Francisco Bulletin.* Both were with the famed "Battalion of Death," composed of Russian women fighters.

Another outstanding woman correspondent of this period was the late Dorothy Thompson, who also began her newspaper career in Europe without benefit of local newspaper experience. Tall and impressive in appearance, she was concerned mostly with the forces that make news rather than with the spot news development. Nevertheless she was on hand for five revolutions in Europe between world wars. She narrowly missed being killed when rioters fired at her as she watched a street battle from her hotel balcony. Learning of a Polish revolution while she was attending an opera in Vienna, she went to the Polish consul for a visa and then borrowed $500 from her friend Sigmund Freud, the noted psychiatrist. Still in her evening clothes she caught a train to Warsaw. A few miles from the city the train was forced to stop because the tracks had been mined. Miss Thompson and other correspondents cast about frantically for transportation to Warsaw, where the action was. Finally she managed to find an old Ford and drove to Warsaw over a hazardous road along which lurked soldiers who were shooting at anything that moved. Another car containing reporters was riddled with bullets. She got to Warsaw but was unable to file her story because of censorship. Thinking fast, she forced her wheezy vehicle to a small village where the local telegrapher let her send her message.

Born in upstate New York, Miss Thompson was educated at Syracuse University. She reported overseas for the *Philadelphia Public Ledger* syndicate, the *New York Herald Tribune* and various magazines. She moved in influential circles, counting among her friends and acquaintances Arnold Bennett, Lord Beaverbrook, Anita Loos,

Sir Hugh Walpole and, of course, Freud. She was once married to Sinclair Lewis, the novelist, himself a former journalist. Miss Thompson was more at home as a reporter in Europe than she was in the United States. In 1929 she wrote from Russia:

"I could not remain in America where I am so ill-adjusted to everything."

World War II produced more women correspondents than all other wars together. Twenty-one lady reporters covered the Allied invasion alone in 1944. Many, like Margaret Bourke-White, the *Time* and *Life* photographer, saw and heard the fighting. Miss Bourke-White shot pictures of the Tunisian campaign and was the first woman correspondent to fly a bombing mission. Other women wearing combat fatigues were Inez Robb, Ruth E. Cowan, Mary Welsh, Marguerite Higgins, Dickey Chapelle, Leah Burdette and Helen Hiett, who had previously covered the Spanish Civil War.

Miss Bourke-White came by her interest in photography quite naturally. Her father was an engineer and an enthusiastic amateur photographer. She was raised in New Jersey but was of a restless nature as early as she could remember. "I knew I had to travel," she said in her autobiography. She put in considerable mileage in getting an education, attending seven colleges before graduating from Cornell, where she began selling her first pictures. About this time, Henry Luce, founder of Time, Inc., sent for her to become staff photographer for his new magazine, *Fortune*. She took the first cover photo for *Fortune* and later went to Russia for the publication. Six years later she joined the *Life* staff.

A self-demanding perfectionist, Miss Bourke-White happened to be in Russia photographing the implementation of its five-year plan when Germany marched into the Soviet Union. She was on the spot of the biggest story in the world and she took full advantage of it. The Russians had an anti-camera ban but she managed to film the bombing of Moscow and later managed to persuade Josef Stalin himself to pose for a picture. In her book *Portrait of Myself*, Miss Bourke-White recalled that Stalin was "stone-like," making it difficult for her to get the shot she wanted.

"As I sank down to my knees to get some low viewpoints," she continued, "I spilled out a pocketful of peanut flashbulbs, which went bouncing all over the floor." Stalin burst out laughing—long enough for her to get two exposures. Then he was rock-faced again.

The Army honored Miss Bourke-White by using her as a model for the design of the first uniform for a woman war correspondent. It included a pink dress for special occasions and slacks and a green blouse with gold buttons and a correspondents' insignia on the shoulders. But Miss Bourke-White's purpose was photographing the war, not being a fashion model. She requested permission to go to North Africa for the Allied invasion. General Jimmy Doolittle agreed but ruled that she had to go by sea because flying was too dangerous. All the planes made it safely but Miss Bourke-White's ship was torpedoed by a German submarine. She was rescued in a lifeboat but kept shooting pictures during the entire operation.

After pleading for months with military authorities, she was permitted to accompany a bombing run. The Signal Corps lent her heavy flight clothing and a Speed Graphic camera. She held her own dress rehearsal for the mission by practicing crawling inside the B-17, dragging her equipment behind her as she sought the right nook for her work. The flight's objective was to destroy the El Aouina airfield at Tunis. Her plane, the lead ship, was hit twice by flak, but the lady from *Life* escaped injury. Six months later she was on the Italian front, where she flew over enemy lines in a Piper Cub spotter plane. Here is how she described this episode:

> We picked our course over the crests of hills which surrounded Cassino Valley like the rim of a cup. Highway 6—the muddy road to Rome—wound between bald rocky mountains, and we almost scraped their razor-blade edges as we flew over. We could see Italian civilians picking through the sickening rubble that once had been their homes. Then the land dropped away sharply, and all at once we were high over Cassino Valley. I was struck by the polka-dotted effect . . . with hundreds of thousands of shell holes filled with rainwater and shining in the sun. It seemed impossible that so

many shells could fall in a single valley. It was as though this valley, in which so many had suffered and died, was clothed in a sequined gown.

Years later Miss Bourke-White photographed the war in Korea, concentrating mostly on guerrilla fighting.

What Margaret Bourke-White did with her camera, Marguerite Higgins accomplished with her typewriter and a compelling determination to be a greater reporter. When she died tragically at forty-five, Miss Higgins had covered three wars and had scored some of the greatest scoops in journalism. She had wallowed in the mud with the infantry in France and had gone in with an amphibious assault force behind enemy lines in Korea.

A tall, attractive blonde, Miss Higgins quickly proved to her male colleagues that she did not intend to get by on looks alone. At the front in World War II she often worked twenty hours a day, filing 1,500 to 3,000 words a night to her newspaper.

Miss Higgins had newspaper work on her mind since her youth in Oakland, California. After graduating from the University of California *cum laude* and editing the campus paper, she followed the path of so many other journalism hopefuls to New York. But this was 1941 and newspaper jobs were hard to get, especially for a woman. While waiting for an opening she enrolled in the Columbia University Graduate School of Journalism, working her way through on a scholarship and as a stringer or correspondent for the *New York Herald Tribune*. The *Tribune* hired her as a city-side reporter upon graduation. In 1944, with the help of *Tribune* publisher Mrs. Helen Rogers Reid, Miss Higgins was dispatched to Europe as a war correspondent. What she lacked in experience she more than made up for in youth and enthusiasm. She said in her autobiography, *News Is a Singular Thing*, "Having no laurels to rest on, I became a cyclone of energy."

Miss Higgins was first attached to the Army Air Corps and later joined ground units. One of her major stories was the Allied liberation of the notorious Dachau concentration camp in Germany. At one point she and her jeep driver were behind enemy lines before the city had been officially taken by American troops. In the midst of the victory celebration a general ordered her to get out of town because of a typhus epidemic threat. When she objected he tried to grab her. "You let go of me," she retorted. "I've had my typhus shots. I'm here doing my job."

For doing her job in this action, Miss Higgins was awarded the Army campaign ribbon for outstanding service and won the New York Newspaper Women's Club award as the best foreign correspondent for 1945. After the war she covered the Nuremburg war criminal trials and got several assignments behind the Iron Curtain, where she was arrested by both the Poles and Russians.

In 1947, at the age of twenty-six, she was named chief of the *Herald Tribune*'s Berlin bureau and became a major by-line writer. One her big stories was the Soviet blockade of Berlin. By her own admission she was a slow writer, having a great fear of errors. But she was thorough, and her questioning in an interview was sharp and incisive.

Socializing is sometimes a part of the news business, and Miss Higgins was aware of its benefits. A bright, attractive hostess, she gave several "purpose parties" in post-war Berlin for military and diplomatic officials. It's a well-known fact that a news source is more likely to part with his information under the pleasant influence of good company, food and wine. But she couldn't control the ground rules at other social functions. She ruefully remembered one at which, in traditional manner, the male and female guests were separated after dinner. As the women around her chit-chatted about minor things, she was sure Drew Middleton, of *The New York Times,* was casually interviewing an important official in the other room. There are some disadvantages to being a woman correspondent and this was one of them. However, there are also compensations. Miss Higgins admitted: "I received far more national acclaim and publicity than many of my male colleagues who did just as fine or better jobs." During her career she received some fifty prizes and awards, including the Pulitzer.

As a correspondent in Korea, Miss Higgins had trouble with military authorities, who accused her and other American reporters of "giving aid and comfort to the enemy" by their dispatches. According to Miss Higgins the journalists' only crime was "telling the brutal story about the licking our troops were taking."

At one point she was ordered out of Korea because the Army said "there are no facilities for ladies at the front." The order was later rescinded and Miss Higgins rejoined her male colleagues in the battle area. As a concession to her femininity she was given a jeep while the newsmen hitchhiked. But, like them, she scrounged for food and lodgings and fought with headquarters to file her stories.

Despite her professional competence, Miss Higgins ran a continual gauntlet of opposition from both the military and some of her male colleagues.

"Realizing that as a female I was an obvious target for comment, I had taken great pains not to ask for anything that could possibly be construed as a special favor," she noted in her book *War in Korea*. She continued:

> Some of the men correspondents . . . had a distinct objection to female invasion of the field of war corresponding. At the actual war front, a woman has equal competitive opportunities. Essentially it comes down to being in the combat area at the crucial time and having the stamina to do the jeeping and hiking necessary to get to where you can file your story. Of course, the GI's whistle and wolf-call as you Jeep down past a convoy on a road. But when the shelling and the shooting starts, nobody pays any attention. No one has offered me his foxhole yet. And they didn't have to. I early developed a quick eye for protective terrain and can probably hit a ditch as fast as any man.

But through it all, Miss Higgins was never anything but feminine. If some reporters resented her presence, others paid her high tribute. Said one competitor: "Maggie was a cross between Alice in Wonderland and Eleanor Roosevelt. She regarded the world with wide-eyed excitement, then rolled up her sleeves determined to do something about it."

Miss Higgins was an outspoken writer, frequently commenting about the events she was reporting. About Korea she wrote: "Politically and emotionally Korea meant far more to me than just another war assignment."

Miss Higgins took an increasingly strong stand against communism and her later books make this attitude clear. She believed Vietnam to be a "front line of freedom" as much as Hawaii or San Francisco.

When Marguerite Higgins went to Vietnam in 1965 she was at the top of her career, a syndicated columnist whose by-line was known throughout the world. She also was married to Lieutenant General William E. Hall, her second husband, by whom she had two children. Somewhere in Vietnam she was bitten by a tiny insect which pumped into her a fatal poison. In January, 1966, she died at Walter Reed Hospital of leishmaniasis, a rare tropical disease. But Maggie Higgins was a combat casualty just as certainly as if she had been felled by a bullet on the front line. After three wars her luck had run out. Her final book, *Our Vietnam Nightmare,* was in the hands of her publisher at the time of her death.

Vietnam claimed the life of another famous woman war correspondent. On November 4, 1965, a tiny, near-sighted reporter was on a patrol in the Vietnam rice paddies. Someone stepped on a land mine and the cries of pain mingled with the sound of the explosion. When the smoke cleared the reporter lay dead. She was Dickey Chapelle, a brave, tough veteran of many campaigns and one of America's best-known newspaperwomen. She was this kind of correspondent: When she was with the United States invasion force in Guam, an officer asked her how far forward she wanted to go. Her reply: "As far forward as you'll let me."

Dickey Chapelle was born Georgette Louise Meyer in Milwaukee, Wisconsin, on March 14, 1918. She described her parents as pacifists "by heredity." A tomboy as a child, she was interested in mechanical things, and after high school she enrolled at the Massachusetts Institute of Technology. But in college she found herself drawn more to writing than engineering. While in school she sold free-lance magazine articles, an accomplishment which apparently did little for her classwork, for she flunked out. She drifted to Florida, where she became a stringer for various newspapers. When she was nineteen she married her photography instructor, Tony Chapelle, a World War I Navy cameraman and twenty years her senior. Chapelle wanted to buy her an engagement ring and asked her to go with him to pick it out. She agreed but at the jewelry store she had a sudden thought.

"I can do without an engagement ring," she told Chapelle. "I'd rather have a new camera." So instead he bought her a Speed Graphic, the leading news photography camera. Six months later she was taking pictures for *Life* magazine, and husband and wife were launched on a busy free-lance career.

"She was quick at picking things up," Chapelle recalls. "It wasn't long before she was a crack photographer." Working as a team, they carried three cameras each, with Dickey doing most of the writing that accompanied the pictures. For a European trip they had built a special truck that served as their base. Neither would go to sleep at night until their equipment had been thoroughly checked. This was a habit Dickey was to carry with her through scores of battle campaigns. She was both a writer and photographer but probably felt closer to her camera.

In 1944, Dickey Chapelle went to the Pacific war theater for Fawcett Publications. She came under fire for the first time in the battle for Okinawa. Except for nurses, she was the only woman in the invasion fleet. At first she floundered, missing pictures and stories. Finally a male correspondent took her aside and said: "Did you ever think of trying to do something yourself instead of asking permission?" She hadn't. She had been afraid to make a move without asking authorization of some officer who most likely didn't know himself. She took her friend's advice, and once on her own she began operating like a veteran newshawk. But later the marine commandant decided that Miss Chapelle had to leave the fighting zone "for her own protection." An "arrest on sight" order was issued for her. She was found on Guam, stripped of her credentials and shipped home.

After the war she and her husband were divorced but remained good friends for the rest of her life. In her book *What's a Woman Doing Here?* Dickey Chapelle said: "Can a woman be both a foreign correspondent and a wife? My answer is—never at the same time."

In 1956, as a *Life* photographer, she was arrested by Russian soldiers on the Hungarian border as she tried to get into that country to cover the brief but bloody revolution. She was carrying a tiny Minox camera taped under her bra in the best spy fashion. She was jailed for more than five weeks in Budapest, undergoing questioning six and seven hours at a stretch. One interrogator told her: "We will hang you as soon as we are able to prove you were a photographer for *Life.*" Two weeks later she was tried and found guilty of illegal border crossing, an offense carrying a five-year prison sentence. Instead, the Communists expelled her in the wake of a strong protest against her seizure by the Overseas Press Club of New York. She sold the account of her experiences to the *Reader's Digest.*

Always restless, she became a woman in search of a war. She found one in Algeria, which was fighting the French. Later, for the *Reader's Digest,* she reported the activities of a Cuban rebel named Fidel Castro, following him to victory. Through all this, Miss Chapelle was developing a philosophy of war correspondence. She wrote:

> Though any correspondent will tell you the significant bits of history he's seen through his life are ultimately dramatic— war, blood, terror—most of the time the job is a great deal like other jobs with highs and lows and even long stretches that are neither. . . . But what matters is that you keep your eyes open. If you call yourself a correspondent, your reason for being is first to see. And then, of course, to tell.

As a writer, Dickey was slow. Tony Chapelle observed: "She rewrote almost everything many times over. She was never quite satisfied with her written work. But she also was scornful of any reporter who used handouts [prepared news releases] as the basis of a story. This was a real thing with her. She had to see it. She had to do it before it was a worthy story in her estimation."

Dickey got along well with other correspondents but she was basically a loner. Unlike Dorothy Thompson, Anne O'Hare McCormick and Marguerite Higgins, she was less concerned with the ideas and forces underlying the news. Her stock-in-trade was the here and now and she constantly hunted the dangerous, the difficult, the physically hard-to-get stories. She worked hard at keeping in top condition and was capable of twenty-five-mile hikes. She made thirty parachute drops in her career.

For such a woman and such a reporter, Vietnam was an irresistible magnet. She went there as a free-lancer, lugging as her only field gear a small Army combat pack with a change of fatigues and socks, soap and towel, a can of "C" rations, her camera and extra film. She used to say, "I can live and work up to three weeks with what I can carry on my back." Her relations with the brass were good; they felt she was doing a needed job of bringing the impact of the war to United States readers.

Dickey Chapelle remained fiercely independent to the end. Once a newsman in Vietnam offered to help her with her gear. "Get your damned hands off that," she commanded. "I lug my own stuff and I take no favors from you or anybody. Leave it alone."

She was the fourth correspondent and the first woman reporter to be killed in Vietnam. In her obituary, *Time* magazine said: She "showed up just about everywhere men were shooting at each other. . . . Dickey never demanded any special treatment. Men did their best to keep her out of danger, but she always managed to find it."

The history of journalism is replete with the exploits of women foreign correspondents. It is not possible to detail all their careers in this book. In 1940, Mary Welsh (later to become Ernest Hemingway's wife) was the first female correspondent with the British forces and saw the German army march into Czechoslovakia. Later she covered the London Blitz. Helen Hiett reported the fall of France in 1939 for the National Broadcasting Company. She also won the National Headliners Award for her clean scoop on the bombing of Gibraltar.

Virginia Cowles and Martha Gellhorn covered the Spanish Civil War, making trips to the battle lines. Wrote Miss Cowles:

"When you wanted to go to the front you just got into a car and went. The most convenient front [was] only two miles from the main shopping district of Madrid. You took a tram halfway, walked the other half, and you were there."

After that conflict, Virginia Cowles became a roving correspondent for the *London Sunday Times, The New York Times* and the Hearst newspapers. In 1940 she was in Finland during its war with Russia, coming under bombardment several times. Her experience there was described vividly in her book *Looking for Trouble.*

> . . . It is difficult to describe indiscriminate aerial warfare against a civilian population in a country with a temperature 30 degrees Fahrenheit below zero. But if you can visualize farm girls stumbling through snow for the uncertain safety of their cellars; bombs falling on frozen villages unprotected by a single anti-aircraft gun; men standing helplessly in front of blazing buildings with no apparatus with which to fight the fires . . . if you can visualize these things and picture even the children in remote hamlets wearing white covers over their coats as camouflage against low-flying Russian machine-gunners—you can get some idea of what this war was like . . .

Sonia Tomara, *New York Herald Tribune,* and Marylla Chrza-nowska, AP, reported from Warsaw during the German blitzkrieg, narrowly missing death. Eleanor Packard and Fay Gillis covered the Italian invasion of Ethiopia. A Boston girl, Frances Davis, filed mail stories from Spain for several American newspapers. Several times she smuggled copy out of Spain by concealing it in her girdle. "I crackle a little, but if I don't move too much it will be all right," she wrote. It was; she went over the border several times with her dispatches.

Edna Lee Booker got the foreign correspondent fever in the 1920s and sailed for China after jobs on the *Los Angeles Herald* and the

San Francisco Call-Bulletin. She worked for International News Service and the China Press in Shanghai when it was bombed by Japanese planes in 1932. Refugees fled the city, but she remained with the other American reporters, including Floyd Gibbons, Karl H. von Wiegand, Peggy Hull and John Goette.

The famed correspondent H. R. Knickerbocker once remarked:

"Whenever you find hundreds of thousands of sane people trying to get out of a place and a little bunch of madmen struggling to get in—you know the latter are newspapermen."

The ladies are still very much around the battle zones. Nearly a dozen newshens are in Vietnam at this writing. They range in age from twenty-four to forty-six. Betty Halstead, a Temple University graduate, runs the United Press International photo desk there. Denby Fawcett, twenty-five, followed her boyfriend from Hawaii to Saigon and then stayed on for the *Honolulu Advertiser.*

Ruth Burns, a petite blonde journalism major at Rutgers University, decided she wanted to be with her husband, a helicopter pilot in Vietnam, on their first wedding anniversary. She made the rounds and got agreements to cover the war there for six newspapers, the North American Newspaper Alliance and various magazines. This got her press accreditation from the Pentagon and she was on her way. Her husband set up interviews for her and acted as her cameraman. She talked to village chiefs, peasants, shopkeepers and soldiers and was in a crowd into which terrorists threw a grenade. Mrs. Burns also rode in a helicopter that was the target of frequent ground fire. She returned to the United States only because her husband said he couldn't keep flying his helicopter and worry about her safety at the same time. Her articles earned her a William Randolph Hearst journalism award.

Catherine Leroy, a twenty-two-year-old, ninety-five pound freelance photographer, was wounded by mortar shrapnel while covering a marine assault. As she was being loaded on a medical evacuation helicopter, she worked frantically to get film out of her camera, which had been damaged by shell fragments. The French girl, whose photos have appeared in leading newspapers and magazines in the United

States, had previously advanced with a marine unit trying to take a heavily fortified hill held by the Viet Cong. In the midst of furious fighting she shot a dramatic scene of a corpsman attempting to save the life of a dying marine. Miss Leroy had gone to Vietnam with no professional photographic experience.

Beauteous Michele Ray, twenty-eight, a former French cover model, is a free-lance journalist in Vietnam and was once captured and released by the Viet Cong.

Few women war correspondents want special treatment and most resent it. Beverly Deepe, who has reported from Vietnam since 1962 for the *New York Herald Tribune* and other publications, wrote:

> . . . American commanders often present a further prob-
> lem for a woman. They are ultraprotective and superchival-
> rous in ruling whether women may accompany their units into
> battle. When I visit front-line units, I'm ordered to return to
> the base camp by dusk.
> "Men get killed all the time," one marine captain ex-
> plained. "But if a woman gets killed it's a big insult to the
> commander and he's asked a lot of questions."

At another point, Miss Deepe observed:

"Maybe it's my feminine outlook but to me the war is not simply a war but a hellish, dancing madness. One of the most difficult of all problems for a correspondent is to twist his mind to 'feel'—one can rarely 'understand'—a foreign culture of a different century."

When one woman correspondent turned up at the headquarters of a marine fighter squadron in the Mekong Delta, the commanding officer thundered: "You'll wear fatigues all the time. We don't want women with legs down here."

She probably had a pair of fatigues in her pack. Today's woman war correspondent is ready, willing and surprisingly able.

14

Reporters
with Microphones

"THIS IS LONDON."

Millions of Americans waited by their radios for these words in the dark days of 1940 and 1941 when Nazi bombers were raining death and destruction on the English capital.

The broadcaster was a lean, dark-haired man with a deep, compelling voice that was to become known the world over. His name was Edward Roscoe Murrow and he brought World War II into the living rooms of countless homes. Murrow and scores of other reporters with microphones added a new and dramatic dimension to war correspondence. Their efforts also signaled the development of broadcast journalism to a position of prominence and importance. Today, you can see the war in Vietnam on your television set.

Radio as a news device was used long before the Second World War. Newspapers had availed themselves of radio reports even before a wireless message was used by *The New York Times* for its story of the sinking of the *Titanic* in 1912.

The first live battle coverage was made during the Spanish Civil War in 1936 by scholarly Hans V. Kaltenborn, who set up his microphone in a haystack as rebels attacked the loyalist city of Irun on the French border. Listeners heard the crackle of gunfire as Kaltenborn, cool and observant, reported the action. Bombs dropped a few hundred feet away and his lines were cut four times by shell bursts. Another time Kaltenborn stationed himself on a rooftop to give his audience a graphic description of a raging battle.

A former newspaperman, the tall, silver-haired Kaltenborn was to become famous as a World War II commentator. His clipped, precise voice was familiar to millions of radio listeners. Like Murrow, Kaltenborn broadcast for the Columbia Broadcasting System. During crises "H.V." lived for days at a time at the CBS studio, sleeping on a cot and eating onion soup. Periodically he broadcast running interpretations of fast-moving military and political events, speaking from sketchy notes or simply ad libbing. Kaltenborn was well equipped for his job. During the 1930s he had roamed Europe, interviewing Hitler, Mussolini and other important figures.

Murrow, however, always considered himself a reporter, not a commentator, even though he had never worked on a newspaper. Born in Greensboro, North Carolina, in 1908, he was the son of a farmer and railroad engineer who moved the family to the Northwest when Murrow was a child. He graduated as a Phi Beta Kappa from Washington State College, where he was active as a debater and in student dramatics. After college he traveled to Europe with the National Student Federation, a job that furnished him with some of the background he later needed as a news broadcaster, a career he took up in the 1930s.

Ed Murrow always wanted to be where things were happening. In 1938 he was in Warsaw lining up a CBS children's broadcast when he got a phone call from his colleague Bill Shirer in Vienna.

"The opposing team has just crossed the goal line," Shirer said.

"Are you sure?" Murrow asked.

"I'm paid to be sure," was the reply.

Murrow immediately flew to London to broadcast Germany's Anschluss of Austria, a historic moment and the prelude to World War II. Then he flew to Berlin, where he chartered the only plane available—a twenty-seven-seat Lufthansa transport—for $1,000 and flew to Vienna. From the airport he took a streetcar into the city's center in time for the arrival of German troops. He got permission to broadcast the event and was on the air for ten days with a full report of the Anschluss.

Using London as a base, Ed Murrow in World War II was the epitome of the dashing war correspondent. Handsome in a movie actor way, a cigarette hanging from his mouth and wearing a trench-coat, he generated an air of excitement and drama that was to carry him to an outstanding career in broadcasting.

But Murrow was no movie-set hero. He earned his reputation as a war correspondent by dangerous on-the-scene reporting. Night after night he stood on the roof of the British Broadcasting Corporation building to watch the flaming air raids that were shattering London. During the blitz the CBS offices were bombed three times. Murrow also flew combat missions with British and American air forces and covered campaigns in North Africa and on the European continent. Here is part of one of his 1943 broadcasts of his experience on a bomber raid over Berlin:

> . . . the sky ahead was lit up by bright yellow flares. Off to the starboard, another kite [plane] went down in flames. The flares were spouting all over the sky—red and green and yellow—and we were flying straight for the center of the fire-works. D-Dog [his plane] seemed to be standing still, the four propellers thrashing the air. . . . And then with no warning at all, D-Dog was filled with unhealthy white light. I was standing just behind Jock and could see all the seams on the wings. His quiet Scot's voice beat into my ears. "Steady, lads, we've been coned." His slender body lifted half out of his seat

as he jammed the control column forward and to the left. We were going down. . . . I was on my knees, flat on the deck for he had whipped the Dog back into a climbing turn. The knees should have been strong enough to support me but they weren't and the stomach seemed in some danger of letting me down, too. I picked myself up and looked out again. It seemed that one big searchlight, instead of being 20,000 feet below, was mounted right on our wing tip. . . . As we rolled down on the other side I began to see what was happening to Berlin. . . . [It] was a kind of orchestrated hell, a terrible symphony of light and flame. It isn't a pleasant kind of warfare—the men doing it speak of it as a job. Yesterday afternoon, when the tapes were stretched out on the big map all the way to Berlin and back again, a young pilot with old eyes said to me, "I see we're working again tonight." That's the frame of mind in which the job is being done. The job isn't pleasant; it's terribly tiring. Men die in the sky while others are roasted alive in their cellars. Berlin last night wasn't a pretty sight. In about thirty-five minutes, it was hit with about three times the amount of stuff that came down on London in a night-long blitz. This is a calculated, remorseless campaign of destruction.

Two newsmen, Lowell Bennett, International News Service, and Norman Stockton, of Australian Associated Newspapers, did not come back from that raid.

Murrow, who died in 1965 at the age of fifty-seven, became a CBS executive after the war and gained new fame as host and narrator for the "See It Now" and "Person to Person" television shows. He also squeezed in another war assignment—Korea, where he went on more bombing missions. In 1961 he gave up a $300,000-a-year position at CBS to become director of the United States Information Agency at $21,000 a year. He brought to his new post all the skill, enthusiasm and sincerity that had made him a great broadcast journalist. Murrow insisted that truth was more effective than propaganda, telling a United States Senate hearing: "We cannot make good news out of bad practice."

Ed Murrow contributed something more to journalism than just reporting. He was able to put the news in perspective and he always showed compassion and understanding of his fellow man. James Reston, *New York Times* columnist and editor, said: "He had courage and he had style." Murrow's colleague, Eric Sevareid, remarked: "He was an original, and we shall not see his like again."

Other CBS reporters also were broadcasting the war. Bill Henry was one of the first radio newsmen accredited to the fighting fronts, and his voice was heard from London almost every day. Farnsworth Fowle, a Rhodes scholar, landed with the Allies at Salerno, Italy, and was the first wireless correspondent to broadcast from conquered Axis territory. In the Pacific, Cecil Brown, a lean Pennsylvanian, was aboard the British ship *Repulse* when it was sunk by the Japanese. A few hours after his rescue from the oily waters off Singapore, he gave the world the first story of the disaster. Later Brown was bombed on the Burma Road and got out of Yugoslavia less than twenty-four hours ahead of the German invasion. A graduate of Ohio State University, Brown won the 1941 George Peabody Award for his eyewitness story of the *Repulse* torpedoing. He also got Sigma Delta Chi's Distinguished Service Award for his description of the German parachute invasion of Crete.

William J. Dunn landed with General MacArthur at Leyte in the Philippines and made the first American broadcast over Tokyo radio in 1945. Dunn was only minutes ahead of the Japanese when he escaped from Java in a small inter-island boat. Seventeen of his fellow passengers were killed by strafing from enemy planes. Once he wrote to CBS:

"Sooner or later every correspondent in the fight zones is asked: 'Are you drafted for this job?' When the correspondent boasts that he chose the work, there is a standard answer from the American soldier: 'You must be nuts.' "

Among those working under Edward R. Murrow was a twenty-three-year-old Cornell graduate named Charles Collingwood, who had began his career as a United Press correspondent in London in 1939. Born in Three Rivers, Michigan, and the son of a college professor, Collingwood had worked as a cowpuncher and a deck hand on a freighter during his summer vacations. He was in Europe on a scholarship when war broke out.

Collingwood's manly visage and well-timbred voice were later to become well known to millions of television viewers. But in 1941 he was a raw cub, frightened of his first radio assignment.

"Ed threw me into the breach the second night," Collingwood said in a *New York Post* interview. "I was an untutored punk kid . . . nervous, panicky. I told Ed he was taking a chance on me. He said, no, I'd learn; I'd find my own niche after a while."

Murrow was right. Collingwood rendered the first eyewitness account of the fall of Tunis, entering the city with the first Allied troops and then speeding back to Algiers, driving all night to be in time for the CBS regular morning "News of the World" program.

"I went in with the first tanks just behind the spearhead," he announced over the air. "In front of us there was fighting and all around was the sound of gunfire as the last Germans were being mopped up, but we had driven a corridor right down the main avenue into the town and the people were out to meet us. They were crazy with joy."

On D-Day, Collingwood, his probationary period over, rode into deadly Omaha Beach on an LST loaded with a half ton of dynamite.

Many of the radio correspondents were enticed away from the newspapers and wire services. One was William L. Shirer, who was hired by Murrow in 1938 after he had covered Europe for several years for the *Chicago Tribune* and Universal News Service. Shirer, born in Chicago, had worked his way to Europe on a cattle boat after graduating from Coe College. He was in Berlin during the first British bomber raid, and at the fall of France he scooped the world with the news of the signing of the surrender agreement at Compiègne. Shirer's book *The Rise and Fall of the Third Reich* became a best seller.

Another newspaperman turned broadcaster was Eric Sevareid, a brawny product of North Dakota who worked his way through the University of Minnesota as a reporter on the *Minneapolis Journal.* He drifted to Europe in 1937, hooking up with the *Paris Herald* and

United Press. Ed Murrow, ever on the alert for bright young talent, offered Sevareid a job for CBS, telling him, "I like the way you write and I like your ideas." The new staffer broadcast from Paris after war was declared; and when Germany invaded the lowlands he headed for the Belgium front, where he and other correspondents were kept from the fighting by military authorities. But Sevareid learned of the Nazi breakthrough to French soil and knew the collapse of France was imminent. He sent his wife and infant twins back to the states and stayed in Paris, beaming his last broadcast hours before the Germans entered the city. The CBS man then fled to Bordeaux, where he continued broadcasting. He left France with a boatload of refugees.

Other CBS correspondents in World War II were Larry Lesueur, who covered the Russian front, Howard K. Smith, Richard C. Hottelet and John Daly, all of whom went on to distinguished careers in broadcasting. In one newscast from London, Daly cracked:

"The sound of guns is terrifying and my first inclination is to dive for the gutter. The only thing that keeps me on my feet is that it takes about three weeks to get a suit cleaned."

Daly engineered a beat on the fall of Messina, Sicily, when General George Patton permitted him and Merrill Mueller, of NBC, to use his personal plane to fly back to Palermo and file their stories. But they found the airfield closed for the night and were told that even if they did take off there was a good chance they would be mistakenly shot down by American anti-aircraft guns in the dark. As if that weren't enough trouble, they learned that the plane's radio operator was sick and could not fly.

Despite these obstacles, Daly and Mueller insisted on going up. Officers at the field telephoned General Patton, who ordered: "Get them through if they are willing to take a chance." Another radio operator was rounded up and the aircraft roared off. Daly said:

"Merrill and I wrote our stories in the bucking, blacked out plane, lighted only by a flashlight held by a crew member."

When they landed, both raced for the censor's office to clear their stories. Daly was swifter and got his story on the air thirteen minutes before all other news sources. It contained the news of the all-out air bombardment of Cassino and an interview with the bombardier of the lead plane. Daly, who became an urbane, witty host of a TV guessing game and other programs, saw additional action in Italy and North Africa during the war.

In December, 1944, Richard Hottelet gave the first report of the German counter-offensive which grew into the Battle of the Bulge. He was also on hand for the historic contact of the American and Russian armies on the banks of the Elbe River in Germany on April 27, 1945. He reported that the long-awaited link-up was something less than spectacular.

"There were no brass bands, no sign of the titanic strength of both these armies," he said. "The Americans who met the Red Army were a couple of dust-covered young lieutenants and a handful of enlisted men in their jeeps on reconnaissance."

The CBS man was soon joined by about fifty other correspondents, who trooped to Russian battalion headquarters. Then still more newsmen arrived. A goggle-eyed Soviet captain asked Hottelet who they all were.

"Reporters," Hottelet replied.

"You have as many reporters as you have soldiers," the Red officer remarked.

Hottelet and other correspondents left shortly for Berlin, entering the ruined city forty-eight hours after it had been taken by the Russian army.

Merrill "Red" Mueller also had his share of journalistic triumphs and war action. Starting his newspaper career in Connecticut at the age of fourteen, he covered the Munich meetings of Hitler and Neville Chamberlain and, as a licensed pilot, shared the controls of a bomber with the Italian dictator, Mussolini, to get an exclusive interview. As an NBC man in World War II he reported the Battle of Britain (during which he was bombed out of two apartments), the Battle of the Bulge, the atom bombing of Hiroshima and the Japanese surrender aboard the U.S.S. *Missouri*. He was wounded by shrapnel in Tunisia, and in the Pacific he was once reported missing and presumed dead in island fighting. All this earned him the Purple Heart, the Order of the British Empire, the French Legion of Honor and numerous journalism awards.

Other NBC war correspondents included Elmer Peterson, Morgan Beatty, Henry Cassidy, Robert Shaplen, Don Hollenbeck, Robert Trout, W. W. Chaplin and John McVane.

Peterson, a one-time AP man, joined NBC after escaping from Poland during the Nazi occupation. A native of Duluth, Minnesota, and graduate of Carleton College, he got his first taste of war in Spain in 1936 and was the first American correspondent accredited to the Japanese army in its invasion of Manchuria in 1938.

Chaplin reported the Allied invasion of Normandy from a landing craft, and NBC's Chester Morrison originated a radio report on one of the attacking boats in the assault on southern France. The broadcast was relayed to the world via the Rome and Algiers radios. He told how the tremendous fire power of fourteen-inch naval guns rattled his typewriter as he wrote his dispatches in the early stages of the landing. His broadcast was made for four major American networks. Hollenbeck went ashore in the Salerno, Italy, invasion and Shaplen, who also worked for *Newsweek,* broadcast the first eyewitness account of the effect of the atomic bombing of the Japanese city of Nagasaki. Shaplen currently writes about Southeast Asia for the *New Yorker* magazine.

Robert Magidoff, a former AP man, was in Moscow for NBC at the time the city was under siege by German forces. He and other newsmen, including Quentin Reynolds, *Collier's* magazine, M. S. Handler, UP, and Henry Cassidy, AP, were evacuated to a small town on the Volga River, along with the diplomatic corps. Magidoff covered the eastern front but recalled that the Russian general staff allowed reporters in the fighting zone only when there had been a Soviet victory.

"Usually we were flown in by plane and then taken by jeep to the battlefield," Magidoff said. "One time the jeep right ahead of the one I was in hit a mine, killing the occupants."

The soft-spoken Magidoff, a native of Russia, was sometimes pressed into service as a translator when Russian officials held press conferences. In 1948 he was ordered out of Russia on what he termed "trumped up" spy charges. Magidoff, who later went into college teaching, turned down an opportunity to take sanctuary in the American embassy while spy charges were being hurled against him. He told the United States ambassador, General Walter Bedell Smith:

"I'm not guilty of any crime against the Soviet Union and I don't want even to *seem* to admit any guilt, no matter how indirectly."

The risk was great because Magidoff was subject to arrest at any moment.

D-Day, June 6, 1944, was also an historic day for radio, which, for the first time, pooled its facilities for newscasts over all networks. One of the memorable broadcasts was made by George Hicks, American Broadcasting System, who recorded it aboard a landing craft under heavy attack by enemy planes. Another momentous pool operation was the broadcast of the Japanese surrender aboard the battleship *Missouri*. In World War II radio got its messages to America by various means, including special radio ships and mobile short-wave transmitters mounted on trucks in the combat area.

A few local radio correspondents also reported from the fighting fronts. Jack Shelley, of station WHO in Des Moines, Iowa, provided hometown and state coverage in the manner of newspapermen. He reproduced the voices of thousands of Iowa soldiers and his broadcasts were eagerly awaited by Iowans.

After 1945, combat reporting by radio continued as a significant news medium. The Korean outbreak drew several World War II broadcasters and some new ones. CBS reporter Bill Downs covered the retreat of United States and South Korean forces to the Pusan perimeter. Later he was assigned to the revolt in Cyprus and the Israel-Arab war. Ed Murrow also broadcast from Korea.

NBC fielded fourteen correspondents in Korea, including such veterans as William Dunn, Ken Kantor and Peter Murray. This news-gathering team was headed by George Thomas Folster, who was assisted by his wife, Helen, a correspondent in her own right, who had covered the Far East in the Second World War.

Among the American Broadcasting Company reporters in Korea was Lou Cioffi, who was wounded in action and was awarded the Purple Heart. Cioffi, a native of New York City, also covered the Suez invasion, the Hungarian uprising in 1956, the French and Algerian fighting and Vietnam.

The 1961 Bay of Pigs invasion in Cuba caught most of the news media by surprise, but NBC's Herb Kaplow got an unexpected eye-witness exclusive on the story. He was in Miami at the time but flew immediately to Cuba, where he talked his way past guards into the Presidential Palace where Fidel Castro was eating lunch. The bearded leader welcomed Kaplow expansively, first telling him about an American plane his agents had hijacked and then inviting him to view the Bay of Pigs battlefield, where a force of Cuban refugees were taking a terrible beating from the Cuban army.

Kaplow accepted with mixed emotions. He knew it would be a great story but he also wondered if he would ever be able to tell it. Kaplow got a ringside view of the abortive invasion and then was returned to Havana, where he waited tensely for permission to leave the country. After an ominous delay the Cuban secret police approved his exit.

An NBC newsman, Richard Valeriani, a Camden, New Jersey, native and Yale graduate, was arrested five times in a twenty-month period in Cuba. This experience taught him that in going out on assignments, it was a good idea to carry not only a pad and pencil but also a toothbrush, candy bar and paperback novel in preparation for an overnight stay in one of Castro's jails.

The late, late show may not be an old movie. It could be a film of a bitter fight for a strip of jungle in Vietnam. Television reporters and cameramen have brought that war more vividly to Americans than ever has been done before. We can see in our living rooms the agony of the wounded, the physical destruction and the unremitting brutality of war. There have been complaints, some from the Pentagon, that the one-dimensional camera has given a distorted picture of the conflict, chiefly in regard to civilian casualties.

Like the combat newspaper correspondent, the TV reporter has sought out the hot spots in Vietnam. Ron Nessen, NBC, was wounded while filming a story of the operation of the 101st Airborne Division in the central highlands. A CBS reporter, John Laurence, went on forty-two combat operations, including four air strikes. "Most," he said, "were the daily routine grind of searching for the elusive enemy—what the G.I.s call long, hot walks in the sun."

Laurence, who has light-colored hair that reflects the sun, was a clear target for snipers. An officer suggested that he wear a hat. The reporter found one and later learned why the officer had pressed the matter. He had been out with another correspondent who had been hit by a sniper's bullet.

The twenty-six-year-old Laurence was injured in a helicopter crash and also suffered facial wounds in a battle. He said that more than one hundred correspondents in Vietnam had been wounded.

"We had to laugh about the danger of death or go crazy," he added. "Surprisingly few of the reporters in Vietnam suffered breakdowns."

Laurence was cited by the Overseas Press Club for his dramatic report on the evacuation of United States troops from a Special Forces camp near Plei Me. As he described the operation, the sounds of Viet Cong gunfire and strafing jet fighters could be heard.

The OPC 1966 award for best television reporting went to a thirty-four-year-old Canadian, Morley Safer, of CBS, who shocked millions of TV viewers with his film story of the American burning of a Vietnam village. The report put him at odds with United States authorities in Vietnam, but Safer insisted he was merely doing his job. Once Safer missed death by inches when a bullet smashed through the plexiglass of a helicopter in which he and other newsmen were riding to a battle. Vietnam was Safer's third war; he had reported fighting in the Congo and Cyprus.

A CBS exclusive was turned out by correspondent Charles Kuralt and cameraman Fred Dieterich—the hard way. They were on the scene for hand-to-hand fighting between South Vietnamese regulars and Viet Cong. At one point the CBS team was surrounded by the enemy and subjected to strafing by Communist aircraft.

Under such circumstances a TV news crew might not be able to move as fast as the pencil reporters. The cameraman is burdened with his equipment and the newsman often carries a microphone. There also is a sound man, who lugs other mikes, audio tapes and a tape machine, most of them on his back.

Howard K. Smith, the distinguished ABC news analyst, had one interview in Vietnam he will never forget. It was with his son Jack, twenty-one, an army specialist fourth class, who was wounded in the Ia Drang Valley battle and was one of the few survivors of that action.

FATHER:

When you were wounded . . . did it hurt?

SON:

The one up here [face] just numbed me; down there, it stung like a bee sting, along my whole leg for a few minutes.

FATHER:

Did you bleed a lot?

SON:

Through my face. I didn't bleed much here, but my face, I lost quite a bit of blood.

FATHER:

What happened after that?

SON:

Well, then I heard them massing for another one, charge the PAVN [North Vietnamese regulars]. . . . I took off to the right, started crawling along the grass . . . and I was crying.

FATHER:

Did you see a lot of Americans around?

SON:

No, they were all—most of them didn't have arms or legs so I was lucky I didn't get torn to pieces. . . . I crawled back.

. . . I was just about out of my mind then, so I crawled back to where the mortar platoon was . . .

FATHER:

What did you think? Did you think you were going to die?

SON:

I thought I was going to die. I lay there awhile, passed out, various other things. By then I was, it was like a big dream. I lost an awful lot of blood and I was half conscious. At nightfall, I crawled out to a bunch of guys, a bunch of guys were lying there . . .

FATHER:

Were these Americans?

SON:

Right . . . And we lay there until midnight, waiting for them to come in and get us because we knew we were all going to get killed, and this guy next to me crawled off and died. Everybody was pretty messy. . . . There were guys who were dying with all their guts hanging out and everything else . . .

The ABC reporting staff in Vietnam included attractive Marlene Sanders, an award-winning television and radio newswoman who has her own program, "News With a Woman's Touch."

"My goals were not to cover combat," she explained. "I didn't feel my job was to prove I was as brave as the men who were. But I did feel other parts of the story were not being done: How Vietnamese conducted their daily lives in wartime, how troops lived in the field, what kind of medical care is available to civilians and so forth."

Nevertheless, Miss Sanders' month-long tour was no garden party. She was tear-gassed twice covering mob demonstrations in Saigon, and in the field she was close enough to the fighting to hear the sound of mortar shells. "One of the first things I learned," she said, "was how to live with apprehension."

Here is how she described her work in Vietnam:

Travel by jeep in the countryside is hazardous but several times we had to do it when helicopters weren't available. The tall brush near the Cambodian border didn't look inviting.

The driver was armed, but we were sitting ducks. The rest of the trip you lug equipment into cattle class accommodations in the back of a C-130 plane or climb aboard a 'copter with open sides and nothing but a seat belt keeping you from going overboard. You sit next to a machine gunner, posed and alert all the way. Then they drop you off in the middle of a field, wind whipped and several feet off the ground.

During my entire stay in Vietnam I was treated like any male correspondent. I could and did take the same risks, stood in the same chow lines, rode the same helicopters, helped the crew carry the equipment, attended the briefings, suffered the same miserable heat and did pretty much as I pleased.

ABC suffered a tragic loss during the Vietnam conflict. Its vice-president for news, Jesse Zousmer, and his wife, Ruth, were killed in a Tokyo air crash while returning from a trip to Vietnam. Zousmer, a broadcast journalist for many years, wanted to find out exactly how his men covered the war and what their problems were.

The death toll of broadcast correspondents must also include the names of George Polk, CBS, and George Clay, NBC.

Polk was murdered in Greece in 1948, a time of trouble between the government and Communist-led rebels. Both sides accused each other of the crime. The correspondent was found dead in Salonika harbor, shot through the head and his hands and feet tied with twine. Three Greeks were convicted of the slaying in 1949.

Annual awards for outstanding achievement in journalism have been established in George Polk's name at Long Island University.

George Clay, South African-born newsman, was ambushed and killed while covering the march of mercenaries into Stanleyville during the Congo war in 1964. The correspondent, who had won an Overseas Press Club award for "Best Radio Reporting from Abroad," was recording news tape when he was shot. He had been under fire many times.

In the Cyprus civil war between Greek and Turkish factions, Al Rosenfeld, NBC, was hit in the face by a bullet as he was driving across "no man's land" after he had passed a Greek outpost. His car was wrecked and he had to wait for four hours for a United Nations armored car to rescue him.

All three men had known what every other war correspondent knows: If you're where the shooting is you run the risk of getting hit. They took their chances, anyway.

I don't believe that any correspondent mentioned in this book would think of himself as a hero. If you asked him, he would probably say he was doing his job—covering the news. No reporter is forced by his boss to go to war. But newsmen do go and many have earned the right to be called heroes.

Suggested Further Reading

American Journalism—A History 1690-1960, Frank Luther Mott, New York: Macmillan Co., 1962.

American Reporters on the Western Front 1914-18, Emmett Crozier, New York: Oxford University Press, 1959.

AP: The Story of News, Oliver Gramling, New York: Farrar & Rinehart, Inc., 1940.

Battle for the Solomons, Ira Wolfert, Boston: Houghton Mifflin Co., 1942.

Berlin Diary, William L. Shirer, New York: Knopf, 1941.

Brave Men, Ernie Pyle, New York: Grosset & Dunlap, 1944. (Copyright 1943-4 Scripps-Howard Newspaper Alliance)

Crusade in Europe, Dwight D. Eisenhower, Garden City, New York: Doubleday, 1948.

Deadline Delayed, by members of the Overseas Press Club of America, New York: E. P. Dutton & Co., Inc., 1947.

Deadline Every Minute, Joe Alex Morris, New York: Doubleday & Co., Inc., 1957.

Dorothy and Red, Vincent Sheean, Boston: Houghton Mifflin Co., 1963.

Famous War Correspondents, F. Lauriston Bullard, Boston: Little, Brown & Co., 1914.

Foreign Correspondence: The Great Reporters and Their Times, John Hohenberg, New York: Columbia University Press, 1964.

Foreign Correspondent, Robert St. John, New York: Doubleday & Co., Inc., 1957.

Good Evening, Raymond Swing, New York: Harcourt, Brace & World, Inc., 1964.

Here Is Your War, Ernie Pyle, New York: Henry Holt & Co., 1943.

I Can Tell It Now, by members of the Overseas Press Club of America, ed. by David Brown and N. Richard Bruner, New York: E. P. Dutton & Co., Inc., 1964.

I Can't Forget, Robert J. Casey, New York: Bobbs-Merrill Co., 1941.

Ladies of the Press, The Story of Women in Journalism by an Insider, Isabel Ross, New York: Harper & Bros., 1936.

Making of a Quagmire, David Halberstam, New York: Random House, 1965.

Mathew Brady, Historian With A Camera, James D. Horan, New York: Crown Publishers, Inc., 1955.

News Is a Singular Thing, Marguerite Higgins, New York: Doubleday & Co., Inc., 1955.

North Reports The Civil War, The, J. Cutler Andrews: University of Pittsburgh Press, 1955.

Once There Was A War, John Steinbeck, New York: Viking Press, 1958.

Portrait of Myself, Margaret Bourke-White, New York: Simon & Schuster, 1963.

Reporters for the Union, Bernard A. Weisberger, Boston: Little, Brown & Co., 1953.

Reporting The Wars, Joseph J. Mathews, Minnesota: University of Minnesota Press, 1957.

Slightly Out of Focus, Robert Capa, New York: Henry Holt & Co., 1947.

Story of The Stars and Stripes, The, Bud Hutton and Andy Rooney, New York: Farrar & Rinehart, 1946.

With Fire and Sword, ed. Quentin Reynolds & Robert Leckie, New York: Dial Press, 1963.

Index